THE ESTABLISHMENT OF EUROPEAN WORKS COUNCILS

The Establishment of European Works Councils

From information committee to social actor

WOLFGANG LECHER
Hans-Böckler Foundation

BERNHARD NAGEL
University of Kassel

HANS-WOLFGANG PLATZER
University for Applied Sciences, Fulda

PROJECT TEAM
Roman Jaich
Stefan Rüb
Klaus-Peter Weiner

AFFILIATED RESEARCHERS
Lionel Fulton, *Labour Research Department, London*
Udo Rehfeldt, *Institut des Recherches Economiques et Sociales, Paris*
Dr. Volker Telljohann, *Bolonga*

Translated by Pete Burgess

Ashgate

Aldershot • Brookfield USA • Singapore • Sydney

Published by
Ashgate Publishing Ltd
Gower House
Croft Road
Aldershot
Hants GU11 3HR
England

Ashgate Publishing Company
Old Post Road
Brookfield
Vermont 05036
USA

British Library Cataloguing in Publication Data
Lecher, Wolfgang
  The establishment of European works councils: from
  information committee to social actor
  1. Works councils - European Union countries
  2. Labour-management committees - European Union countries
  I. Title II. Nagel, Bernhard II. Platzer, Hans-Wolfgang
  331' .094

Library of Congress Catalog Card Number: 98-73886

ISBN 1 84014 886 1

Printed in Great Britain

Contents

Tables and figures

Abbreviations

AEEU	Amalgamated Engineering and Electrical Union (UK)
AG	Aktiengesellschaft (Public Liability Company) (D)
AMPS	Association of Managerial and Professional Staffs (UK)
ASAP	Associazione Sindacale Aziende Petrolchimiche (Association of Petrochemical Enterprises) (I)
BAVC	Bundesarbeitgeberverband Chemie (Federal Chemical Employers Association) (D)
BDA	Bundesvereinigung der deutschen Arbeitgeberverbände (Federal Association of German Employer Organisations) (D)
CBI	Confederation of British Industry (UK)
CEFIC	European Chemical Employers Association
CFDT	Confédération Française Démocratique de Travail (Democratic French Confederation of Labour) (F)
CFTC	Confédération Française des Travailleurs Chrétiens (Christian French Confederation of Labour) (F)
CGC	Confédération Générale des Cadres (General Confederation of Managers) (F)
CGIL	Confederazione Generale Italiania del Lavoro (General Italian Confederation of Labour) (I)
CGT	Confédération Générale de Travail (General Confederation of Labour) (F)
CIA	Chemical Industries Association (UK)
CISNAL	Confederazione Italiana Sindacati Nazionali Lavoratori (National Italian Union Confederation of Workers) (I)
CISL	Confederazione Italiana Sindacati Lavoratori (Union Confederation of Italian Workers) (I)
COBA	Comitato di Base (Grass roots committee) (I)
CONFINDUSTRIA	Confederazione Generale dell'Industria Italiana (Confederation of Italian Industry) (I)
DGB	Deutscher Gewerkschaftsbund (German Trade Union Federation) (D)
ECJ	European Court of Justice

EEA	European Economic Area
EEC	European Economic Community
EEF	Engineering Employers' Federation (UK)
EESA	Electrical and Engineering Staff Association (UK)
EMCEF	European Mine, Chemical and Energy Workers Federation
EMF	European Metalworkers Federation
EMU	Economic and Monetary Union
ETUC	European Trade Union Confederation
ETUI	European Trade Union Institute
EU	European Union
EWC	European Works Council
FGMM	Fédération Générale des Mines et de la Métallurgie (General Federation of Mining and Metallurgy) (F)
FILCEA	Federazione Italiana Lavoratori Chimici e Affini (Federation of Chemical and Refinery Workers) (I)
FIM	Federazione Italiana Metalmeccanici (Federation of Italian Engineering Workers) (I)
FIOM	Federazione Impiegati Operai Metalmeccanici (Federation of Engineering Staff and Operatives) (I)
FLERICA	Federazione Lavoratori Energia Risorse Chimica e Affini (Federation of Workers in Energy, Resources and Refining) (I)
FNV	Federatie Nederlandse Vakbeweging (Dutch Trade Union Confederation) (NL)
FO	Force Ouvrière (Workers' Force) (F)
FULC	Federazione Unitaria Lavoratori Chimici (United Federation of Chemical Workers) (I)
FUC-CFDT	Fédération de la Chimie - Confédération Française Démocratique de Travail (Chemical Workers Federation - CFDT) (F)
GMB	General and Municipal Union (UK)
IG CPK/IG BCE	Industriegewerkschaft Chemie Papier Keramik (German chemical workers' union) (D) - since renamed Industriegewerkschaft Bergbau Chemie Energie.
ILO	International Labour Organisation
INTERSIND	Intersindicale (I)
IRRU	Industrial Relations Research Unit, Warwick University

MSF	Manufacturing, Science, Finance (UK)
plc.	Public Limited Company (UK)
RSU	Rappresentanza Sindacale Unitaria (Unified Union Representation) (I)
SA	Société Anonyme (Limited Company) (F)
SEA	Single European Act
SNB	Special Negotiating Body
TEU	Treaty on European Union (Maastricht Treaty)
TUC	Trades Union Congress (UK)
TGI	Tribunal de Grande Instance (District Court) (F)
TGWU	Transport and General Workers Union (UK)
UIL	Unione Italiana del Lavoro (Italian Union of Labour) (I)
UILCER	Unione Italiana del Lavoro Chimica Energia Risorse (I)
UIMM	Union des Industries Métallurgiques et Minière (Employers Association in Metalworking and Mining) (F)
UILM	Unione Italiana Lavoratori Metalmeccanici (I)

Preface

This study of the establishment and development of European Works Councils (EWCs) in four European Union countries presents the results of a research project carried out between September 1996 and September 1997. It sets out, for the first time, to anchor a number of qualitative case-studies of EWCs in a systematic, nationally comparative approach. This called for a special type of project organisation and division of labour, and in particular for close co-operation with colleagues across Europe.

The project was led by Dr. Wolfgang Lecher, Economic and Social Research Institute (WSI) at the Hans-Böckler Foundation; Prof. Bernhard Nagel, University of Kassel; and Prof. Hans-Wolfgang Platzer, University for Applied Sciences, Fulda. The research team in Germany consisted of Roman Jaich (an economist), Stefan Rüb (a sociologist) and Klaus-Peter Weiner (a political scientist). Affiliated researchers outside Germany were Lionel Fulton, Labour Research Department (London); Udo Rehfeldt, Institut des Recherches Economiques et Sociales (Paris); and Dr. Volker Telljohann (Bologna).

The backgrounds and locations of these team members made a substantial contribution to the project's capacity to draw together data on a systematic basis and come to a well-founded assessment of its significance. They organised, prepared and attended interviews, evaluated the results, and added their interpretation of ongoing developments, both in the field of EWCs and more broadly in national systems of industrial relations - all of which enhanced the eventual outcome of the study. Obtaining and evaluating secondary material on EWCs and the structures and strategies of the selected companies, together with the task of making an overall assessment of the case-studies and putting the empirical material into a publishable form, was undertaken by the members of the team working independently within an agreed division of labour. In addition, all contributed to the preparatory theoretical phase of the project and offered substantive contributions to a range of issues raised in the research. Their specific backgrounds - economics, sociology and political science - also played an important role in facilitating interdisciplinary work and theoretical reflection on the results.

Each stage of the research was reviewed in joint project meetings. The chapters and sections of the final report were prepared by individual team members and discussed and reworked collectively within these meetings.

Acknowledgments

This project would not have been possible without the willingness of the numerous interviewees to speak in both detail and with frankness about the processes and practices of European Works Councils. All are owed a debt of gratitude.

A conference held in Brussels at the conclusion of the empirical stage of the project, attended by representatives of all those EWCs covered by the study, aimed at reviewing and deepening the initial results would not have been possible without the organisational and financial support of the Friedrich Ebert Foundation (Bonn), to which we also extend our heartfelt thanks.

Finally, we wish to thank the Hans-Böckler-Foundation which financed the research, its publication in Germany and the English translation.

Wolfgang Lecher
Bernhard Nagel
Hans-Wolfgang Platzer   Kassel, January 1998

PART I: INTRODUCTION

1 Scope and Method of the Research

The first decisive steps towards the establishment of European Works Councils (EWCs) were taken in the mid-1980s with a number of voluntary agreements - initially in French undertakings - which provided for the setting up of European information committees. Barely a decade later, in September 1994, the European Union (EU) Directive on the establishment of EWCs was adopted by the Council of Ministers. The origins and effects of this Directive were innovatory in a number of respects.

For the first time in the field of social policy, European legislation had created a primary European institution. In contrast to the - relatively few - previous Directives in the employment field, the EWC Directive went much further than merely requiring national implementation of a common set of framework conditions. The issue was also the first to be dealt with under the new procedures for qualified majority voting provided for by the 'Social Protocol' to the Maastricht Treaty. This required that negotiations on the Directive be held between the social partners at European level as a first stage; following the breakdown of these negotiations, the Directive became law via a decision of the Council of Ministers. And finally, the Directive was innovative in that it linked the introduction of an novel institution - the European Works Council - with a judicious blend of *subsidiarity* (national transposition in accordance with local law and custom), *shared responsibility* (joint action by governments, employers associations and trade unions in transposition into national law and practical implementation) and *flexibility* (the Directive allows a number of options for transposition).

All this would appear to offer extensive scope for research. And one might be forgiven for thinking that a good deal of quantitative and - given that some EWCs have been operating for more than a decade - qualitative research into the impact and forms of social interaction of EWCs would have already been completed or be in train, and that parallel research into national implementation would be under way. Surprisingly, however, there have been few empirical research projects on voluntary EWC agreements and, at the time of writing, no discernible flood of proposals for research into the problems of implementation.

Moreover, as yet, there has been no '*comparative* provisional assessment of existing research at a meso-theoretical level' (Höland, 1997, p. 74).

In setting out to locate the present study within the broader landscape of research on EWCs, we therefore begin with a short overview of current activity, and specifically of the positions and research strategies associated with some of the principal approaches. Of particular note here are the research and wider activities of the Dublin 'European Foundation for the Improvement of Living and Working Conditions' which, in collaboration with the Industrial Relations Research Unit (IRRU) at the University of Warwick has completed several studies on the current state of voluntary EWC agreements and the national implementation of the Directive (Bonneton et.al., 1995 and subsequent studies). Most recently, the Foundation has prepared an analysis of some 390 of the estimated 430 agreements along such formal criteria as geographical scope, exclusion and/or inclusion of particular subsidiaries, composition of employer and employee sides, existence of smaller sub-committees, competence and frequency of EWC meetings, support from external experts, financial and other resources provided by the employer, language problems and training (Marginson et.al., 1998). Since 1996, the IRRU and Industrial Relations Services (London) have also published the bi-monthly *European Works Council Bulletin*, which combines reports on current developments and documentation with detailed analyses across the entire field of practice and research.

A second branch of research has looked at the effect of EWCs on the shape of European industrial relations. Two strands - a 'Euro-sceptic' and a more 'Euro-optimist' - can be distinguished, although these terms are not used here in the sense usually associated with the UK debate on European integration. The 'sceptics' argue that EWCs could commend themselves to employers as a suitable instrument for a Europeanised human resource management strategy which would, at most, promote and stabilise the movement towards the Europeanisation of corporate functions (Schulten, 1997). Such a new company-based European-level of regulation would also fit well with the trend towards the decentralisation of industrial relations, further weakening supra-company levels of regulation at either national or branch level (Streeck/Vitols, 1993).

This contrasts with the 'optimistic' position which postulates the establishment of a close relationship between transnational trade unionism and the new institution of the EWC (Buda, 1998). On this view, were the trade unions to succeed in creating close and stable networks around EWCs, at both national and European level, then 'favourable' - that is better than average - company agreements (measured against the European dimension of multinational corporations and the countries they embrace) at group-level with EWCs could provide an impetus to the emulation of such agreements within national collective bargaining, with an associated multiplier effect (Lecher/Platzer, 1996, *idem*, 1997), at least on consensual issues such as health and safety, training, and environmental standards (Schmidt, 1997). This position starts from the premise that the existing level of Europeanisation, which will now be strengthened by European Economic and Monetary Union (EMU), has already largely blocked the prospect of any return to national self-containment for the actors in national systems of industrial relations (the state, trade unions, management and employers associations). For good or ill, these actors have no choice but to widen their radius of action to the international and supra-national level, including in the field of industrial relations. As a consequence, EWCs could prove to be more important in establishing the foundations of an enduring system of European industrial relations than the 'compensatory' Social Dialogue between the umbrella organisations of employers and employees at European level or the first observable and tentative steps towards the international co-ordination of collective bargaining (Keller, 1997).

The third, and given the novelty of the institution, possibly most interesting and potentially fruitful area of research, concerns the 'inner life' of the EWC: that is, the structures and processes of communication and patterns of interaction within EWCs. This not only covers formal arrangements (frequency of meetings, trade union preparations for formal meetings, feedback between EWCs of different nationalities and relations between parent companies and subsidiaries, and links to their own national 'substrate') but also *informal* networks of information and communication within and between EWCs.

This network of communication can be looked at in terms of four tracks. In terms of the *modus operandi* of the forum, the first critical link is that between the EWC and national structures of employee representation and the feedback from the latter to the former. The work of the EWC can only achieve a genuine life of its own and establish its legitimacy if there is a steady, but also informal, exchange of information between these two poles.

The second track concerns the relationship between management and the EWC, not only at European level but also with its foundation at national level - whether parent company or subsidiary. Many processes of change at workplace level can be detected earlier at national level than would be possible through a formal request for information to be supplied at transnational or European level at official meetings of EWCs and central management.

The third track concerns the relationship between EWCs and trade unions. This relationship, especially within the dual systems which predominate in the EU (exceptions include UK, Sweden and Italy), is crucial for the role and status of EWCs. Only through the external support of trade unions can EWCs acquire the resources in depth which will allow them to function either as an instrument for information and consultation or in any possible future role as a negotiating body. As with national patterns of industrial relations (in Germany, as the paradigm: workplace bargaining via works councils and industry bargaining, crucially on pay, via trade unions) such a bi-polar relationship serves to both strengthen and secure the status of EWCs within corporate structures.

The fourth track concerns the relationship between different national EWC representatives. In particular, the structural privileging of parent company representatives means that the relationship between EWC representatives from parent companies and from subsidiaries merits particular attention. Should this privileged status become entrenched, it can lead to a national appropriation of the entire EWC institution, compromising its transnational, pan-European character and detracting from what marks it out as an institutional innovation.

An analysis of the processes of interaction which characterise EWCs, both formal and informal, might then also allow some conclusions to be drawn on the issue of the Europeanisation of industrial relations. Compared with the 'Euro-sceptic' or 'Euro-optimist' positions set out above, such conclusions would have the advantage of no longer being based ultimately in speculation - as well-informed as it might be - but on empirical research. The conclusions and prospects at the end of this volume are based on this research.

Leaving aside case-studies of individual EWCs (Deppe/ Hoffmann/Stützel, 1997) and studies of earlier information and consultation initiatives in international companies (Gold/Hall, 1992; Guariello/Jobert, 1992; Martinella et.al., 1992; Nagel et. al., 1996), there are surprisingly few published studies in the field of qualitative-comparative research into EWCs (Coëutoux/DiRuzza, 1990; Jobert, 1990; Rehfeldt, 1992; Lecher, 1994b). This may well be explained by the small number of available instances and the initial predominance of French companies. What is less surprising is the fact that the bulk of these studies was conducted in the first half of the 1990s; the burgeoning number of 'voluntary' agreements since 1994 under the provisions and options set out by the Directive has meant that research since then has been preoccupied with structuring and charting the quantitative growth of this rapidly expanding field.

Framework, Approach and Course of the Study

The European Works Council (EWC) is a recent institution in industrial relations, novel in its transnational character, and unique in international comparison. Both its origins and its potential for future development have a dynamic quality which is reflected in the approach and methods employed in this study. The contradictory and, at times, speculative character of current research into the scope and preconditions for the development of EWCs is not only the product of the diversity of the theoretical approaches and value-judgements brought to bear on this subject: it also reflects the sheer lack of empirical material, as well as a number of methodological shortcomings.

This can be seen, for example, in the conceptual confusion surrounding the terms used to describe employer-employee bodies and employee-only bodies. In this study, we use the abbreviation 'EWC' to refer to the employee side, irrespective of whether this is part of a body or the entire body. This corresponds with the conceptual approach used in the Annex to the EWC Directive.

The project has three main objectives. *Firstly,* it sets out to offer a qualitative investigation into the ensemble of processes of communication and interaction which condition and influence the constitution and shape of EWCs through a systematic, case-study based analysis of the 'subjective' factor of the interests, motives, expectations and perceptions of the actors involved and of the conditions of and barriers to socio-cultural interaction which characterise the realities of the operation of EWCs. *Secondly* it seeks to remedy the lack of a transnational and comparative approach directed at the 'objective' - that is, structural - framework conditions and parameters set by national systems of workplace industrial relations. And *thirdly,* it aims to redress the lack of any approach which links these internal factors and their national foundations with those external parameters set by the specific forms of economic integration and political regulation which occur within and via the framework of the European Union.

Finally, the object of the research - the EWC - demands a linking of, or at the least a degree of cross-fertilisation between, a variety of academic disciplines (law, sociology, economics, political science) and the integration of a number of different relevant research fields, in particular comparative research into industrial relations and processes of European integration. However, meeting the demands of such an interdisciplinary approach through an integrated research programme is inevitably a challenging undertaking. Nonetheless, the diversity of disciplinary backgrounds of the members of our research team did allow us to move towards this goal, if no more than in the context of our internal discussions. And the design of the research and the interpretation of the results represented at least an attempt to link these various disciplines with the aim of extending the current frontier of empirical research and analysis and widening the range of possible theoretical explanation.

In adopting a simultaneously national and company comparative approach, this study consciously follows the strategy pursued by the qualitative studies carried out in the early-1990s, with the added aim of meeting the objectives set out above. In all, eight undertakings – in each case a parent company and a subsidiary – in the metalworking and chemical industries in four EU member states were examined.

Table 1.1 Companies in the study by country and branch

Branch	Undertaking	Location of registered HQ	Location of subsidiary
Chemicals	ENI	Italy	France
	Hoechst	Germany	Italy
	ICI	UK	Italy
	Rhône Poulenc	France	UK
Metalworking	Bull	France	Germany
	GKN	UK	Germany
	Merloni	Italy	UK
	Schmalbach-Lubeca	Germany	France

This both corporate and nationally comparative dimension also defines the potentially creative character of the study. The dual focus locates the empirical material and its evaluation at the intersection between three key areas of research into EWCs.

• The field of 'national industrial relations systems and EWCs' encompasses an investigation into the specific prerequisites, problems and probable consequences of the establishment of EWCs in the four selected countries (compatibility research).

• The field of the development of transnational industrial relations embraces an analysis and assessment of the relationship of EWCs to each other and to central managements at European level and their likely influence on the Europeanisation of industrial relations (Europeanisation theory).

• Finally, generalising the results of the case-studies offers some empirically-based pointers to 'best practice' in the setting up and operation of EWCs -

which must now be established across-the-board in line with the requirements of the Directive (implementation research).

The choice of countries – France, Germany, Italy and the United Kingdom – was determined by the overall research strategy. The selection not only embraced the four largest members of the European Union, with comparable levels of economic development and performance, but also encompassed four countries whose national systems of industrial relations are representative of the spectrum of systems found in Europe, both in their variation and the specific configuration of their variables. For example: trade union pluralism vs. (limited) principle of a single trade union confederation; diversity of representative institutions at workplace level vs. representation via a single institution (such as German works councils); diverse structures of representation at group level; highly juridified vs. voluntaristic systems; traditionally conflictual vs. consensus-based systems; and finally dualist vs. monistic systems.

Moreover, the earliest and longest experience in the operation of European information committees has been gained in German and in particular in French transnational companies. At the same time, the development of EWCs in the UK in the context of the 'opt out' from the Maastricht Treaty's Agreement on Social Policy is instructive in other respects. The specific theoretical premises underlying this comparative approach, together with the categories and questions specific to EWCs, are set out in Part III below.

In addition to the criteria of country of origin and industrial branch, the choice of companies for the study was primarily guided by the criterion of the date at which the European information and consultation body was first established. The sample focuses on and is restricted to companies in which bodies were established at a sufficiently early point in time to allow for an analysis both of the origins and evolution of the institution.

The process of the constitution and development of EWCs encompasses around a decade from the first voluntarily agreed information committees in the mid-1980s to the transposition of the EWC Directive. This period also demarcates the boundaries of this study. Over this period, the origins and development of this new institution of workplace industrial relations were also subject to a variety of economic, political and social factors, acting individually and in combination, and all subject to shifting patterns of feedback and interaction.

The developmental process of EWCs is divided into and analysed on the basis of three main phases:

1)   The 'pioneer' phase of voluntarily agreed EWCs embraces the period from the mid-1980s up until the adoption of the EWC Directive in September 1994. It can be sub-divided into two periods: the first, from the mid- to late-1980s, in which the initial pilot projects were agreed and established; and a second, from 1990 to 1994, which can be designated as the phase in which voluntary EWC agreements were concluded against the background of material and institutional EU support. The processes of negotiation and the establishment of voluntary EWCs have been described as negotiation 'in the shadow of the law'.[1]

2)   The phase between September 1994 and September 1996, when the Directive was adopted and transposed, might be described as the phase of 'Directive-driven voluntary agreements' (that is, those concluded under Article 13 of the Directive).

3)   September 1996 marks the beginning of the final phase of the mandatory establishment of EWCs (under Article 6 of the Directive) – a phase which will continue at least until September 1999 (the date set for reviewing the operation of the Directive).

The choice of case-studies accords with this periodisation of developments. The Bull Information Committee was one of the pilot projects established in the early stages of the 'pioneer phase'. The first meetings at Rhône-Poulenc also took place during this stage; however, a formal agreement was only concluded once the Directive was imminent. In the case of the German companies Hoechst and Schmalbach-Lubeca, information committees were set up in the second stage of the 'pioneer phase' and were further developed and sealed by a written agreement during the period of 'negotiation in the shadow of the law'. At Merloni a decision was made to set up an EWC at the end of the 'pioneer phase' within the framework of a company-level agreement: however, the constitutive meeting did not take place until three years later, shortly before the Directive was adopted. Developments at the two British companies ICI and GKN, where voluntary agreements were agreed despite the 'opt out', and at ENI took place during the period of the 'Directive-driven' establishment of EWCs. To some degree, the date at which institutions were established reflects the general drift of EWCs on a country-by-country and branch basis: first France, then Germany, and then other European countries, and first metalworking followed by chemicals.

Table 1.2   Order of developments at case-study undertakings

Company	Preliminary developments since:	Constitutive meeting:
Bull	mid-1980s	1988
Rhône-Poulenc	1990	1990
Hoechst	1990	1991
Schmalbach-Lubeca	1991	1992
ICI	1990	1995
ENI	1994/5	1995
GKN	1990	1996
Merloni	1993	1996

Such a diachronic perspective within a period of observation extending over a decade does, however, make comparison more difficult because of the overlap of internal and external events. For this reason, we sought to capture the interactions between the internal factors shaping the constitution of EWCs and the changing external environment, with the aim of arriving at some generalisable propositions as to the logic of constitution and the dynamics of development of this new institution in transnational industrial relations.

The focus of the empirical study is on the four dimensions of communication and interaction which determine the development, character and efficacy of EWCs and in turn also affect each other. These are:

- those internal to EWCs (formal and informal co-operation between EWC members),

- EWCs and management,

- EWCs and national structures of employee representation,

- EWCs and trade unions.

The theoretical assumptions which underpin this approach are set out in Chapter 8 below. The research took place in two successive stages. In the first, formal and quantitative data was collected on each EWC using questionnaires together with secondary data on the companies, their structures and strategies. This created the basis for a second stage in which the relevant actors were interviewed. These included: EWC representatives (parent company and subsidiary); representatives of management; representatives of national trade unions and employers associations, and the corresponding European trade union federations – using an interview schedule tailored to each interviewee, with the interview conducted in the interviewee's mother tongue.

Research teams were set up on a country basis, consisting of a project supervisor and a German project worker together with a corresponding local national specialist whose linguistic competence and academic and policy experience within each national system guaranteed a high degree of reliability as far as the qualitative data and interpretation of the perception of the actors was concerned.

This systematic and comparative data was supplemented by interviews with the representatives of national and European employer associations, the European Parliament and the EU Commission together with a Brussels-based management consultancy: the views and assessments of all these actors were incorporated in our overall interpretation. In all, some 80 interviews were carried out between December 1996 and April 1997: the list of companies and organisations at which interviews were held is set out in the Appendix.

This research formed the basis for the preparation of initial results which were presented at a three-day conference seminar held in Brussels in May 1997, with the participation of representatives of the EWCs in the study and of the European trade union federations. Following this further additional empirical work was undertaken and theoretical refinements added to the final report.

Note

1. Based on a quantitative evaluation of voluntary agreements concluded up until 1995 Rivest (1996, pp. 236f) arrives at a different periodisation. Phase 1: 1985-1989 the 'pioneer phase' (with four agreements in France and one in Sweden). Phase 2: 1990-1992, in which the expectation of a Directive led to some four agreements a year being concluded (in all four in Germany, seven in France, one in Switzerland). Phase 3: 1993-95, in which the number of agreements rises significantly (42).

PART II:
THE CONTEXT FOR THE DEVELOPMENT OF EUROPEAN WORKS COUNCILS

2 Political Europeanisation - Economic Globalisation?

Between Globalisation and Regionalisation - on the Political and Economic Structure of Transnational Social Formation[1]

The establishment of cross-border structures of representation in European companies touches on a number of questions which transcend the scope of the individual undertaking. The reason is that the emergence of functioning and strong EWC structures also poses the question as to how transnational structures of industrial relations and the social dimension of the European Union might develop. Although in a purely legal sense, EWCs are inconceivable without the institutions of the EU, they are also closely bound up with these institutions in practice via the social dimension to economic integration, understood here as the manifestation of an, at least, partial recognition of employee rights. And because EWCs are simultaneously an expression of increasing political and economic globalisation, this also raises the question of the possible impact of globalisation on the future shape of national and supra-national frameworks of action.

The social effects and political consequences of globalisation continue to be disputed. Three – to some extent overlapping – positions can be identified. The first does not view globalisation as novel. Measured in terms of world trade and direct investment, it sees no recent qualitative leap, noting that a comparable degree of economic integration was already evident before the First World War (Roth, 1984). Consequently, globalisation should be seen primarily as an overemphasising of familiar processes of internationalisation which neither seriously weaken the regulatory capacity of the nation-state nor exert distinctive or wholly new pressures on the welfare state. On this view, the globalisation thesis principally occupies an ideological role within national debates on international competitiveness (Küchle, 1996). Moreover, social conflicts continue to be located in a national political framework, albeit one which is no longer closed but subject to growing interdependence (Armingeon, 1996; Elsenhans, 1996).

A second position, which accepts the quantitative arguments for globalisation, does not see this as representing any universalisation of the capitalist world-economy but rather – via regionalisation – has identified a growth of trade and investment which is concentrated within the Triad of North America, East Asia and Europe (Zürn, 1996; Weidenfeld/Turek, 1996; Huffschmid, 1994). This newly-configured geo-economy is characterised by intensified competition and interstate rivalry (Luttwak, 1994). What is required, on this view, is the development of a sufficiently robust system of regulation at regional and inter-regional level to re-anchor a 'debordered' capitalism either within civil society and/or structures which stabilise existing patterns of governance. Problems previously resolvable within national frameworks must now be tackled at regional or international level. Although the nation-state remains a key political arena, it is not the only one. In Europe, for example, it is being complemented by the growing range of powers of the European Union.

In contrast, a third position, influenced by the regulation school, emphasises the transformational power of globalisation (Altvater/Mahnkopf, 1996; Hirsch, 1995; Jessop, 1992). The remoulding of production (the end of Taylorism, systemic rationalisation), of the regime of accumulation and mode of regulation (crisis of Fordism and transition to post-Fordism) and of the international division of labour (global value-creating chains) is not matched by any corresponding globalisation of politics. Rather, the power and capacities of the state (including the European Union) are being squeezed between global competition and the locality (Altvater/Mahnkopf, 1996; Junne, 1996). The dislodging of economic processes from their social and political linkages – previously mediated via the nation-state – corresponds to the construction of new links in the form of local networks for the establishment of productivity pacts. The state is losing its authority over territorial space and is undergoing a transformation from the traditional, Keynesian nation-state into a national, neo-liberal 'competition state'. The disjuncture between economic globalisation and political regulation means that economic competition on the world market is being translated into a competition between individual locations, with competition between locations translated, in turn, into political competition between states. And since international or macro-regional regulatory instances exist only in an embryonic form, politics continues to be tied primarily to the nation-state (more optimistically in relation to the EU, see Jessop, 1992).

From Nation State to Multi-Tiered System of Governance

In the post-war Keynesian state, industrial relations were embedded in a network of social rights and safety nets. Moreover, by setting rules and arbitrating conflicts the state was able to reconcile the income interests of wage earners and the valorisation interests of companies. In the wake of globalisation, this reconciliation has been shattered by the transformation of the state and of established patterns of industrial relations. This process of transformation took varying forms. In addition to the 'competition state' – 'Wettbewerbsstaat' (Hirsch, 1994) or 'Konkurrenzstaat' (Narr/Schubert, 1994) – there was also the neo-liberal 'nightwatchman state' (Wilke, 1992) which largely withdrew from the task of regulating the conditions of competition to exercising a supervisory role. What all these analyses share is their identification of a loss of state autonomy and sovereignty in the fields of monetary, finance, and economic policy which, in conjunction with the renaissance of neo-liberal supply-side policies in the 1970s and 1980s, has led to a decline in the social-welfare component of the state's activity.

The dismantling of external economic borders in the wake of globalisation has been accompanied by growing domestic social fragmentation. The gulf has widened between 'private affluence and public squalor', between incomes drawn from the ownership of capital and from waged employment, and between the winners and losers from modernisation. Social polarisation has brought about a recommodification of labour-power (Neyer/Kaiser 1995), which becomes exposed to the pressures of a Schumpeterian 'performance state' (Jessop, 1992). The welfare state is subordinated and finally sacrificed to world market competition as social policy becomes perceived solely as a cost factor (Koch 1995).

In contrast, there is an alternative perspective which sees the welfare state as a necessary prerequisite for globalisation. Only through the social cushioning of world market competition via state guaranteed and mediated mechanisms to secure incomes can national economies truly be opened up. Accordingly, the dichotomy between global economy and national statehood is qualified through a structural similarity in the welfare states of those countries most deeply integrated into the world economy. Efforts to counterpose the exigencies and functional requirements of globalisation and those of the welfare state are, of necessity, condemned to fail and will merely provoke new forms of protectionsim and mercantilism (Leibfried/Rieger 1995). Instead, tackling the problems of social inequality must be tied to the establishment of competitiveness in a global economy as a precondition for a social welfare state. The example of the EU represents one appropriate regional framework for a new synthesis of economic prosperity and social security.

Although the process of European integration has limited the sovereignty and autonomy, and hence the national scope for autonomous action, of national states through a transfer of powers to the institutions of the European Union, it has not eliminated it entirely. National governments continue to set the direction and scope of the powers which are to be exercised at European level by the institutional actors – and in particular by the European Commission in the first pillar of the EU, the European Communities. However, the growing political power of the EU not only feeds back on to the political institutions and decisions of the Member States but is leading to a transformation of statehood into a comprehensive multi-tier system embracing regional, national and supra-national levels (Jachtenfuchs/Kohler-Koch, 1996). During the 1990s, this change in the character of statehood (Héritier et.al, 1994) has increasingly embraced the social policy and social regulative dimensions of national-state policy and been expressed in a shift in powers in the field of social policy from the national to the supra-national level, although it has not been able to put in question the predominance of the Single Market and EMU projects, and their associated objectives of deregulation and increased flexibility.

The Neo-Liberal Mode of Integration and the Social Dimension

The dominance of neo-liberalism in the EU has found expression in the establishment of the Single Market and the programme for Economic and Monetary Union (EMU). Social measures to parallel the development of the market have, as yet, not gone beyond limited and selected EU initiatives in the field of social, employment and labour market policy. The dynamics of the social dimension have lagged behind those of economic globalisation. As a consequence, the growing power of transnational undertakings in the EU in relation to national states can continue to reproduce itself institutionally largely uninterrupted. And whereas the differing interests of national states, based on the associated distributional effects of these processes, act to block the development of a European social policy, the diminished regulatory capacity of the state means that nationally-oriented trade union activity is also losing effectiveness. One conclusion drawn from this is that what is emerging at European level is a 'neo-voluntarist' framework rooted in 'soft' modes of regulation which ultimately serve to stabilise neo-liberal policies (Streeck/Vitols, 1993).

The view that the social dimension is essentially a stabiliser for neo-liberal policies is countered by the argument that social policy interventions at European level have created structures through which national welfare states have become parts of a larger multi-level social policy system. As such, welfare states are no longer sovereign nation states in the classical sense. And the EU's social dimension is not a corrective to the market but rather an element in the extension of the internal market. Social policy is not the expression of a protective reaction to the extension of the market but is part of the development of the internal market (Leibfried/Pierson, 1995, 1997). As a result, it seems entirely consistent for the EU Commission to pursue a policy of Europeanising interest associations as actors in the social dimension (Kohler-Koch, 1996; Martin, 1996; Platzer, 1991).

Admittedly, the extension of the EU's welfare state structures and capacities, effected through the transfer of regulatory powers in the various Treaty revisions and the shaping of areas of social policy through the provision of resources and procedures, is still in its infancy. Set against the economic processes observable at Community level, the trailing development of the social dimension represents the 'undefended flank' of EU integration (Leibfried, 1996). It is a manifestation of the EU's endemic inability to offer a positive, market-correcting form of integration as a counterweight to the prevalent negative, market-liberalising form of integration. Social policy – including labour-market and employment policy – constitutes one of the few virtually intact bastions of national sovereignty, and for this reason alone national governments will do all they can to cling onto it (Majone, 1996). However, an even stronger force than the resistance of Member States to a transfer of social policy powers is the hope that the benefits of deeper economic integration via the Single Market and EMU will induce social progress in a quasi-automatic fashion. In reality, the conflicts over the EU's social dimension, which range from employee participation in enterprises to employment policy, are evidence that economic interdependence and the growing weight of social problems are leading Member States to look for supra-national procedures for co-operation and concertation.

Social Regulation in the European Social Model

Compared with the USA, Japan, or East Asia, Europe possesses a distinctive European social model (Albert, 1993). Western European societies have converged a good deal in the post-war period, although not initially in the field of industrial relations (Kaelbe, 1987). However, during the 1980s – prompted by the emergence of similar social problems and promoted by the Single Market programme – Western Europe's trade unions have exhibited a growing degree of willingness to pursue co-operation and concertation (Platzer, 1991; Deppe/Weiner, 1991). This development has corresponded with a convergence of national practices in the field of industrial relations (Lecher, 1992; Fulton,

1996). On the other hand, the persistence of distinctive national paths of development has meant that the transition from Fordist to post-Fordist capitalism has taken widely differing forms (Kastendiek, 1990), each with its own specific impact on the scope and capacities of national trade unions.

A glance at the development of the EU's Member States reveals the extent of these differences over the past two decades. For example, whereas the UK has undergone a radical programme of deregulation, this trend has been less marked in Germany. And while the statutory framework for trade union representation has been strengthened in France and Italy, this legal advance has been accompanied by a liberalisation of the labour market, an increase in working time flexibility which has undermined the concept of the 'normal working day', a decentralisation of collective bargaining and losses in union membership (Crouch, 1995, 1993). Hence, a second glance might show that there are indeed a number of fundamental basic common processes at work in all the Member States: deregulation at the level of the state, decentralisation of collective bargaining, and greater flexibility in corporate organisation. But because these developments are associated with a new degree of diversity at national level, this development could be interpreted as implying greater heterogeneity in industrial relations (Flecker/Schulten, 1996).

The EU's social dimension – built around the Social Fund, Social Action Programme, mandatory minimum standards and the Social Dialogue – is scarcely in a position to offset the effects of these fundamental national and transnational processes of deregulation, decentralisation and flexibilisation, especially as it was initially merely intended to legitimate 'negative' market integration. Moreover, the growing displacement of the principle of solidarity by the doctrine of subsidiarity does not offer a propitious terrain for social initiatives at European level. In addition, the development of relations between the social partners at European level continues to lag behind political integration, with no legal and institutional foundation for the construction of a system of European collective bargaining.

Although the employment and social policy dimension of the EU may, provisionally, be no more than the political and institutional expression of efforts to cushion the impact of the dramatic changes in the economic and political environment, and hence still some way off being a truly social and democratic 'European social model', the dynamic of social integration does conceal a potentially transcendent moment: the more that social conflicts go beyond the national framework – either in terms of the issues or directly geographically – the stronger will be the pressure on the institutional actors at European level to redefine their problem-solving competences and extend their problem-solving capacity. Against this background, the new dynamic injected into European industrial relations and the EU's social dimension by the adoption of the EWC Directive can be viewed as a clear sign of forward movement (Keller 1996a; 1997). Under the pressure of globalisation and regionalisation, the social actors and EWCs have been given an arena in which conflicts over the shape of the social dimension can now be acted out.

Note

1. *Vergesellschaftung*: the formation of societies, social forms and social intercourse, literally translatable as 'societalisation' or 'sociation'. See *The Sociology of Georg Simmel* (Glencoe, 1950), trans. Kurt H. Wolff.

3 The Transformation of Corporate Strategies

The process of the internationalisation of business has been judged very differently, depending on the viewpoint of the observer. This section does not set out to add to these judgements, but rather to look at the internationalisation of corporate activities on the premise that transformations in the internationalisation strategies of companies are likely to have an impact on European Works Councils.

One initial observation in this context is that most large European companies and groups carry out the vast bulk of their activities and transact the majority of their cross-border trade within Europe. More than two-thirds of their investment is carried out in Europe. There are, however, good reasons to suppose that this European variant of globalisation is a temporary phenomenon and will weaken as companies grow – that is, the European market will eventually prove to be too small (Dörre 1996). The main reason for the continuing overwhelming focus of European companies on Europe is their adaptation to the creation of a large domestic market. The intensification of competition which this gives rise to offers long-run survival only for those companies which can grow beyond the European economic zone. Nonetheless, the European market remains a very large one and will continue to exercise a powerful force, tying European businesses to Europe – given the importance of market proximity in location decisions. Some 85 per cent of global production continues to be sold on domestic markets (Burchard 1997).

In addition to the economic orientation of European businesses towards Europe, corporate cultures are also being Europeanised. Many companies are seeking to establish unified human resource approaches for each of the three regions of the Triad, irrespective of any overarching global business strategy, with the aim of lowering transaction costs. For management, EWCs have a value in this context because they favour the alignment of European HR policies.

From an economic standpoint, the principal agents of internationalisation are multinational corporations[1] which extend their business activities beyond national borders with the aim of boosting profitability. The cost advantages which accrue to the pioneers then force other companies to follow suit. Neo-

20

classical economics views this entirely positively – with the rider that the free movement of goods and capital is not a zero-sum game. An increase in the international division of labour allows national comparative advantages to be deployed, producing a competitive situation which leads to a more efficient use of resources. The result is an increase the supply of goods and services and hence a rise in incomes and wealth.[2] According to neo-classical theory, factors of production will, under ideal conditions, continue to be shifted abroad until the marginal productivity of factors of production in foreign and domestic sites are equal. This leads to a deployment of factors of production which maximises (global) economic welfare. What this approach overlooks is the possibility of disparities of power between the factors of production. For example, the dismantling of trade barriers allows capital to become more mobile than labour, lowering the cost of the export of capital and shifting power in favour of capital. This power allows the owners of capital to realise increases in productivity through changes in the institutional framework.[3]

Seen against the background, one might ask whether EWCs can develop at all in an environment characterised by cuts in and relocations of production. Although the discussion of a few years ago was dominated by fears that, as far as the developed nations of Western Europe were concerned, internationalisation would mean a rundown of existing sites in favour of low-wage countries, more recent literature has come to the view that the relocations of production occasioned by globalisation are only partly the outcome of lower wages and deregulated labour markets.[4] For example, the study by Wortmann and Dörrenbacher (1997) has shown that direct investment by German companies is only associated with a export of jobs in a small number of cases. This also broadly applies to other European countries. The main reason for setting up production facilities abroad continues to be the desire for market proximity. However, this argument needs to be qualified by the observation that even if direct investment abroad is not associated with relocations of production, it may imply a reduction in investment at the domestic site, leading to rationalisation and job cuts. The argument that wage costs are of secondary importance in most branches in determining whether production should be carried out abroad is also bolstered by the fact that one key motive behind globalisation is the desire to take advantage of increasing returns to scale, both in marketing and production. However, the key element in cutting unit costs in most capital-intensive areas of manufacturing is fixed cost: labour remains essentially a variable cost.[5]

Hence, the image of the 'footloose enterprise', ready at any time to shift production to a new site if this will lower costs, is only rarely encountered in reality. Most internationally operating companies continue to carry out the bulk of their value-added in their home countries or regions. This is often underpinned by strategic alliances in the political and scientific sub-systems rooted in common cultural orientations and much lower opportunity costs.[6]

What is critical, however, for the influence of global companies on workplace representatives and national politics is less how mobile companies actually are than their potential for mobility.[7] The mere threat of relocation is often sufficient to induce employee representatives, as well as political decision-makers, to be more responsive to employer demands for more overtime working, pay cuts and a lowering of social standards. This is evidently a key area for EWC activity, as exchanges of information between employe representatives at European level could allow a more realistic assessment of the plausibility of such threats.

Irrespective of any assessment of the effects of the internationalisation of production, changes in the strategic orientation of companies will have a direct impact on industrial relations, and through this on EWCs. A change in the reactions to globalisation can be seen in the following behavioural changes in transnationally active companies and their managements.

One new variant of globalisation discernible since the early-1990s, and attributable to the acceleration in the pace of change in the economic environment, is the increase in internationalisation via foreign acquisition. One reason for this is the faster rate of change in the economic environment, leading to a higher valuation being put on the opportunity costs of the time entailed in setting up a new plant abroad than on the acquisition costs of an existing business. At the same time, globally active companies also pursue market leadership in each of their business streams. The acquisition of plants abroad can serve both to open up a new markets and simultaneously eliminate a potential competitor. EWCs can be useful for corporate managements in such circumstances as foreign acquisitions usually create particular problems of integrating acquired businesses which are not encountered when setting up a company from scratch. Acquisition means not only taking over physical assets but also changing a corporate culture. Existing structures are broken up, leading to uncertainty on the part of national managements and employees. In such a situation, an EWC might offer some additional options for integrating the acquired business into a unitary corporate strategy.

Whereas corporate growth in the 1970s and 1980s was characterised by a marked diversification of activities (horizontal integration), since the early-1990s companies have been seeking to re-focus on their core businesses, retain fields in which they can exercise market leadership and dispose of the rest. One factor behind this development is the rising cost of research and development which is unsustainable across a large number of fields. The shortening of product life-cycles is also adding to the pressures to concentrate on core businesses. Reducing uncertainty is also important: focus on core businesses leads to an increase in productivity and opens up possibilities for rationalisation. This transformation in the profile of companies also has an impact on EWCs. Restructuring often pitches companies into a permanent revolution, with waves of acquisitions and disposals of business streams and divisions. This leads to constant change in the composition of the EWC, making it more difficult to establish a steady and effective pattern of operation.

The growing importance of conglomerates and holding companies is also having an effect on EWCs. The problem for EWCs is that the Directive only envisages them being established at one level in the organisation. This leads to the dilemma of having to decide on and negotiate over which level this should be. Installing an EWC at the level of a holding company offers the benefit of access to the most senior levels of management, with the associated advantage of enabling EWC representatives to gain access to information on group strategy as a whole. However, in most cases, locating an EWC at holding company level creates additional heterogeneity – that is, on top of 'normal' national heterogeneity. Seeking to embrace the differing interests of different businesses can diminish the effectiveness of the EWC. However, if – in contrast to the model envisaged by the Directive – the EWC is installed at business or divisional level, the interests represented on it will be more homogeneous, but direct contact to top group management will be lost. This can become especially problematic if employee representatives from the parent company's national base are unable to establish contact with group management through their own national structures, as is typically the case in the UK.

The prospects for EWCs also depend on the group's overall strategy. Medium-sized undertakings, which have a reached a scale which requires them to have an EWC but which remain strongly regionalised or tied to one principal national location, often pursue a 'national' strategy of internationalisation characterised by a concentration on the activities of the parent company. Communication usually takes place in the form of instructions and directives which travel from the parent to the subsidiaries, and in which 'head office' procedures, practices and organisation are transferred to the subsidiaries. The strategy is characterised by a low level of differentiation and integration. Headquarters' managerial practices are often transferred to subsidiaries through the assignment of parent company managers to local businesses. Foreign subsidiaries are not linked horizontally to any great degree and remain highly dependent on corporate headquarters. The consequence of this strategy for

EWCs is that the strong position of the corporate headquarters and its ties to the home country base carry with them the problem of 'nationalisation' - that is, the domination of the EWC by the industrial relations practices of the parent company. In such circumstances, employee representatives from the foreign subsidiaries have a particularly strong interest in the EWC. What is doubtful, however, is whether they can prevail over the lack of interest on the part of employee representatives from the parent company's headquarters who usually dominate EWCs where such national strategies are being implemented.

Another form of internationalisation is built around a country-specific strategy. This is characterised by a low degree of integration and a high degree of differentiation, and builds on the recognition that the unknown environment of another nation-state requires particular care and attention. The driving force is usually the desire for market access. Country-specific oriented companies seek to give their foreign subsidiaries an image which will enable it to be accepted as a domestic firm, enlisting the knowledge and experience of local managers. Group HQ seeks to optimise each individual national strategy – usually without any particular effort to align them within an overall strategy. That is, there is no integrated strategy for the group as a whole, management is decentralised and there is a low level of linkage between the individual companies in the group. This offers a more favourable terrain for the EWC. Foreign production facilities are directed at serving nationally or regionally limited markets and the individual sites are not technically linked or part of the same supply chain. The consequence is that there is usually no competition between different national sites. The dominance of the parent company is not so great that the EWC is at risk of being 'nationalised'. Moreover, further internationalisation of the group is likely to take the form of a shift from a multinational to a global strategy. The EWC can use this phase to establish communications and high-trust relationships between its members which will facilitate 'efficient' EWC activity in the event of corporate restructuring.

Such transitions from a country-specific strategy to the integration of groups' subsidiaries into a group global strategy can be observed. This approach aims to draw together the national perspective of the parent company on the one hand and the multinational focus on local integration of subsidiaries on the other, to produce a global strategy leading to greater efficiency on the world market for the group as a whole. A global strategy is intended to reflect both the overarching aims of the group and the local objectives of the subsidiaries. This leads to a management of information in which the flow not only runs from parent to subsidiary but also includes intensive communication between individual subsidiaries. These subsidiaries are closely linked – in part through supply chains and in part as competitors. In the literature, the transition to globally-integrated networks can be read off by the fact that there is no longer any clearly discernible corporate headquarters (Flecker, 1996). Such strategies are characterised by the following:

1) The ranking of the individual corporate units in the group is no longer the same on all dimensions.
2) Rankings can change over time.
3) Management is not only vertically but also horizontally integrated.
4) Cohesion is primarily achieved through normative integration.

However, a countervailing trend is also observable in which the integration of foreign subsidiaries into a global strategy takes place via an increase in central control, with a growing dependence of the subsidiaries on the centre. This development is favoured by technical progress in communications which allows central control even where business units are highly dispersed. In this context, the EWC takes on an additional significance. The transition from a decentralised to centralised structure leads to a weakening of national information and codetermination rights. National managements are not informed about group strategy, and as a consequence cannot inform employee representatives about it. Moreover, where conflicts arise, national managements can point to their own inability to resolve problems. The EWC offers a possibility for obtaining important information about group strategy, and also offers some benefits to group management. Because the pursuit of a global strategy via a centralised approach requires a high degree of control, the EWC can be used by central management as a second tier of control, giving it access to unfiltered information about the situation at local level.

Overall, both national employee representatives and central managements can draw advantages from the existence of an EWC. This creates favourable preconditions for establishing EWCs as a European employee representative body.

Notes

1. See the position taken by Dörre et.al. 1997 which refers to 'key undertakings' in this context.
2. Cf. Simons, 1997. The positive effects of globalisation have also been emphasised by the EU's Economic and Social Committee (Economic and Social Committee, 1997).
3. See North, 1992.

4. See, for example, Härtel et.al., 1996.
5. For example, Müller 1997 (p. 34), referring to Kenichi Ohmae, designates fixed costs as a driving force behind globalisation because of efforts to spread them over as broad a market base as possible.
6. Hirsch-Kreinsen (1997, p. 489) refers to the barriers to the internationalisation of companies. These raise considerable doubts as to whether 'footloose' companies can emerge at all. As barriers he cites high managerial and organisational costs and effort, organisational limits to internationalisation and resistance, which should not be underestimated, to international linkages and ties by national managements and employee representatives.
7. See too Dörre (1996, p. 22) who notes that employee representatives frequently cannot assess whether there any is any reality to the threat of a relocation.

4 The Legal Context for European Works Councils: The Directive and its Precursors

Legal and Practical Problems in the Establishment of EWCs

The EEC Treaty (the Treaty of Rome) contained a number of provisions and powers in the employment and social policy field which pre-date the social measures of the Maastricht Treaties. As well as the basic provision on 'close co-operation... in the social field' in Article 118, Articles 48ff established freedom of movement for workers as one of the four market freedoms, Article 119 provided for equal pay between men and women, Article 123 established the European Social Fund, and Article 128 provided for the setting out of basic principles in vocational training. The 1987 Single European Act (SEA) introduced a number of changes: Article 118a allowed measures to improve the working environment to be adopted by a qualified majority on the Council of Ministers, and Article 118b provided for social dialogue at European level.

Although the Maastricht Treaty (Treaty on European Union, TEU) extended these competencies, the UK government excluded itself initially through the 'opt out' provided for in the Social Protocol. As a consequence, the measures adopted under the Agreement on Social Policy only applied to 11 of the 12 member states (or 14 out of the 15 once Austria, Finland and Sweden joined the EU in 1994). According to Articles 1 and 2 of the Agreement on Social Policy, the Council decides in accordance with the 'co-operation procedure' (Article 189c, SEA) and by qualified majority, provided the European Parliament does not withhold agreement, in the following areas (Article 2.1):

- improvement in particular of the working environment to protect workers' health and safety;
- working conditions;
- the information and consultation of workers;
- equality between men and women with regard to labour market opportunities and treatment at work;

- the integration of persons excluded from the labour market, without prejudice to Article 127 of the Treaty establishing the European Community.

In contrast, unanimity is required on the following (Articles 2:3 and 6):

- social security and social protection of workers;
- protection of workers where their employment contract is terminated;
- representation and collective defence of the interests of workers and employers, including co-determination:... this Article shall not apply to pay, the right of association, the right to strike or the right to impose lock-outs;
- conditions of employment for third country nationals legally residing in Community territory;
- financial contributions for the promotion of employment and job creation, without prejudice to the provisions relating to the Social Fund.

The initial condition for the adoption of the EWC Directive was, therefore, the possibility under the Maastricht Treaty of adopting measures with qualified majority, and without the UK, on employee information and consultation in contrast to the unanimity required for measures on co-determination.

Prior to the May 1997 UK General Election, the Labour opposition pledged itself to abandon the Conservatives' antagonism to the Agreement on Social Policy, and at the June 1997 Intergovernmental Conference the newly-elected Labour government stated that it would end the opt-out, allowing the Agreement's provisions to be integrated into the body of the new Treaty of Amsterdam. Pending ratification of the Amsterdam Treaty by national legislatures, steps were taken to allow EWC agreements to be concluded which could include UK employers and employee representatives through the adoption of a 'mini' extension Directive on 15 December 1997. For those undertakings and groups which only fall within the scope of the Directive because of the inclusion of their UK workforces, a new transitional period is allowed along the lines of Article 13 of the Directive. Member States must make some adjustments to their own transposing legislation in order to facilitate the inclusion of British parts of their national undertakings, with their workforces.

The Directive on Collective Redundancies as a Precursor of the EWC Directive

In 1975 the European Community adopted the Directive on the Approximation of the Laws of the Member States relating to Collective Redundancies

(75/129/EEC). This can be seen as a forerunner to the EWC Directive in a number of respects. It is based on Article 100 of the EEC Treaty and merely provides for a minimum level of procedural protection. Improvements are possible by means of national legislation or collective agreement. The Directive creates two procedural safeguards. Prior to any collective economic dismissal (UK: 'redundancy'), employee representatives must be consulted.[1] Collective redundancies must be notified to the appropriate authorities and can only be implemented in general 30 days after such notification has taken place.

The concept of a 'collective redundancy' is set out in Article 1 of the Directive. For example, a collective dismissal would be deemed to be taking place where, in any establishment with at least 500 employees, at least 30 employees are to be dismissed on economic grounds within a period of 30 calendar days. According to the case-law developed by the German Federal Labour Court, this would also be sufficient to be considered an 'alteration' in the running of an establishment sufficient to trigger the co-determination and consultation rights of works councils in Germany, which can entail the agreement of a social compensation plan *(Sozialplan)* with the employer.

In 1992 the Directive was amended in a number of respects (92/56/EEC). For example, individual terminations together with voluntary terminations at the employer's instigation were brought under the definition and within the threshold of the Directive. The content of information and consultation was also more precisely defined. In particular, connections between companies were dealt with such that subsidiaries which carry out dismissals can no longer hide behind the fact that they have not been sufficiently informed by the parent company.

The Directive on the Establishment of European Works Councils

The earliest deliberations on European Works Councils, which were based very much on the German model of employee representation, date back to the draft for a regulation on a European Company Statute in 1970 - a proposal which has still not been implemented, despite numerous reworkings and attempts at political compromise. The Commission made a second attempt in 1980 with a proposal for a Directive on employee information and consultation in undertakings with complex, and in particular transnational, structures. The draft Directive, named after the responsible Commissioner – Vredeling – was rejected by companies and employers' associations from the outset. The third attempt, which ultimately succeeded, came in 1990 with the draft EWC Directive. The proposal, which like Vredeling was confined to information and consultation rights, was to have an eventful destiny. In view of the opposition of the then UK government, there was no prospect of obtaining the unanimity required under Article 100a: Para 2 of the Single European Act.[2] Following the agreement of the Social Protocol to the Maastricht Treaty, the Commission was soon able to press ahead. In the first instance, efforts to negotiate an agreement on the proposal between the social partners came to nothing. After consultation with the Economic and Social Committee and the European Parliament, the Council moved to a common position on 18 July 1994, subsequently largely ignoring the changes called for by the Parliament. The outcome was EC Directive 94/45/EC, 22 September 1994, on the establishment of a European Works Council or a procedure in Community-scale undertakings and Community-scale groups of undertakings for the purposes of informing and consulting employees. Article 14, Para. 1 required Member States to transpose the Directive into national law by 22 September 1996.

One key factor behind the success of the proposal was a 'paradigm shift' (Höland, 1997, pp. 60, 67ff) in relation to the Vredeling draft. The EWC Directive is not a highly prescriptive instrument, and allows considerable scope for negotiated solutions. Its key points are as follows. It covers undertakings and groups of undertakings with at least 1,000 employees and with at least 150 in two Member States (including EEA members). In essence, it sets out a procedure for establishing the consultative body, the European Works Council. Since employment law differs greatly as between the Member States, the largest single area of the Directive is devoted to electoral procedures and the assignment of powers to the 'Special Negotiating Body' (SNB) which has the job of agreeing the procedures and powers of the proposed EWC with the group's central management. EWCs can consist of employer and employee representatives or be employee-only. In order to prevent central management from blocking or delaying negotiations, and hence preventing the establishment of an EWC, Article 7 of the Directive provides for a set of 'subsidiary requirements', set out in an Annex, which will apply automatically after three years. These would require EWCs to be established with certain minimal rights. Although an EWC does not have to be set up if the workforce does not want it, or if the SNB accepts a decentralised solution, the mandatory requirements can supervene or serve as a back-up to negotiations. In contrast, Article 13 of the Directive 'rewarded' companies which negotiated a voluntary agreement with employee representatives before the transposition deadline.[3] Such an agreement may continue in force after the transposition date of the Directive in the country in which the central management is located provided it covers all employees in the group and provides for transnational information and consultation. If there is no voluntary agreement under Article 13, then under Article 6, agreement on the establishment, composition and powers of the EWC will be reached via negotiation between central management and the Special Negotiating Body. As far as the political approach of the Directive is concerned, it is a mixture of carrot (Article 13 'voluntary' agreements) and stick (application of the subsidiary requirements, under Article 7).

The legal sanctions which apply if central management fails to inform an EWC correctly are not specified. The Directive merely requires that Member States provide for 'appropriate measures' should the Directive not be complied with; in particular, they must ensure that administrative and judicial procedures are available through which compliance can be ensured (Article 11, Para. 2). However, given that, according to the case-law developed by the European Court of Justice based on Article 5 of the EEC Treaty, Member States are obliged to impose effective, proportionate sanctions with a deterrent effect to ensure compliance with the requirements of a Directive,[4] then one cannot really speak of a lack of enforceability of the Directive even if it 'only' makes provision for information and consultation. However, one evident weakness of the Directive lies in the fact that it does not provide for the protection of the rights of individual employees who fail in an attempt to obtain information via a request to the EWC. There is also no protection for minorities.

As noted above, the Directive, which was passed unanimously with Portugal abstaining, originally only applied to the 11 Member States who were allowed, under the Social Protocol, to make use of the provisions of the Agreement on Social Policy, with the UK opting out. Following the accession of Austria, Sweden and Finland, the '11' became '14' out of 15 Member States. Following the Treaty of Amsterdam, the UK government also moved to 'sign up to the Social Chapter' – that is, to comply with those Directives passed under the Agreement on Social Policy and end the opt-out. In the case of EWCs this was accomplished via a special Directive adopted in December 1997. In addition to the EU member states, Norway, Iceland and Liechtenstein – as members of the European Economic Area (EEA) – are also covered by the Directive.

The Enforced Voluntarism of British and Swiss Undertakings

One novel feature of Community law is the 'favourability' principle embodied in Article 13 of the Directive which guarantees the continuing validity of 'voluntary' agreements provided they meet certain minimum criteria. It is still too early to make any definitive judgement as to the success of this approach, which encourages and accepts diversity. However, the initial results have been noteworthy.

But how voluntary have these EWCs actually been? Has the vision of the philanthropic 'aggregate entrepreneur' been realised: namely that workplace representation, if recognised as efficient, will be set up voluntarily by employers and employees? Or has the record on EWCs confirmed the historical experience that managers will not voluntarily cede power because they accord this a greater value in the present than the uncertain efficiency gains achievable through co-operation in the future? In particular, what led to the fact that by 1996 57 voluntary agreements had been concluded in the UK and 28 in Switzerland?

It is no secret that Swiss and British companies sought advice from their own national and from German experts as to the value (or lack of value) of EWCs before embarking on the process. One British management consultant, who had previously worked for the UK Engineering Employers Federation, recommended that UK companies should pursue a strategy of 'going early' - that is, anticipating developments by concluding Article 13 agreements. If one does the simple calculation that since 1994 a large number of companies expected the Labour Party to win the coming General Election, and end the UK opt-out, then the dream of the voluntary realisation of the efficiency gains of co-operation begins to recede, especially since, at least according to the text of the Directive, voluntary agreements would no longer be possible in the UK after 22 September 1996: that is, there was an expectation that the UK might be 'punished' for its tardy application of the Directive via an immediate application of the more complex and less flexible provisions of Article 6. Or put differently: the fact that the prospect of a 22 September 1996 deadline also applied to the UK created a powerful incentive for voluntary agreements. In fact, under a special Directive passed in December 1997 companies which only fall under the scope of the Directive because of the end of the UK's opt-out have been given an additional two-year period during which they can conclude voluntary agreements.

However, in itself this is not sufficiently analytical about the respective interests of employer and the employee side in the establishment of EWCs. And in particular, it does not explain why voluntary agreements were concluded in Switzerland, where there is no immediate prospect of any obligation to set up EWCs. A US-owned company, for example, might well have played for time. There are evidently national differences which may be crucial in determining the assessment of advantages and disadvantages in such a situation.

What is certainly the case is that many Swiss companies, notably the big chemical undertakings (Ciba, Sandoz, Roche) but also engineering companies such as ABB, Bucher, Bühler, Georg Fischer, Sulzer and others, went beyond the narrow legal requirements of choosing either Article 13 or 6 for those parts of their operations located within the EU in that they have included their own national employees in the new bodies. The same applies to most British companies. Moreover, the inclusion of their UK workforces by six British managements which were not required to set up EWCs can be attributed to the fact that they expected a Labour victory. We now know that they calculated 'correctly'. However, more than half of the Swiss companies potentially affected by the Directive, and just about half the UK companies, spurned the 'carrot' offered by Article 13 and continued to play for time. In their eyes, the advantages of not having to inform or consult their employees at group level for an estimated three years or showing 'toughness' in their industrial relations is greater than the alternative benefits derivable from 'going early'.

The Transposition of the Directive

The period by which the Directive had to be transposed into national law ended on 22 September 1996. (The table overleaf indicates the state-of-play of transposition, as of July 1998.)

The extent of the differences between the Member States as far as transposition is concerned can be seen in the case of Italy, where the Directive was initially implemented via an agreement between the two employers' associations CONFINDUSTRIA and ASSICREDITO (banking and insurance) and the three main trade union confederations CGIL, CISL and UIL. Their agreement, concluded on 27 November 1996, then set the basis for draft legislation to extend the agreement. According to this provision, the Italian members of EWCs consist of one third trade unions which are signatories to the national agreement which applies in the undertaking, and two thirds from workplace employee representatives (the *Rappresentanza Sindacale Unitaria* - RSU). The share of employee representatives which corresponds to the RSUs also gives the trade unions a strong position based on their workplace status within the RSUs. Central management also has a strong position, as do the employers' associations who negotiate on a national agreement every four years with the central trade union confederations. Such a link between workplace interest representation and the parties to national and industry-level collective bargaining is not provided for by the Directive, but is also not excluded.

Belgium is also an example of where the Directive could be directly transposed by means of national collective agreement – albeit one which required supplementary statutory measures to rectify one or two omissions.

Table 4.1 Transposition of EWC Directive into National Law, July 1998

Austria	Legislation adopted on 17 October 1996
Belgium	National collective agreement of 6 February 1996, extended by Royal Decree, March 1996. Legislation resolving some outstanding issues passed in Spring 1998.
Denmark	Legislation adopted on 22 May 1996
Finland	Legislation adopted on 9 August 1996
France	Legislation adopted on 12 November 1996
Germany	Legislation adopted on 28 October 1996
Greece	Presidential Decree, No 40 enacted 20 March 1997
Irish Republic	Legislation adopted on 10 July 1996
Italy	National collective agreement concluded on 6 November 1996. Extending legislation pending.
Liechtenstein	Legislation pending
Luxembourg	Legislation pending
Netherlands	Legislation adopted on 23 January 1997
Norway	National collective agreement concluded on 30 November 1995, made generally binding in August 1996
Portugal	Legislation pending
Spain	Legislation adopted on 24 April 1997
Sweden	Legislation adopted on 9 May 1996
United Kingdom	Following end of 'opt out', regulations must enter into force by December 1999.

Source: Roberto Pedersini, 'The impact of European Works Councils', EIRO, July 1998.

The 'Vilvoorde Shock'

At a point when most of the newly-agreed voluntary European Works Councils had just held their first or second meeting and when the national legislation of the Member States transposing the Directive was barely a year old, a spectacular conflict arose which led to three court rulings dealing, amongst other things, with the issue of the applicability of the national legislation transposing the Directive to voluntarily agreed EWCs.

On 27 February 1997, Renault S.A. announced at a press conference in Boulogne sur Seine (Paris) that it intended to close the Vilvoorde (Brussels) plant of its Belgian subsidiary, which employed 3,100 workers, by 31 July 1997.[5] On hearing this information, the Vilvoorde workforce occupied 'their' plant. On 7 March the first 'Euro strike' took place in the company's Belgian and French plants, with some participation in Renault's Spanish plants. And on 11 March there was a demonstration of Belgian, French and Spanish Renault employees in Paris to accompany the meeting of the Renault EWC. Following legal proceedings instituted by one Renault Vilvoorde employee on 25 March 1997, with trade union support, the Brussels Labour Court[6] ruled on 3 April 1997 that Renault had to restart the procedure for consultation and the conclusion of a social compensation plan.

On 4 April 1997, following an application for an injunction by the Renault EWC, the Nanterre District Court *(Tribunal de Grand Instance)*[7] ruled that Renault had failed to respect the EWC's rights to information and consultation, and breached basic employee rights both at national and European level. The company was instructed to pay FF 15,000 to the EWC. This decision was in essence upheld on 7 May 1997 at the Court of Appeal for the Yvelines Departement in Versailles.[8] Renault was required to call an extraordinary meeting of the EWC and release all the documentation needed to elucidate the reasoning behind the closure and its impact at least eight days ahead of the meeting. Renault was instructed to pay a further FF 15,000 to the EWC. The EWC was supported in the appeal by the European Metalworkers Federation.[9]

The ruling by the Brussels Labour Court was also issued in response to a request for an injunction, based on the fact that the Belgian works council *(Ondernemingsraad)* had to be given information and consulted on such far-reaching measures while they were still in the planning phase. This followed from the national Belgian collective agreement (no. 24), of 20 October 1975, which transposed the collective dismissals Directive into Belgian law.

The Nanterre court's decision was also issued in an accelerated procedure. The court had to consider a voluntary agreement establishing the EWC concluded between Renault and the trade unions represented there on 3 April 1993. This agreement was renewed and extended on 5 May 1995 following the adoption of the EWC Directive and 'in cognisance' of the imminent transposition of the Directive into national law. Because this was a voluntary agreement under Article 13, which preceded transposition, the court had to decide whether it could draw on the legal principles of the Directive to interpret the voluntary agreement which took precedence over it. It resolved this problem by looking at the December 1989 Community Charter of the Basic Social Rights of Employees (the EC 'Social Charter'), which was not binding because of the refusal of the British government to sign it. The court solved this problem in that it viewed the agreement of 5 May 1995 as taking over what the Directive had understood by information and consultation. Although there was no basis in the agreement itself for such an interpretation, the text of the agreement did not rule this out. In turn, the court took from the Directive that, according to Article 17 of the Social Charter, the basic social rights of employees to information, consultation and co-determination were to be developed in accordance with the customs and practices of the Member States. Although the agreement only committed Renault to one EWC meeting each year, extraordinary meetings could be held if events merited it. At any event, the court regarded it as impermissible to announce the closure of Vilvoorde on 27 February 1997 and hold an EWC meeting on 11 March at which neither dialogue nor an exchange of views could take place, but rather at which the closure was simply announced as an irrevocable and incontestable fact. Renault should have informed the EWC and consulted with it over the closure before the decision was announced, but failed to do so.

The Versailles Court of Appeal qualified the requirements of the Nanterre court that consultation had to take place beforehand. Article 18 of the Social Charter and the EWC Directive required that consultation take place 'in good time' or 'as soon as possible' (Annex 3:3). According to Article 2, Para 1f and Article 6 Para 3 of the Directive, in association with Article 17 of the Social Charter, information must be given on 'transnational questions which significantly affect workers' interests'. This includes information, consultation and participation by employees in the event of collective dismissals. For Renault the 5 May 1995 agreement implied an anticipated adjustment to the Directive. The dispensation offered by Article 13 of the agreement was confined to procedural provisions which could be replaced by an alternative information structure. The content and timing of information were not affected by Article 13. Of direct relevance is the injunction in Community law that the provisions of Directives had to be given proper effect *('effet utile')* by transposing legislation.

It was not only the French transposing legislation which had to be interpreted in the light of the requirements of the Directive, but also the Renault agreement. In any individual case – and here the Versailles court weakened the judgment of the Nanterre court – it would need to be decided in the light of all the circumstances whether the requirement that information had to be provided 'in good time' and the Directive given *effet utile* implied consultation in advance.

This would require consideration of the importance of the reservations, objections, and criticisms of any decision, the scale of the prejudice to employee interests, the provisional character or finality of the proposed measures, and finally the sequence of events which might have allowed for effective measures or reactions, perhaps even a change, to the original proposals. The decision also had to demonstrate a minimum degree of 'flexibility' *(souplesse)*, acceptance and agreement.

None of these conditions had been met in the case of Vilvoorde. As a consequence, Renault breached its obligation to inform and consult 'in good time'. The closure could not proceed until these commitments were met. That is, the court supported the call for Renault to desist from the closure.[10] It rejected Renault's objection that a French court could not prohibit measures which affected a subsidiary in another country (ex-territoriality). The effect of the decision on the closure, for which Renault S.A. was responsible, was not confined to the Belgian subsidiary but had implications for the entire European level of the group.

Both rulings have avoided submitting legal issues to the European Court of Justice for a preliminary ruling. 'On their own competence' they established the substantive validity of Community law on an instance in which, under Article 13 of the EWC Directive, the precedence of an autonomous agreement on the part of the social partners should have held good. This precedence, offered by Article 13, was confined to the procedure for information and consultation. Both rulings can be seen as elements in a growing practice of case-law which accords precedence to Community law, although the significance of this extension is only little realised. These cases also imply that transposing legislation should be interpreted 'in the light' of the underlying Directive.

Is there a Fundamental Community Right to Information and Consultation?

Both French court rulings relate to basic European rights. As yet there has been no adoption by the EU of an explicit, common catalogue of basic rights. The European Parliament adopted a resolution on basic rights and freedoms in 1989,[11] the 24 articles of which included classical freedoms such as freedom of worship and expression, freedom of movement, property, freedom of association and right to practice an occupation and some social rights such as the right to education, basic judicial rights, a ban on the death penalty, the principle of democracy and principles of environmental and consumer protection. And in

December 1989, the Council adopted the Community Charter of the Fundamental Social Rights of Workers (the 'Social Charter'), which set out a number of basic social aims such as the right to fair remuneration, a right to social protection, freedom of association, equal treatment for men and women, and the protection of children and young people. However, neither catalogue had legal force, but was rather a declaration by those Member States which endorsed them. No more could be achieved in the face of resistance from the UK government, which had refused to sign the Charter. Article F, Para. 2 of the Maastricht Treaty on the European Union, states that the EU will respect fundamental rights, as guaranteed by the European Convention for the Protection of Human Rights and Fundamental Freedoms and as they result from the *en bloc* application of the 'constitutional traditions' of the Member States as general principles of Community law. However, the issue of ensuring respect for these basic rights by the institutions of the European Union is not sufficiently specified. As the ECJ established in 1996,[12] the EU cannot accede to the European Human Rights Convention as there is no suitable basis in Community law. The Treaty of Amsterdam included a preamble on the TEU in which the significance of basic social rights was confirmed, as set out in the 1961 European Social Charter and the 1989 Social Charter.

In its decisions, the ECJ has referred, if only briefly, to the written and unwritten fundamental rights provided for in Community law. A number of such rights are expressly stated in the Treaty of Rome. Firstly, there is an express prohibition on every form of discrimination on grounds of nationality, including discrimination against nationals, in Article 7. Article 119 provides for the principle of equal pay for men and women for work of equal value, which has been considerably developed by the courts. Based on these proscriptions, the ECJ has developed a system of case-law which is tantamount to a recognition of the general principle of equality at European level.[13] Further fundamental rights include the freedoms required for the Common Market, such as the free movement of labour in Article 48 of the EEC Treaty, the right to free establishment, and the freedom to offer services, set out in Articles 52 and 59 of the EEC Treaty. Finally, a number of basic procedural rights are also guaranteed, in particular in the case of proceedings under competition law.

The ECJ has, however, gone far beyond this. Even before the Treaty was agreed in Maastricht, it recognised a number of unwritten general fundamental principles within the Community's legal order. In addition to the general principle of equality, it has recognised property and freedom of occupation as fundamental Community rights. In addition, the ECJ has recognised the protection of a right to a dwelling, to religious freedom, to a fair trial and to effective legal protection. As well as individuals, the ECJ also recognises companies as the bearers of basic rights.

The development of fundamental rights in the law of the European Union has been favoured by the fact that Article F, Para. 2 of the Maastricht Treaty requires the Union to respect fundamental rights as set out in the European Human Rights Convention and as they result from the constitutional traditions of the Member States. This raises the question as to whether this is sufficient to derive a collective or individual right to information and consultation at the workplace and at company level. The French courts in Nanterre and Versailles did indeed recognise such a right in Community law – primarily based on the fact that the 1989 'Social Charter' was referred to in the EWC Directive. Both courts viewed this fundamental right not in the sense of a right which can be asserted via proceedings to enforce a constitutional principle before a jurisdiction's highest court but rather as comparable, in terms of its possible development, with the freedom of movement of workers and equality between men and women provided for in the Treaty of Rome. In both cases, Community law and ECJ case-law have, starting from modest beginnings, developed legal positions which are now seen as constituting a body of basic rights. A similar development can be seen in the sphere of basic collective rights, following the reference to the Social Charter of an increasing number of Directives. The development of the Charter from a mere political programme to directly applicable law is still at an embryonic stage. However, the more that Regulations and Directives, as well as the ECJ, make reference to the Social Charter, the greater will be the prospect of its development into such a code.

The EU's Power of Sanction in the Sphere of the EWC Directive

Considering the skill with which EU institutions arrived at the voluntary transposition of a Directive which was not binding on the UK, even in a field in which the UK sought to obtain competitive advantage via lower standards through the opt out, it would appear to be worth exploring the thesis that – short of a disaster which destroys the very foundations for the gradually emerging union of Europe's citizens and given the relative neglect of employment law issues compared with liberalising markets and fostering competition – the political unification of Europe will continue to press forward, slowly but surely. This stands in contradiction to the view that European-level institutions are only suitable as vehicles for economic deregulation. In this respect, one can be reasonably optimistic about the solidity of the legal basis for EWCs. It is hardly surprising that following the Renault Vilvoorde case, there have already been calls for the EWC Directive to be amended.

The view that the EU has a growing capacity and authority to intervene in the social field should not be interpreted as implying that the call for 'legal progress via trade union countervailing power' in the sphere of employment law and specifically of EWCs should be replaced by a new maxim - 'legal progress via bureaucratic manoeuvring and creative judicial interpretation'. However, through a practice of making law which looks to the long-term and which has proved capable of riding out numerous efforts at obstruction, the institutions of the Community have succeeded in initiating a number of legal advances in the employment and social sphere which have now been bolstered by ECJ decisions on the precedence of Community law and the extent of the rights to freedom and equality enshrined in the Rome Treaties. The rulings made by the French courts on the Vilvoorde issue can also only add to the reasons as to why there is some scope for optimism on this issue.

Notes

1. The difference between the definition of a dismissal in the Directive and 'redundancy' in UK law has caused a number of problems over the years, and ultimately required an amendment in UK law to ensure that the meaning of the Directive was properly transposed. However, this is not an issue of relevance to the current discussion.
2. Article 100a introduced the principle of qualified majority voting in the Council of Ministers for measures related to the completion of the Single Market, but expressly ruled out of this any provisions on the rights and interests of employees.
3. Companies only brought under the scope of the Directive because of the 1997 'extension' Directive have until December 1999 to conclude voluntary agreements under Article 3 of this measure.
4. See ECJ 1994 I-2479, C, 383/92.
5. For a documentation of the court rulings (in German) see Höland 1997, pp. 82-96.
6. Arbeidsrechtsbank van Brussel - Rep. No. 97/08228.
7. Nr. BO: 97/00992.
8. Arret No. 308, 7 May 1997, R.G. No. 2780/97.
9. See Kolvenbach/Kolvenbach, NZA 1997, 695ff.
10. See the report in Euro/AS 5/1997, pp. 68ff.
11. 15 March 1989, OJ C96, 17 April 1989.
12. ECJ, 28 March 1996.
13. Cf. Feige, *Der Gleichheitssatz im Recht der EWG*, 1973.

5 The Establishment of European Works Councils: Process and Course of Development

The Pioneer Phase

The Pilot Projects

The first 'European company council' was set up at the French undertaking Thomson Grand Public in October 1985, followed by a number of other French companies including Bull (1988) and Rhône Poulenc (negotiations conducted in 1990). Up until the formal establishment of a European Works Council at Volkswagen in 1990, all the initiatives were either in or by French firms.

The preponderance of French companies in these pilot projects is attributable in the first instance to the political environment, but is also rooted in a number of broader processes. The French 'Auroux laws', passed in 1982, required the establishment of 'group committees' *(comités de groupe)* in all large undertakings, the structure and functioning of which was closely followed in the newly-created European bodies. The first European information bodies were established in public or nationalised French undertakings. For example, in 1989 Prime Minister Rocard called on the presidents of public corporations to 'behave in an "exemplary" way on the issue of social dialogue and to set up European group committees' (Rehfeldt, 1998, p. 210). The fact that such undertakings were in public ownership, with the corresponding management and political influence, was an important - but not the only - factor in explaining the initiatives taken by their managements, or the latter's willingness to negotiate. They were also motivated by new managerial approaches prompted by economic and technical developments (such as the significance of the telecommunications branch and of human resources in the value-added chain) as well as transformations in the structures of these undertakings, the declared aim of which was to 'use European agreements and dialogue arrangements to promote a common awareness of the problems and a European "corporate identity" amongst employees and their trade union representatives. Indirectly, European consultative committees should also

41

contribute to the harmonisation of management practices within the group and, especially, to help to shape a common "style" for dealing with industrial relations' (Rehfeldt, 1998, p. 219).

The interest on the part of the French trade unions in voluntarily-agreed European group committees was the product of employer resistance to European legislation in the field, the tactical consideration that agreements with 'dissident' employers would create precedents, and the strategic expectation that impetus could be given to a medium- and long-term process of workplace and trade union transnational communication and co-operation. Although this view was shared by the CGT trade union, there was some hesitancy on its part following the rejection of its application to the join the European Trade Union Confederation (ETUC) and the consequent worry that it would be further marginalised within European trade union circles by the creation of European group committees.

One further relevant factor during the pioneer phase - both in policy and logistical respects - was the role of the trade unions at European level. The European Metalworkers Federation (EMF) initially played a leading and innovative role within the European industry federations during the first stages of the pioneer phase. Its efforts to create company-based European consultative arrangements reflected a number of specific historical experiences, strategic judgements and organisational interests.

The historical experiences include, first and foremost, its coming to terms with the failure of autonomous trade union initiatives to establish so-called 'world company councils' in multinational companies during the 1960s and 1970s. Drawing support from the International Trade Secretariats, these were intended to construct a system of international trade union countervailing power to the multinationals. Although some 50 bodies were established following the creation of the first world company councils in 1966, the refusal of employers to recognise them meant that they remained purely trade union bodies, unable to match the hopes invested in them of being able to conduct co-ordinated international collective bargaining. They led a largely formal existence with infrequent meetings, usually only once every three years to coincide with international branch congresses. One central reason for the failure of this global initiative was the absence of any international political or legal framework. Despite a prolonged debate about codes of conduct for multinational companies, it was not until 1977 that the 'Tripartite Declaration of Principles concerning Multinational Enterprises and Social Policy' of the International Labour Organization was agreed: this, however, was non-binding in ILO Member States and hence - in contrast to the later EU process - could not draw on institutional support and resources to achieve political effectiveness.

This failure, combined with further developments in European integration and institutional changes within the European trade union movement, led to a number of more pragmatic efforts to establish regional – that is, European – structures of multinational industrial relations at group level within companies.

In the trade union sphere, the foundation of the ETUC in 1972 and of the EMF as an independent European regional organisation of the international trade union secretariat in 1971 (cf. Platzer, 1991, p. 117) meant that by the early-1980s what had been an initially difficult period of policy development and organisational consolidation had been concluded. Specific projects were needed to strengthen the European level of trade union organisation and raise its public profile. One of the tasks which the EMF had taken over from the International Metalworkers Federation was the co-ordination of trade union work in multinational companies at European level, for which it had established company-level working parties in which trade union representatives from European subsidiaries regularly met each other (Platzer, 1991). One of these working parties – for Thomson Grand Public – constituted the strategic link between the European and national trade union levels in negotiations over the first pilot project (Rehfeldt, 1998, p. 208).

The voluntarist strategy, which characterised the pioneer phase of the establishment of EWCs, can be explained ultimately by the specific context for European social policy in the first half of the 1980s: these stand out more clearly in a broad periodisation of the sweep of EU social policy from its inception. This can be divided into five phases.

1) The 'modest' start: 1958-1972: measures in the social insurance field to underpin free movement; the provision of funds from the European Social Fund.

2) The first 'dynamic phase' following the 1972 Paris Summit: the 1974 Social Policy Action Programme which the summit inaugurated led to new activities on the part of the Commission and the adoption of numerous Directives and Regulations in the employment and social sphere.

3) The 'phase of stagnation' 1980-1986: the 'Thatcherite Blockade' of EC legislation and the advance of neo-liberal policies of deregulation and raising flexibility.

(4) The 'unhurried departure' towards the Social Dimension to the Single Market with the passage of the Single European Act 1986/7 up until the

Maastricht Treaty in the early-1990s: reform of the structural fund, the 1989 'Social Charter' and its associated Social Action Programme with significant regulations in the sphere of health and safety at work, themselves prompted by the desire to ensure equal competitive conditions within the Single Market.

(5)   Social policy since 1993 following the 'Agreement on Social Policy' in the Maastricht Treaty: uprating of 'Social Dialogue', agreement on parental leave (1996) and part-time workers (1997), adoption of the EWC Directive in 1994, and the Directive on Posted Workers in 1996.

The voluntaristic approach to EWCs in the first stage of the pioneer phase was, on the one hand, a reaction to the preceding years of stagnation in the field of social policy regulation, most vividly and significantly expressed in the failure of the Vredeling Directive (draft 1980, revised version 1983, abandonment 1986). And on the other, it marked a response to the paradigm shift in economic and social policy which began in the early-1980s (supply-side policies and deregulation) and which manifested itself at EU level in the 1986 White Paper on the Single Market. As a consequence of this new overall constellation – including the departure from the principle of *ex ante* harmonisation and hard regulation – voluntaristic approaches appeared to the trade unions to be an admittedly second best, but at least feasible approach.

The Phase of Voluntary EWCs with Institutional and Material EU Support

The key impetus for the establishment of EWCs during this phase, which extended from the beginning of the 1990s up until the adoption of the Directive, can be primarily explained by the interaction of two factors. The stage of the initial pilot projects was followed by a stage in which material and institutional support was offered by the EU. The trade unions pursued a dual strategy: on the one hand, national and European trade unions worked together to push forward more voluntary EWC agreements in order to create precedents which were intended to facilitate a legislative regulation; and on the other, they called directly for such an instrument. The regulatory approach was regarded by those trade unions with highly legally-regulated national systems, and in particular by the German metalworkers' union IG Metall, as central and indispensable. Nevertheless, following its earlier reservations about the voluntaristic approach to EWC agreements, IG Metall changed its strategy and subsequently mobilised considerable resources in this field.

One important initiative which gave additional impulse for further agreed solutions at the beginning of this period was the voluntary accord concluded in August 1990 between the social partners in the German chemical industry at the instigation of the chemical workers' union IG Chemie (now IG BCE) which was concerned about the implications of the Single Market. These 'Guidelines for Works Councils Contact at European Level' (see Klak, 1998, pp. 150ff) did not have the status of a formal and binding collective agreement but were adhered to in practice by larger companies in the industry. Within a relatively short period, all large German chemical undertakings had established European forums. Based on the strong influence of the German associations within the corresponding European bodies, this national and consensual approach also had an impact in the wider transnational context of the European chemical industry, and beyond.

> The approach adopted by the German chemical industry has often been designated as a 'third way' of achieving autonomous industry-specific solutions to the problem of how to establish European-level arrangements for informing employees. The models established exhibit varying degrees of formality (Klak, 1998, p. 151).

One second important influence, which provided political and material support to trade union and company-level initiatives in this phase, can be found in the changes in the broader shape and direction of policy at international level. The 'unhurried departure' towards the European social dimension (see Däubler's periodisation above) was promoted and supported by the Commission and the Centre-Left majority in the European Parliament. This offered fertile soil for European trade union lobbying, for example via the inter-party trade union group in the European Parliament. As far as the principle of strengthening the Social Dialogue and creating social measures to cushion the impact of the Single Market was concerned, this also coincided with the aims of the European Commission, and in particular with those of Commission President Jacques Delors.

The role of the Commission as an 'activist bureaucracy', which initiated and directed these processes, can be seen in the 1990 draft EWC Directive, which coincided with the establishment of a new budget line (4004), supported by the European Parliament, to promote social partner activity by financing meetings.

This financial support allowed hundreds of European meetings to take place between employee representatives: these were organised by the European trade union industry federations, in line with their strategic objectives, and served the aim of creating the preconditions for subsequent voluntary negotiations and agreements via the establishment of transnational communications. This control of the process by the Commission also reflected a fundamental change in regulatory approach since the beginning of the 1990s, which was also evident in other policy areas such as environmental policy, and which ran from a concrete and specific regulation towards the creation of procedures and options in European framework legislation. In contrast to the efforts at substantive harmonisation seen in the approach of the Vredeling Directive,

> virtually nothing was regulated. The provisions offered legal and financial support for Community-wide forms of co-operation as a well as maximally company-specific and 'flexible and practicable' representation in the form of European Works Councils or decentralised 'procedures for information and consultation of workers' (Keller, 1996, p. 472).

In some of the individual voluntarily agreed EWCs established in this period, such as Renault in 1993, direct reference was made to the draft Directive.

It was the joint action of international trade union activity and supra-national control of the process by the Commission which explains the growth of EWCs in terms of numbers, branches and national HQs of the parent companies in the second stage of the 'pioneer phase'.

The Phase of 'Directive-driven' EWC Negotiations

The continuing resistance of both national and European employer associations and a number of governments (notably the UK) to any form of statutory provision on EWCs - despite the dynamic process in train which had seen the establishment of around 40 voluntarily agreed EWCs - meant that any decisive move in the direction of the general establishment of EWCs through the adoption of a Directive would require a change in the political and institutional context. The key factors in this phase were both the pressure and the specific effect exerted by the Directive (creation of procedures and options via Article 13). In turn, the Directive only became a political possibility because it was included amongst those issues deemed suitable for qualified majority voting under the Maastricht Treaty, combined with the fact that the UK government had opted out of this procedure through the Social Protocol.

One early upshot of the 'new style of politics' (Falkner, 1996) created by the extension of the treaty foundations emerged even before the adoption of the Directive in the 'enforced willingness' of the European employers, faced with the threat of legislation, to negotiate on the EWC issue under the new procedures for Social Dialogue (Articles 3 and 4 of the Agreement on Social Policy). The phase of 'enforced voluntary' agreements which followed the failure of these negotiations and the adoption of the Directive was accompanied by intense efforts by national and European trade unions to support negotiations, and by the diverse national processes of negotiation and institution-building which marked the implementation of the Directive.

In this dynamic phase of the establishment and development of EWCs, around 120 EWCs were agreed in the metalworking and chemical sectors covered by this study prior to the transposition deadline of 22 September 1996. In contrast to the initial possibility, which had not been ruled out by the trade unions, that this might lead to a proliferation of 'quick and dirty deals', the systematic support of these negotiations by the trade unions, tied to a number of standard provisions (the subsidiary requirements of the Directive), produced results which the European Metalworkers Federation summed up as follows – and which reflects the experiences of our own study:

> In free negotiations between the metalworking trade unions and EMF, on the one side, and leading industrial undertakings on the other, agreements have been concluded which meet the basic requirements of the EMF and its member organisations. The key points of these agreements are: participation of external experts in the work of EWCs, and in particular of representatives of the metalworking unions and EMF; the requirement that meetings should be held at least once annually; that a preparatory meeting of employee representatives should be held; consideration for all the relevant languages in translation and interpretation; and a central role for employees in preparing and organising meetings.

> Such important companies as Airbus Industries, Bosch-Siemens Domestic Appliances, British Steel, Daimler Benz, Fiat, Ford, Hitachi, ITT-Cannon, Krupp-Hoesch, Mitsubishi Electric, Siemens (...) have chosen the path of negotiation and agreement ahead of their statutory obligation from 23 September 1996. The majority of these companies are characterised by high turnovers, large numbers of employees and a modern product range. Moreover, they are companies which shape their environments with a high capacity for innovation and investment. They are a decisive part of Europe's economic strength and successful as 'global players'.[1]

The motives and strategic conceptions which animated corporate behaviour in this phase yielded the following picture, according to the assessment of a Brussels-based management consultancy which advised some

50 undertakings in the establishment of EWCs, in some cases offering draft agreements and conducting negotiations. The strategic conception varied. The wish for a 'minimalistic' solution (that is, generally below the minimum requirements of the Directive) was offset by a larger number of 'pro-active approaches' (new information strategy, improvement in corporate image, development of a European corporate identity, transnational human resource management). Compared with the structure and corporate profile of companies, national origin played only a minor role as far as negotiating aims were concerned. What was significant, however, was the specific and clearly substantial need for advice on the part of non-European companies affected by the Directive (primarily Japanese and US American). As far as the conduct and aims of the negotiations was concerned, whether the voluntary agreement was concluded before or after the adoption of the Directive was largely immaterial.

The main aim of the companies covered by the Directive during the phase of 'enforced voluntarism' was to achieve made-to-measure solutions - that is, a good fit between the proposed information and consultation structures and their existing in-house strategy, in many cases with a need to establish an EWC-related structure of 'bottom up' communication within and between decentralised management layers (subsidiaries) and group HQ.[2] The fact that employers associations were stretched when confronted with company calls for tailored solutions also explains why these played only a minor or even no role in negotiations and in the implementation of EWCs, compared with the service and advice offered by the trade unions, and why their lobbying role was confined to the legislative process.

Overall, the patterns of interaction and negotiating outcomes in the established EWCs observable in this phase fit with the broader findings on corporate internationalisation and its implications for management of companies' political and social environment.

> Accordingly, the particular quality of international restructuring in the 1990s would be that key undertakings have initiated experiments in the structuring of their negotiating relationships in more or less all policy arenas, but especially in the control of industrial relations, which in practice amounts to a restructuring of their negotiating arrangements. Whether matters remain at incremental regulatory changes or whether the changes in industrial complexes will culminate in a change of path and far-reaching transformations in national industrial models, cannot be determined with certainty in advance (Dörre et.al., 1997, pp. 58f).

State of Voluntary Agreements in the Study Countries

Some 430 voluntary agreements were concluded by the 22 September 1996 transposition deadline under the provisions of Article 13 of the Directive. Of these around 130 were agreed in the European metalworking industry and 150 in the chemical industry. The country breakdown of voluntary agreements, and the total number of companies in each country expected to be covered is set out below.

In Germany, approximately 350 undertakings are covered by the Directive. The first EWC in a German company was established in 1990 at Volkswagen. In all, 150 voluntary agreements had been concluded by 1996 - 20 in the chemicals industry (according to information from the German chemical employers association, BAVC) and 30 in engineering.

In France, some 200 undertakings are covered by the Directive. As already noted, the first EWCs were established in French companies in the mid-1980s, and the phase of EWC 'pilot projects' was dominated by agreements in French undertakings. However, this trend has slackened considerably. Overall, a total of 41 EWC agreements had been concluded in French headquartered companies by the time the Directive came into force (including the agreements at the Franco-German joint ventures Europipe and Eurocopter). Of these, 17 agreements had been signed in the metalworking industry and eight in the chemical industry.

Taking into account the end of the UK opt out, in all 238 British undertakings are covered by the Directive. There have been problems in gauging the exact number of voluntary agreements, as some EWCs have been established without trade union involvement and have not been made public.[3] The first voluntary agreements were concluded later than in France and Germany, with the earliest at United Biscuits in November 1994. Nonetheless, the total of 59 agreements at UK headquartered companies is fairly high. Of this total (which is in fact 57 because of three separate agreements at BP), 11 were in metalworking and nine in chemicals.

On 31 December 1996, a total of 38 Italian companies or groups of companies met the criteria for inclusion under the Directive. As in the UK, agreements were struck at a fairly late date. The first EWC agreement was concluded as part of the collective agreement at group level at Merloni (see case-study below). In all 15 voluntary agreements were agreed, four in metalworking and three in chemicals.

The Phase of the Mandatory Establishment of EWCs

During this phase, which follows the period covered in this study, a further 1,000 EWCs remain to be established via formal negotiation, assuming their employees wish it - and subject to the mandatory imposition of the Directive's subsidiary requirements where firms delay or refuse negotiations.[4] This period will also see a review of the Directive's operation, due to take place no later than September 1999. It is likely that the dynamic of development and experience accumulated in the developmental phases analysed here in existing voluntarily-agreed EWCs will also continue into the phase of mandatory compliance – both in terms of how employers and trade unions assess practical experience in the light of the impending review of the Directive and in terms of gathering and disseminating best practice. This creates serious challenges for the trades unions, if only because of the sheer number of EWCs to be negotiated.

Overall, the development of EWCs so far has significantly raised the role and importance of the trade unions at European-level – the ETUC during the negotiations in the Social Dialogue, and the industry federations during the pioneer phase and Article 13 agreements during the phase of 'Directive-driven' negotiations. In many cases, the European industry federations were directly involved as negotiating partners with companies, which saw this as one means of lowering their transaction costs. In the current phase which runs until 1999, the emphasis will move increasingly to the national level. The steering and clearing functions and the, by now, mostly formalised networks of information at the European trade union level will probably, however, not diminish in strategic importance.

Notes

1. EMF Press Notice 8/1996, p. 1.
2. Interview with J.M. Didier, Didier Business Consulting, Brussels.
3. For example, the TGWU - the largest union contingent at BP - only found out from the German chemical workers' union that an agreement had been signed in the company.
4. UK companies not previously affected by the Directive have a longer period in which to conclude voluntary agreements.

PART III:
INDUSTRIAL RELATIONS
IN
WESTERN EUROPE

6 National Industrial Relations and the Context for EWCs in Italy, France, the United Kingdom and Germany

The social forces, institutions and procedures which structure the field of industrial relations in Western Europe have undergone several episodes of profound change since the Second World War. These were initially attributable to the changing balance of forces between the state, employers (and their associations) and the trades unions, together with the strategies pursued by these actors. At the same time, these phases of transformation represented a reaction to economic conditions which were increasingly set by the world market. And although the economic cycle is an important variable in industrial relations, the strategies and actions of the actors in this field have been impelled more by the broader changes which have taken place in the overall economic, social and political context. In turn, the adaptation of the actors serves to modify existing industrial relations arrangements.

The profound changes in the field of industrial relations since the mid-1970s have not only been determined by developments in their broader social and political environment but were also subject to the structural economic changes in the social formations of the highly-industrialised countries. Whilst the 'minor crises' of the economic cycle can challenge and even raise the adaptive capacities of regulatory political institutions, 'great crises',

> may be interpreted as a structural breaking of forms of social accumulation and regulation, when disturbances to equilibrium can no longer be overcome without a change in the regulatory institutions (Altvater, 1993, p. 45).

On this analysis, the crisis of the Fordist mode of regulation was the outcome of the exhaustion of the productive reserves of the traditional Taylorist organisation of labour, with consequent feedback effects on productivity growth, of a decline in the profitability of capital and lower economic growth, of the shift in the balance of forces in the late-1960s and early-1970s to the disadvantage of labour, and of the growing aggregate costs of environmental destruction and the stress on individual psychological structures generated by a hypertrophied division of labour. In contrast, 'post Fordism' represents a new economic and political regime which restructures the Fordist system. The key element in this new pattern of development is the introduction of new technologies which save on both capital and labour and which require a change in 'production concepts' - in turn posing new challenges to the organisation of work and to workers. It produces new structures of capital through the drive to concentration, centralisation and globalisation, with corresponding corporate strategies and management philosophies. In particular, the new information and communication technologies serve to foster the globalisation of finance and value-adding chains. At the level of political regulation, there is a switch from Keynesianism to neo-liberalism, the economic and social yardstick of which is increasingly that of transnational competition.

State support for this structural transformation, through the restructuring of the framework for economic activity via privatisation, deregulation and flexibilisation, has undoubtedly generated a new economic dynamic. Growth has stabilised – albeit at lower levels than before. Profitability has risen enormously since the late-1970s, and the trade unions have been weakened. And despite persistently high unemployment the political stability of the system remains high. This restructuring of the social environment has extended beyond the national framework, with particular impacts and feedbacks effects in Europe.

The impulse towards the restructuring and modernisation of the European Union entailed by the Single Market Programme has initiated a new phase of fundamental change for industrial relations. The *leitmotiv* of the Single Market project – competitiveness – has lent enormous strategic force to moves towards economic integration in Europe. In contrast, the regulation of industrial relations within the EU continues to lag considerably behind this: binding regulations exist only in minimal or embryonic form. Those forces in the EU Commission and Member States which advocate greater deregulation not only expect that the greater mobility of goods, services, capital and labour will lead to a general increase in welfare but will also require an adjustment on the part of national states to those regulatory institutions and political structures which have proven to be the most functional and efficient within the framework of the EU. 'Convergence through competition' will render regulation at the level of EU superfluous and will ensure a 'reasonable' level of approximating social standards in the Member States.

The realisation of the Single Market project remains, however, tied to diverse national structures within which the process of integration is carried out and which themselves are reproduced through this process. In Italy, the United Kingdom, Germany and France, the relevant actors in industrial relations have reacted in similar ways to the new constellations in global politics, to changes in the international division of labour and to the new trends in technical-economic and socio-political restructuring. This has also led to changes in the national formations of political and social forces. In particular, power relations have shifted markedly within the field of industrial relations, and in a noteworthy parallelism in all these countries, against 'labour'. However, although the actors are responding to the same challenges in the formulation of their strategies, the position of each country in world politics, its industrial make-up, economic strengths and weaknesses, its position in the European and international division of labour together with its unique inherited social and political system have led to very different national responses.

National Framework Conditions for Industrial Relations and EWCs in the Case-Study Countries

The success of EWCs is highly dependent on their fit with national systems of industrial relations. An especially key role is played by the relationship between workplace and supra-workplace structures of employee representation (Lecher/Platzer, 1996). In the countries presented below the trade unions have sought to create a structure of binding regulations for the employment and incomes of employees using both workplace- and company-level representation and formal structures of collective bargaining. There are considerable differences in the manner of negotiation, the form of agreements and not least the substance of collective agreements (Ruysseveldt/Visser, 1996). Whereas in Germany, for example, collective bargaining takes place between employers (or their associations) and trade unions free from state intervention, in France the state plays a key role. And whereas in Germany, industry collective bargaining is still the main form of collective regulation, company-level bargaining is predominant in the UK. In Germany, although trade unions retain the sole competence in the field of collective bargaining 'proper', with an increasingly important role in the German 'dual system' for works councils to negotiate workplace agreements *(Betriebsvereinbarungen),* the national federation, the DGB, merely exercises a co-ordinating role. In contrast, in France the national confederations negotiate directly. The possibility of concluding workplace agreements varies considerably between countries, both as regards the institutional framework and procedures and the substance of such agreements. Whereas DGB-affiliated unions in

Germany overwhelmingly negotiate independently and on their own, Italy and France continue to be characterised by a plurality of political trade unions, although the extent of differences varies and the degree of rivalry is generally diminishing. In the UK there is still often competition between trade unions at the workplace.

All this is of importance for the positioning and power of existing and prospective EWCs, both within their national industrial relations settings as well as from the standpoint of Europeanisation. The following description and analysis of developments in industrial relations in the 1990s in the four countries included in this study look at how these national specificities have manifested themselves and what significance they have for the capacity of EWCs.

Italy

Without doubt the most important development in the Italian industrial relations system in the 1990s consisted in the replacement of a traditionally conflictual system, the outcomes of which were determined essentially by the respective balance of power between the two sides, to a form of institutionalisation which has demonstrated a powerful participative effect and which is characterised by adherence to a framework of binding rules for the conduct of negotiations. In the past, the central guarantor for the continuity and development of industrial relations lay in the existence of a set of national industry collective agreements. It was only with the tripartite negotiating rounds in the early-1990s, which sought to reform pay structures, restructure the system of collective bargaining and set express objectives for employment, labour market and industrial policy, that this situation began to change. These negotiations culminated on 23 July 1993 in the so-called 'Accord on Labour Costs' which has since entered the literature as the 'Social Pact' because of the breadth of its provisions (Telljohann, 1995).

In addition to the restructuring of collective bargaining, the 1993 accord also paved the way for a national-level agreement on workplace industrial relations which was concluded in December 1993. In a change from the system which had prevailed since works councils and workers delegates had been created during the 'hot autumn' of industrial militancy in 1969, a new structure of workplace representation – the RSU *(rappresentanze sindacali unitarie)* or 'unitary union representation' – was established as the institution for workplace employee representation, in a construction unique in Europe. Under the newly-agreed provisions, those trade unions which are signatories to the national industry agreement and which have proposed candidates for workplace elections to the RSU have the right in aggregate to nominate one third of the RSU's members. As a rule, this embraces the industry unions affiliated to the three main national confederations, CGIL, CISL and UIL.[1] The remaining two-thirds are elected from trade union lists by all the employees at the workplace. As well as nationally representative trade unions, trade union organisations which are formally constituted, which have their own rule-book and articles of association and whose nomination is supported by at least 5 per cent of the workforce, may also enter the elections for the RSU.

This is the beginnings of a structure of representation which links trade union representation with a need for broad workplace representative legitimation. This aspect of the overall 1993 settlement has been subsequently implemented in greater detail in industry-level agreements, with RSUs now overwhelmingly elected in accordance with these provisions. The RSUs are just as much a legitimate negotiating partner for employees at workplace level as local trade union organisations. As yet structures of workplace representation have not been put on a formal statutory footing.

One gap which this agreement did not close concerns the area of employee participation at workplace level. As a result, trade union codetermination rights, principally over workplace restructuring, continue to be based on agreed, not statutory, provisions – with the associated problem that these rights are not guaranteed on an enduring basis. It also means that the practical exercise of codetermination is confined to a few innovative companies. These isolated and somewhat random experiences are unlikely to be enough to ensure the emergence of a real culture of codetermination in Italian industrial relations.

The Italian system of industrial relations may arguably be regarded as still in a transitional phase, with current arrangements likely to constitute a provisional solution. Recent advances should not conceal the fact that the present structure, especially of workplace employee representation, cannot yet be viewed as fully developed, in particular in the field of mandatory rights to elect workplace representatives. A statutory solution, but one rooted in preceding practice, would appear to be indispensable. Only such a solution would provide the effective protection of rights from external interference.

In the past, the anomaly of the Italian industrial relations system consisted in its lack of institutionalisation of the system of collective bargaining. For example, there were no binding provisions on the procedures and timetable for negotiations. In this respect, the 1993 accord represents a decisive step forward as, for the first time, it lays down binding provisions for the conduct of negotiations at the various levels in the system. The restructuring of the system of collective bargaining confirmed and consolidated the scope and power of the trade unions. Nonetheless, it should be remembered that the accord only creates a general system of rules which require interpretation – and which create scope for such interpretation – at the various levels at which it is applied in practice.

Four main lines of development of industrial relations can be discerned in recent years. Firstly, the threat to the three principal trade union confederations through a 'tertiarisation of conflict' as a result of the decentralised industrial action of the so-called 'basis committees' (COBAS) and autonomous groups was taken very seriously and led to an unprecedented readiness to accept legal regulation of strikes and to work constructively on draft legislation in this field. A certain degree of 'juridification' of industrial relations was no longer seen as an attack on individual autonomy but as collective protection from hasty deregulation under crisis conditions. There was a willingness to grant new – and divergent – organisational activities, especially the COBAS, a degree of legitimacy, as evidenced by the 5 per cent representation clause in the RSUs. Secondly, and in the same broad direction as greater legal regulation of industrial relations, has been the willingness of the trade unions to introduce more formality into structures of workplace representation and finally bury the myth of the factory councils, which had already become obsolete over the course of the 1980s. As noted above, clear agreed procedures were established for the election of workplace representatives.

The rapid expansion of very small enterprises (often suppliers in the black economy), especially in the north east and central regions, has created a third area in need of regulation on employment protection, health and safety, minimum pay rates and hours of work. Legislation passed in 1990 on employment protection in small enterprises represented a major effort to improve legal regulation in this area. Fourthly, and finally, the collapse of 'actual existing socialism' in Eastern Europe led to an accelerating 'de-ideologisation', especially of the Italian Communist Party (PCI) and the Communist wing of the CGIL, a process already in train for some years. Against this background, the coalitions needed to form an administration in Italy, normally a factor for instability, and the necessary capacity to come to compromises might also exercise a positive influence on the never entirely abandoned hopes for merger between the main trade union confederations. How the mixture of socialist, social democratic and Christian and secular/ humanist strands in the Italian trade union movement might function will depend not least on the progress of Italy's integration into the EU. The pressures exerted by European integration have already obliged trades unions, and not only in Italy, to step up co-operation to defend the development of their national interests within a broader European perspective.

These developments will have an impact on how EWCs will work. At present, there is no statutory obligation on employers to disclose information to employees or their representatives. In this respect, EWCs will create pressures for change which could run in parallel with the broader trend towards more legal regulation within the Italian system. Moreover, the new structure of workplace industrial relations - the RSU - represents a combination of employee representatives which are elected by all employees, and not just those who are trade union members, with a proportional share reserved for the trade unions. This structure could endow EWCs with greater legitimacy than was the case in the former system of trade union delegates. In most workplaces elections have not been held for years - if at all in some cases - with a corresponding loss of legitimacy of the old structures of representation. In contrast to the old system, there are aspirations to put the RSU structure on a statutory footing.

France

Despite all efforts at reform, industrial and social relations in France have still not reached the degree of 'normality' which characterises most other Western European industrialised countries. Key elements of France's 'special path' can still be discerned: the centrality of the state, weakness and fragmentation of intermediate organisations, low level of importance attached to autonomous regulation, low level of procedural formalism in collective bargaining and poor articulation between the levels of bargaining. In short - a marked degree of uncontrollability of social conflict and an unpredictability to the 'eruptions' which tear at the tissue of industrial relations.

The trades unions are recognised by the state and employers as the representative of employees and an unavoidable interlocutor, and they have a legally enshrined status and protection in this role. Since the Auroux laws, introduced in the early-1980s, employees have enjoyed the status of 'citizens' at the workplace and enjoy direct consultation rights which are hardly matched elsewhere. Regular collective negotiations at workplace and branch level are mandatory, and the right of employee representatives to be consulted on economic and technological change is firmly legally protected. This structure of state regulation was and is, however, not sufficient to check a number of developments which are deeply rooted in the political and cultural traditions of the French trade union movement, and which have led to a crisis of regulation and representation in the context of the economic and employment crisis of the 1980s and 1990s.

Such a diagnosis of comprehensive crisis is not shared by all the socia actors and academic observers. Many representatives from the reformi modernising current would argue that social regulation has been strengthened i a number of areas in recent years and can cite several indicators, such as a fa in the number of strikes and a quantitative increase in collective bargaining at a levels, as evidence. This impression of a growing density of social regulation an protection through collective agreements is deceptive, however, as it conceals th widely differing substance of these agreements, the growing heterogeneity o social position of employees, and the spread of ever-larger islands of socia deregulation.

Moreover, the erosion of the position of the trade unions has not proved t be stoppable in recent years. Trade union density is currently around 10 per cer and only 6 per cent in the private sector. It would only be a slight exaggeratic to say that effective trade unions, especially at workplace level, represe 'islands' in an otherwise unstructured ocean of industrial relations. Five trac union confederations are nationally recognised as representative negotiatii partners. Representatives of these five can sign collective agreements which the apply to all employees in a sector or region. Such agreements will be regarde as valid even if the signatory trade union only represents a small minority employees in that bargaining unit. Moreover, the signature of one recognise union is sufficient to render an agreement valid (Dufour, 1993).

At workplace level, up until 1995 only trade union delegates were formal entitled to negotiate. Based on the difficulty which all the trade unions have ha in achieving any representation at all at workplace level, there was a growir trend towards works committees *(comités d'entreprises)* signing agreements informally and in a departure from the law. This is not unproblematic as Fren works committees include employee representatives but meet under th chairmanship of a representative of management. On the other hand, not to much should be read into this as management representatives often do no mo than prepare the agenda. However, such a situation does not guarantee genuir independence from the opposite side. This is also the reason why employ associations proposed in the early-1990s that so-called 'staff delegates' *(délégu du personnel),* which consist solely of employee representatives, should be ab to conclude agreements where there is no trade union representation. This w categorically rejected by the trade unions. Instead, three trade uni confederations - CFDT, CFTC and CGC - concluded a collective agreeme which allows negotiations and settlements at workplace level without direct tra union involvement via non-organised employees nominated or elected by t trade unions. This was converted into legislation in 1995.

Recognised organisations have the right to nominate candidates in workplace and other elections, such as those for joint management of the social security system: these do not have to be trade union members themselves. Only if these organisations are not able to find candidates or if their representatives win fewer than 50 per cent of the votes in the first ballot, can non-union trade candidates be nominated in the second ballot. In this way, they obtain a limited representativeness (Lecher, 1994a). Numerous non-trade union candidates and also some representatives of so-called 'autonomous trade unions' have been able to achieve a degree of representativeness at workplace level, especially in some areas of the public sector but also increasingly in private companies.

As in the German system, French industrial relations has formalised collective agreements. However, their practical significance is different. Although such agreements are legally possible at national, regional, local and workplace level, for some time the company level has been gaining in importance at the expense of the other levels. This trend has been promoted by the fact that annual negotiations at company level have been required by the Auroux laws since the mid-1980s (Javillier, 1984). Moreover, collective agreements in France are less important than in Germany because there is practically no guarantee that they will be complied with. This is one indirect consequence of trade union pluralism. Typically, not all representative trade unions sign a collective agreement. The main reason is inter-union competition, a focus on sub-groups within workforces and the use of discontent to promote individual trade union organisations. A strike can be called at any time by a trade union which has been a signatory to an agreement. In addition, clauses prohibiting strike action are legally banned - the right to strike is seen as an individual right. Put somewhat polemically, collective agreements are only in practice binding on companies but not on employees or their representatives.

Aside from that, the state itself also occupies important areas of supra-workplace level collective regulation, such as minimum wages and working time: the regulation of these areas by the law has meant that they have lost practically all significance as attractive issues for collective bargaining. Finally, all French trades unions are clearly more workplace-oriented than is still the case in Germany, for example. One reason for this is their political concentration on the grass roots; another is the fact that French trade unions have more rights at workplace level, especially in the field of collective bargaining. In addition, French trade unions do not have full-time officials at local, regional or national level in sufficiently large numbers to enable them to co-ordinate trade union activity to any satisfactory degree. Trade union officials are in many cases effectively part-timers. In particular, the local sections of the trade unions are led by employees who continue to be employed by their companies and who are merely granted a few hours off for trade union activity, either by law or local agreement. In turn, this is not only a function of the high degree of politicisation of the trade unions but is also a direct consequence of their financial difficulties which have been massively exacerbated by the drastic loss of members.

The trade unions have been finding it difficult to renew their organisations and approach; the number of abstentions in elections to work committees and staff delegates has continued to grow in recent years. Non-trade union candidates have been winning increasing numbers of seats, displacing candidates from even the largest confederations and assuming the leadership of strikes in such weakly organised sectors as the health service, and also in such traditional union bastions as the railways, once discontent with trade union representation takes hold.

Although France played a pioneer role in the voluntary establishment of EWCs, academic discussion has lagged behind these developments. The reasons for this lack of interest are manifold. In the first place, there has been a lack of empirical research into the phenomenon. The studies by Couëtoux/Di Ruzza (1990), Jobert (1990) and Rehfeldt (1992) provide the only analyses based on reasonably detailed case-studies. According to Rehfeldt, a number of phases of trade union reaction to the process of internationalisation can be distinguished. On this analysis, the adoption of the EWC Directive, after years of debate, in part signifies a concession to a long-standing trade union demand, and in part an attempt to compensate for the failure of autonomous trade union initiatives at the level of multinational companies.

In order to support trade union information exchanges and coordination, the International Trade Secretariats had promoted the establishment of 'World Company Councils' since the mid-1960s. The rapid growth of such councils in France initially seemed to confirm the correctness of this analysis and the action which flowed from it. However, in practice, most such company councils represented only fleeting and weakly institutionalised bodies. In contrast to the view suggested by their names, only very few consisted of elected employee representatives from subsidiaries, but rather only of formal structures. In no case were they able to move on to their next planned objectives – the inauguration of co-ordinated collective bargaining.

The collapse of this strategy was first and foremost the result of the absence of a legal framework at international level. This negative experience led French trade unions to re-direct their efforts towards achieving European legislation, a process which culminated with the adoption of the EWC Directive in 1994. The Directive and its national implementation were the precondition for the widespread extension of this instrument, and with this a growth in academic interest into its implications. In particular, the involvement of legal specialists culminated in the two court rulings in the Renault-Vilvoorde affair, which substantially raised the public profile of the issue of information and consultation in European companies and of EWCs.

United Kingdom

As with France, the main actors in the British system of industrial relations are the trade unions, individual employers and the state. Two other elements which play a major role in other EU countries – independent elected employee representatives and employers' associations – either barely exist (in the former case) or exercise a radically different role (in the latter). There is currently no formalised and widespread system of independent employee representation and employer associations have lost a good deal of influence in recent years. The most visible expression of this development is the fact that the erosion of collective bargaining in the UK has been the most far-reaching of any of the EU Member States. The years of Conservative government (1979-97) saw a steady weakening of the trade unions, paralleled by efforts on the part of employers at corporate level to reshape industrial relations.

The Labour administration, elected on 1 May 1997, has not sought to restore the *status quo ante* as far as trade union legislation is concerned, and has been eager to minimise the institutional ties between the Labour Party and the trade union movement. However, two measures have held out the possibility of an improvement in the scope and status of collective employee representation. Firstly, the 'opt-in' to the social policy provisions and mechanisms of the Maastricht and Amsterdam Treaties, anticipated by the specific 'extension' Directive on EWCs, means that EWCs will be established in all UK-headquartered companies which meet the criteria, together with companies located elsewhere for which the inclusion of their UK workforces will bring them within the scope of the Directive. And secondly, the government's 1998 White Paper on employment policy and industrial relations *Fairness at Work* envisages mechanisms for achieving union recognition and facilitating union representation of individual employees. Although not meeting all the hopes of the trade union movement, the White Paper was seen to be more 'union-friendly' than many observers expected.

More clearly than in other countries, the example of the UK offers an illustration of the deregulation of employment as a reaction to economic and social crisis – but at the same time also a case-study in what was a highly ideologically-driven purge of 'encrusted structures' in the market economy. Following the election of the Conservative government in the 1979, policy was driven by a desire to control the trade unions, make labour markets more flexible, reprivatise state industries, and restructure and deregulate the economy (Wendt, 1991). This 'economic' approach, aimed at recasting structures of employment and production, was coupled with a 'political' strategy of excluding intermediary organisations - most notably the trade unions - and of using populist methods to establish a direct, if fictive, link between government and people.

The trade union structure is characterised by a diversity of organising principles, at least in theory – industrial unions, craft unions, and general unions: the most dominant form is a hybrid of these options, dominated by general unions which have emerged from continuing process of mergers. Although the process of mergers both between large and small numbers has led to some reduction in the degree of union fragmentation, in the early-1990s this ran in parallel with a continuing fall in the number of union members: however, union density, at some 32-35 per cent – comparable with Germany and Italy – now appears to have stabilised somewhat. It is also worth noting that this level of union membership has been achieved without legislative support, and often in the face of opposition.

Industrial relations in the UK are traditionally described using the concept of 'voluntarism'. This means that employee organisations settle pay and conditions directly through negotiations with the employer, without state intervention and to a large degree without statutory regulation, at least on substantive terms and conditions. This does not mean that voluntarism offers a guarantee to complete freedom of collective bargaining. On the contrary, as the experience of the 1980s showed, the state actively sought to shape industrial relations: although the influence of the package of trade union legislation in the 1980s is still a topic of debate, the susceptibility of non-legally regulated and guaranteed arrangements to severe erosion in the face of determined action by a neo-liberal government served to convince the TUC that there could be merit in workplace bodies possibly existing independently of and in parallel to trade union representation.

The withdrawal of state support for tripartite arrangements in the 1980s and early-1990s and the weakening of the power of the trade unions has gone hand in hand with a decline in the influence of the main British employers' organisation, the CBI. With few exceptions, industry-wide collective bargaining has declined dramatically, and the function of employers' associations has become more one of lobbying and offering advice to their members, especially in the legal field.

The practice of workplace industrial relations depends very much on the branch of industry, the level of union organisation and the country of origin of the employing company. US and Japanese firms have had a marked influence on the climate of industrial relations over the past two decades. And whereas a number of US firms refuse any form of trade union recognition (following their native traditions), several Japanese companies pursued a different approach, especially in the mid-1980s. Although generally willing to accept collective bargaining at company level, they have insisted on recognising only one union - again analogous to Japanese traditions. This led in the past to competition between unions for representative rights, often exercised through so-called 'beauty contests' in which concessions were made to managements, including - most notoriously but in a small minority of cases - no-strike agreements and final offer arbitration ('pendulum arbitration').

Although it is correct to speak of a weakening of British trade unions, this needs some qualification and specification. The British trade union movement remains one of the largest employee organisations in Europe with almost seven million members organised in a single confederation, the TUC - with a few exceptions. Trade unions have sought to win members in fields which have traditionally been very difficult to organise. This applies in particular to the recruitment of women and part-timers, where the TUC has been able to mount fairly successful campaigns in recent years.

At workplace level, shop stewards - or their functional equivalents with varying titles - remain the main institution for employee representation in manufacturing and the public sector and hence form the backbone for EWCs. Their role can summarised as follows:

- representatives of their section, and with this an element in the formation of a group identity vis-à-vis management and other sections,

- mediators between sections within workplaces and in some cases between different plants of the same company,

- key recipient and distributor of information,

- actor in informal and formal workplace grievance procedures,

- key figure in workplace collective bargaining, either directly or by delegation, and also by delegation to company-level bargaining and consultation.

The organisation of the business of information, consultation and negotiation at workplace level depends critically on the company and the branch of the economy. In some cases, joint shop stewards committees bargain together (single table bargaining) – a growing trend urged by employers; in others, negotiation takes place for individual employee groups, or at least with a broad division into blue- and white-collar employees. The abrupt decline in employment in manufacturing in the UK has had serious consequences for the strength of the trade unions. However, although the new strategies of human resource management may have changed and weakened the role of trade unions, there are few signs that where collective bargaining is well-established companies wish to derecognise shop stewards and eliminate trade union activity entirely (Millward et. al., 1992). This marks a clear distinction to 'union busting' in the US. And in some respects the decentralisation of collective bargaining in the UK has strengthened the role and importance of workplace union representatives.

More contentious and less well-known are those aspects of TUC policy which set out how information and consultation rights are to be exercised where majority support in the trade unions is uncertain. This question is of particular current interest, as a number of European initiatives presuppose a top-to-bottom system of representation which can also operate in non-organised workplaces. Not least on these grounds, the establishment of EWCs has a particular importance for British trade unions. The TUC has proposed that such rights should operate via the trade unions wherever possible, but where trade unions have fewer than 10 per cent of the workforce, an elected forum should be established for eventualities such as collective dismissals or relocations of production, where information and consultation are vital. As noted above, such an approach, which envisages direct workforce elections as the last resort, has far-reaching significance because it marks a break with the long-held view that only trade unions should represent employees. In this connection, the establishment of the new institution could have a profound effect on the previously strongly voluntarist make up of British industrial relations.

Germany

We turn finally to the German system of industrial relations. How has the German system of industrial relations, with its dual structure of free collective bargaining between employers and trade unions combined with a statutory system of employee codetermination, stood up in recent - critical - years? At first glance, the trade unions do not appear to be in too difficult a position. Union density stands at some 35 per cent - about the same level as in Italy and the UK. More than half of all employees regard trade unions as 'indispensable'. However, the structure of union membership does exhibit a number of problems. Whereas the share of white-collar employees has risen to some 60 per cent of the labour force, they account for only 23 per cent of the membership of the main confederation, the DGB. And whereas women account for some 40 per cent of the labour force, their share of DGB membership is also around one quarter. The situation is even more problematic as far as young workers are concerned. Only around 10 per cent are trade union members and the number of young workers in most DGB affiliated unions has been falling steeply for several years. The proportion of full-time workers has also been falling steadily, with an increase in the share accounted for by part-timers, pensioners and the unemployed - implying a steady erosion of the 'standard employment relationship'.

This negative development can also be read off in the finances of the trade unions - where there has been a steady reduction in the number of full-time officer posts over recent years. Equally alarming is a second structural weakness. Union density in smaller workplaces with fewer than 30 employees, in which around half of employees work, is below 10 per cent. The manufacturing sector is also oversized, reflecting the extremely high export dependency of the German economy: the expected shift towards services in the coming years will mean that manufacturing will continue to shed jobs - with a further weakening of scope for trade union recruitment.

Official measures in the field of de-regulation have added to the internal organisational problems of the trade unions: the regulation of working hours and other terms and conditions, social security, labour law and a number of aspects of workplace employee representation have all been targeted for change since the mid-1980s.[2] The trade unions have reacted to official measures, which have been taken up immediately by the employers as bargaining objectives, with a dual strategy. Firstly, they have sought to create or retain full-time jobs through cuts in weekly working hours with no loss of pay. Secondly, they have tried to counter statutory and employer notions of flexibility with an alternative approach of widening the scope for individual working time flexibility. Such individual preferences for 'working time sovereignty' could embrace, from the trade union standpoint, guaranteed time-off for further training, more individual freedom over time-off, time-off in lieu when overtime is worked, phased retirement and a more 'social' organisation of the relationship between working hours and the growth in productivity.

The instrument of free collective bargaining - as the free negotiation of working conditions in the broadest sense between employers associations and trade unions - has proved to be both productive and flexible in international comparison, although much of the flexibility embodied in recent agreements is not made use of at workplace level (Bispinck, 1995). Moreover, the erosion of employers' associations has proved to be more of a problem for the maintenance of free collective bargaining than the fairly stable level of trade union organisation. Nonetheless, industrial relations are undergoing a profound process of restructuring as far as the system of collectively agreed regulation is concerned. Globalisation, intensified international competition and new corporate strategies have placed massive pressures on the established system of collective bargaining. The abandonment of collective agreements and of employers' association by companies, a pattern of structural transformation which favours the growth of weakly organised sectors, and the problems of economic transformation in the new *Länder* have undermined the effect of industry-wide agreements. The differentiation and decentralisation of collective regulation is leading to an increase in the strategic status of the individual firm and workplace - and the institutions associated with it - and not least prospectively the new institution of the European Works Council.

In contrast, the separation of parties and trade unions as different pillars of the labour movement (in contrast to the party affiliations which characterise many other union movements) is firmly established in Germany and is seen as having proved itself over time. Politically-oriented trade unions have - as can be seen in recent years - had greater problems in gaining social acceptance than formally independent unions. An over-intimate relationship between trade unions and political parties can damage both organisations - as has been seen in many countries, and not least in the UK. The dual system of employee representation via trade unions (collective bargaining backed up by the right to strike) and works councils (works agreements and workplace obligation to refrain from industrial action) has also proved to be broadly successful, both in institutional terms and measured against the yardstick of productivity. In addition to the problem of the erosion of 'extensive' collective agreements covering industries and regions, and the consequent revaluation of the workplace level in collective bargaining, there are also constant latent problems created by the distance between the workplace grass-roots and the trade unions - problems which will be exacerbated in the wake of more workplace orientated co-determination. However, overall the dual structure of the system with its separate legitimacy for each pillar guarantees a fairly flexible mechanism for solving problems and achieving compromise.

The legally-based system of codetermination is principally and formally located in the workplace *(Betrieb)* and undertakings or groups *(Unternehmen)*.

In view of the greater need for employee consultation at the immediate workplace on the one hand, and the need to extend European, and especially branch-related, structural policy on the other, both these as yet uncovered levels of codetermination will certainly attract the attention of the trade unions in the future. Complex, highly-developed societies such as Germany must learn and accept that their system of industrial relations and the associated level of motivation is a central socially productive force (Giddens, 1994). What will be decisive for social stability and economic efficiency in Germany is whether this bridge between productivity and codetermination can be developed and consolidated or whether, under neo-liberal pressure for deregulation, it will be deemed obsolete. In view of the economic strength of Germany in the EU, how these matters develop will also have major implications for other countries in a future common Europe characterised by a growing European structure of industrial relations. Social productivity (previously the characteristic feature of the 'Rhine Model' (Albert, 1993) could become a characteristic feature of the European model of industrial relations and hence of a European identity distinct from the great neo-liberal competitor on the world market, the USA (Lecher, 1997).

Notes

1. The three confederations have political or confessional roots: the CGIL, the largest of the three, was formerly but not exclusively closely aligned with the Italian Communist Party (PCI), now the Party of the Democratic Left; the CISL is the Christian Democratic trade union; and the UIL was aligned with the Social Democratic Party. Following the dramatic restructuring of Italian politics in the mid-1990s, which saw the collapse of the Social Democrats and the dispersion of the Christian Democrats, all the trade unions are now nominally non-politically aligned.
2. Among the main measures have been liberalisation of fixed-term contracts, cuts in unemployment benefits, the promotion of working time flexibility, and changes in the law on the negotiation and conclusion of 'social plans' in the event of economic dismissals.

7 EWCs as a Catalyst for European Industrial Relations

Are National Systems of Industrial Relations Converging?

Despite the differing national paths of adjustment outlined above, and the continuing extensive divergences in national systems of industrial relations and political frameworks, is there any discernible trend towards a convergence between these structures? In our view, three factors suggest that – in the longer term – there might be.

Firstly, the process of integration is not only rooted in the existence of functional parallelisms but also in a historical process of convergence between Western European societies over the course of the twentieth century, and especially in the period since 1945. In turn, this has influenced political integration. The social integration of Western European society is surprisingly robust (Kaelble, 1987), evidenced in comparisons of social, family, and employment structures, social mobility and social security, patterns of education and training, industrial disputes and urban development (on health, for example, see LeGoff, 1997). This process has lent an important dynamic to the direction of European integration. It can be expected that the 'wheels of history' will continue to grind even more rigorously with the full realisation of the Single Market.

Secondly, there has been a change in the internationalisation of the structure of capital. For several years, this has no longer been the most important force driving forward Western European integration. Up until the early-1980s, the process of Western European integration, centred on trade liberalisation, had essentially only stimulated a process of *national* concentration; there were few European corporate structures and the impulse for integration was primarily political. It was only with the Single Market Programme and the pressure to establish European Economic and Monetary Union that economic integration crossed the critical threshold. This raised the prospect of a new stage of integration - that of production and corporate organisation. The figures show that the process of concentration and centralisation triggered by the Single Market and EMU processes began to exhibit unambiguously 'European' features.

Thirdly, the process of integration established a level of supra- and inter-state co-operation, to which national policies were tuned and which led to the development of a Community policy, in part complementary to national policy issues. As a consequence, regulation via nation states was supplemented by a regionally structured model of regulation. Problem issues such as the breach with Fordism, economic globalisation, the dissolution of post-war structures or environmental crises were increasingly posing Western Europe's nation states with tasks which were no longer amenable to regulation or solution within national frameworks (Münch, 1993). New demands were formulated for the policies of the EU and the Commission – strengthened through the mechanism of majority voting – has been increasingly placed in the role of a true 'policy maker'. In addition, the attempt to extend the powers of the nation state via the EU had unintended and unanticipated consequences. Within the EU, European interests are often realised only via the incorporation of divergent national interests. As soon as the 'fundamental exchange' has been accomplished, the Commission is entrusted with the task of implementing the policy. As a consequence, it then becomes removed from the scope of direct intervention by the Member States. The implementing provisions decreed by the Commission lead to these mutually compensating interests achieving a degree of autonomy and constituting themselves as relatively autonomous policy spheres vis-à-vis the Member States. Finally, the EU together with the Commission shapes the national practices of the Member States in a reciprocal process, as can be seen not least in the implementation of EWCs.

EWCs - a Catalyst for European Industrial Relations?

Whereas as up until the late-1970s, there was a continuing theoretical and political debate which sought to develop broad countervailing political and trade union strategies to corporate internationalisation, such debates virtually petered out in the 1980s. Supply-side economics, which saw the globalisation of national economies as an expression of a high degree of competitiveness, achieved increasing dominance (Elsenhans, 1996). It was the transnationalisation of companies in Europe, especially in the wake of the Single Market project, which began to effect a change. This has impacted on a changed landscape of debate in which trade union identities are no longer unambiguous (Hyman, 1996) and in which a greater strategic orientation towards Europe - at least in Germany - has played a larger role. At the same time, systems of workplace employee representation and codetermination have been seen to have come under great pressure for reform (Streeck, 1996). Against this background, the response to the question posed as to the developmental conditions and direction of EWCs is of central importance (Lecher, 1996c). And this answer will differ, depending on the theoretical and analytical instruments. Three approaches – presented here in ideal-typical form – can be observed.

Neo-corporatism

Corporatist approaches make the determination of the prospects for EWCs dependent on the institutional capacity of the EU to establish a political and legally-binding framework for social policy and collective bargaining. Because this capacity is not sufficiently developed, it is sceptical about the prospects for the development of a coherent system of industrial relations. Based on the dominance of national states and the fact that neo-liberalism is unable to construct corporatist structures, the EU will remain fragmented and pluralist. As a consequence, collective bargaining at the macro-level, as well as the establishment of EWCs, will have an importance for the trade unions but no political future. Politically, the emphasis is put on the sectoral meso-level, the Europeanisation of which – sometimes with reference to the German model of branch-level agreements – is regarded as difficult, (Traxler, 1996; Martin, 1996; Streeck/Vitols, 1993) and oriented to the defence of national social standards (Streeck, 1996).

Critical modernisation theory

The Directive was not intended to establish a functioning and autonomous system of employee representation. Rather, it created a framework in which company-based productivity coalitions could be established. Previous agreements and experience show that the employee side will only be granted very limited fresh scope for exercising influence. Experience also shows that the establishment of EWCs will not automatically lead to the emergence of an autonomous system of employee representation, but will rather take on the character of a European corporate forum (Schulten, 1996). EWCs are at risk of becoming divorced from pan-employer systems of solidarity and regulation, and of weakening national systems of regulation. Against the background of an absence of regulation of the multi-sectoral level within the EU, EWCs are expected to develop into a company-oriented transnational form of employee representation (Keller, 199b, 1997).

Dynamic modernisation theory

The new impulse lent to European integration since the mid-1980s has not only extended the radius of action for the state and for purely economic actors, but has also created comparable opportunities for the trade unions. If the – late-coming – trade unions want to have a future within the multi-tiered EU system they will be forced to pursue transnational co-ordination (Platzer, 1991). EWCs can serve as a driving force for such co-operation (Lecher, 1996b) and also strengthen the European industry trade unions (Martin, 1996). EWCs are seen as potential seeds of a complex system of European industrial relations, provided the trade unions succeed in establishing and securing their links to EWCs and on the condition that the political capacities of the EU in the employment and social field are expanded (Lecher/Platzer, 1996).

PART IV:
EIGHT CASE STUDIES ON THE ESTABLISHMENT OF EUROPEAN WORKS COUNCILS

8 Fields of Interaction of EWCs

In the preceding chapters we set out the framework conditions for the establishment and development of European Works Councils. This revealed that these conditions do not constitute a set of constants but are themselves subject to change and development. This chapter now moves on to the real focus of our study: the practice of EWCs in terms both of their 'inner life' and their relevant external relations. At the centre is the EWC, constituting itself as a new actor in the representation of employee interests within a corporate framework.

The significance of EWCs is often underplayed - especially within debates in Germany - because they are endowed only with rights to information and consultation, but not codetermination. This view both *overestimates* the importance of the rights which are formally and expressly accorded to an institution and neglects the fact that such rights are only one source of power amongst several. But it also *underestimates* the importance of information and neglects the fact that conflicts of interest are primarily conducted over and through information. And finally, such a view fails to grant the organisational function of such a body the significance which it should have. The establishment of an EWC creates the precondition for the entry of a new political actor into the corporate realm. However, EWCs will only acquire this status over the course of a protracted process of constitution - with no guarantee in advance that every EWC which is established will succeed.

EWCs are constituted through the actions of its members both internally and externally. The pace, direction and course of this process are not only determined by these actions, however: they are not autonomous. Rather, they are also shaped by the related actions of others, in which each action is determined by the structure in which it takes place, and in turn serves to shape this structure. Each EWC is constituted in such a process of interaction and it is this which endows it with its specific shape. Interaction is seen here as a process of mutually-related action, in which actors respond to and anticipate the actions of others. Four different principal fields of interaction can be distinguished in the case of EWCs:

1)   Interaction between the EWC and management.

2)   Interaction amongst EWC members.

3)   Interaction between the EWC and its national sub-structure (existing national employee representative institutions and employees).

4)   Interaction between the EWC and trade unions.

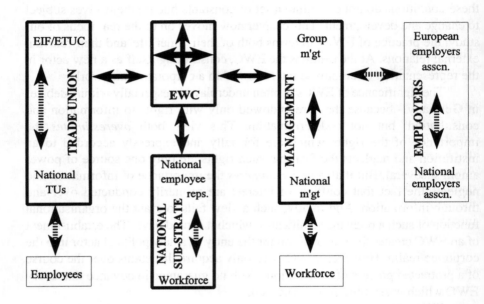

Figure 8.1 Fields of interaction of European Works Councils

Other fields of action have an indirect, though still important, influence on the operation and policies of EWCs: for example, those between European and national trade unions, between national employee representatives and employees, between central corporate management and management in national subsidiaries, and between corporate managements and employer associations. The fields of interaction which play a role for the EWC are set out in the above diagram: this excludes the political level, the significance of which we have already referred to in preceding chapters.

Although the conclusion of an EWC agreement marks the first step in the creation of a European forum for interest representation it is only an intermediate step in the process of constituting an EWC. At this stage, the exchange relationships remain weakly developed in all the above fields. It is only through interaction that learning processes and exchanges begin to take place, and it is these which drive forward the process of the constitution of the EWC. The fields of interaction are differently structured and are subject to different logics of action: each is characterised by a specific 'relationship of tension' which can promote or stunt the development of the EWC.

A: Interaction between the EWC and Management

The relationship of tension in this field of interaction is between the economic interests of the company, as represented by management, and the social interests of the employees, represented by the EWC members. It is concretely manifested on such issues as information, consultation, and the provision of resources.

That management should inform employees at all ought not to be at issue. What is contentious is the question of the topics on which information has to be disclosed, the extent of this information, and when it has to be disclosed. According to the Directive information must be provided on 'transnational questions which significantly affect workers' interests' (Article 6:3). Article 2 of the subsidiary requirements sets out a detailed list of the issues on which information is required.

In contrast, the meaning of 'consultation' has already become a matter of dispute. In the Directive 'consultation' is defined as 'the exchange of views and the establishment of dialogue between employees' representatives and central management or any more appropriate level of management' (Article 2:1 f). The Directive does not state at what stage of the decision-making process consultation must take place, nor even whether it must take place before any decision is taken. Whether consultation can delay a decision is also unresolved. The consultation rights in the Directive lag far behind what is enshrined, for example, in French law. Here 'the obligation to consult with the group committee is mandatory: consultation must be preceded by detailed information in writing, and the committee must have sufficient time to examine the issue. Management cannot make a decision before consultation has been concluded' (Danis, 1996, p. 59).[1] However, even given such extensive rights, the right to consultation only represents a procedural guarantee that employee representatives can set out their views to a company's central management: it does not impinge on management's decision-making prerogative. However, the mere fact that employee representatives may not be confronted with management *faits accomplis* but must be informed beforehand implies a considerable enhancement of their capacity to influence policy and mount a defence if necessary. Because of the broad range of what can be understood by 'consultation', differences between EWCs and managements as how this right is to be interpreted and met are almost inevitable.[2]

The issue of resources will almost certainly prove to be a further area of friction between EWCs and group managements. On the one hand, EWCs - with their costs for interpreting, travel and accommodation - are certainly an expensive item compared with customary forms of employee representation. On the other, there are often no other costs apart from those incurred in holding one joint meeting. As EWCs establish themselves, other expenses – such as for committee meetings, infrastructure, administration, time off and training – can all be expected to increase considerably.

Managements will undoubtedly seek to make active use of the scope for information and consultation to ensure that EWCs also meet their objectives (cf. Schulten, 1995, p. 356). This could yield areas of overlapping interest which might offer EWCs scope to secure regulations which are of benefit to both sides within a corridor of common interests.

B: Interaction between EWC Members

The establishment of an EWC creates a formal structure for the mutual exchange of information, for tackling mutual prejudices and reservations, for a mutual reconciliation of interests, and for the elaboration of common demands. This comprises the organisational, 'inner-directed' function of the EWC. Only practice will reveal the extent to which EWCs prove successful in moving through a process of internal constitution from a heterogeneous forum to a cohesive unity.

One particular relationship of tension may well be that between EWC representatives from the parent company's home base and those of its foreign subsidiaries. In fact, the quality of work of an EWC can be read off from the extent to which EWC representatives from subsidiaries are actively included in the EWC and feel that their interests are represented by it. This thesis rests on two suppositions: firstly, that despite all the rhetoric of decentralisation and networking, foreign subsidiaries remain highly dependent on the strategic planning and decisions of group managements – leading to a correspondingly high level of interest on the part of EWC representatives from foreign subsidiaries in information in this area; and secondly, that – with the exception of the UK – EWC representatives from the home base can obtain information about the group via national representational arrangements, and that, as a result, their interest in such information via the EWC will be correspondingly less.

In building internal strength and cohesion – on our assumption – three dimensions will play a critical role: the communicative, the socio-cultural and the institutional.

As far as the communicative dimension is concerned, this entails the creation of both formal and informal relationships for communication. The establishment of EWCs as institutions capable of representing employee interests can only succeed if these relationships flourish between EWC representatives in the periods between formal meetings.

The socio-cultural dimension aims at the individual ability of EWC members to commit themselves to a transnational forum, to respect and consider the interests of others, and to operate in a situation characterised by very different political styles and forms of conduct: in short, to contribute to the cohesiveness of the body as a whole.

And finally, the institutional dimension focuses on the manner in which the institution is formed – and critically the question of internal democracy.

C: The EWC and National Structures of Employee Representation

This field of interaction is characterised by the relationship of tension between the national and European levels of workplace employee representation. At the time of its establishment, the EWC is initially a body cut loose from national structures of representation. The process of the constitution of an EWC must then also be a process through which the national and European levels of representation are integrated and intermeshed. In other words: in order to prevent EWCs becoming isolated and marginalised – and hence delegitimised – a link must be established both in institutional and communication terms between the EWC and national structures of representation.

This process embraces, firstly, the exchange of information between the two levels of representation and, secondly, the inclusion of employees so that they can form their own, well-founded, judgement on the work of the EWC. Understanding the significance of the EWC is not something likely to emerge spontaneously. Rather, one key task for EWC representatives will be to generate interest in the work of the EWC amongst employees and workforce representatives at national level and persuade them of the necessity for such a body.

Because of the possibility that the EWC will advance from being simply a committee for information exchange to an institution for interest representation at European level, it is crucial for the EWC to be acknowledged as a legitimate forum by employees and their representatives – with a corresponding importance for the choice of procedure for determining EWC representatives.

Moreover, in establishing the interrelationships between European and national levels, questions of capacity and competence are bound to play a part, reflecting the capacity problems already apparent at national level attributable to factors such as a lack of time-off for duties or multiple office-holding.

D: Interaction between EWCs and Trade Unions

The field of interaction between EWCs and trade unions centres on the relationship of tension between the 'internal' and 'external' dimensions. Trade unions as organisation act from outside the corporate sphere and seek, from this position, to exert influence over representational issues within companies via the EWC.

Whilst trade unions have been a key factor in drawing forward the development of EWCs, EWCs for their part could also play a decisive role in the Europeanisation of trade union strategies and the development of European collective bargaining. In other words: interaction between EWCs and trade unions could strengthen both. This interaction could also be a source of problems. There are two, equally likely, scenarios: the risk that EWCs might be 'appropriated' by trade unions or the reverse case in which EWCs become decoupled from the trade unions.

As far as the interrelationships between EWCs and trade unions are concerned, three issues are of relevance:

- The extent to which an exchange of information is provided for: what will be decisive is the degree to which trade unions have access to information on the day-to-day activities of EWCs to ensure that they do not become decoupled from the task of interest representation at company-level.

- The extent to which trade unions support EWCs in practical respects – that is, whether they succeed in building up an extensive, sectoral structure for servicing EWCs and a training programme which gives EWC representatives the appropriate competencies.

- And thirdly, the question of the strategic orientation of the EWC will become more important as their practice advances.

All this will place new demands on the trade unions themselves - demands for greater Europeanisation and for closer integration between European and national trade union structures.

Concluding Observation

Only long-term practical operation, going beyond the scope of this study, experience and actual developments, together with the interaction between EWCs once established on a broad basis will demonstrate how the 'inner' shape and efficacy of EWCs will develop and what their 'external' role might be in the structures of national and transnational European industrial relations. Two – polar – developments could come about. In one, an autonomous development, driven by EWC representatives themselves; in the other, a process directed from the outside, either by management, trades unions, or national employee representative structures. The case-studies which follow for the most part are located midway on this spectrum. They show a high degree of diversity and exhibit a varied pattern of development and progress.

Notes

1. Owing to the weakness of workplace employee representation in France, this right is, however, only observed to a limited degree.
2. See the conflict in the case of Renault, outlined above.

9 Schmalbach-Lubeca: Countervailing Power through Information

Schmalbach-Lubeca AG is a part of the VIAG group of companies. Since 1991 VIAG AG has owned 100 per cent of Continental Can GmbH Europe, which in turn owns 61.4 per cent of Schmalbach-Lubeca. The remaining shares are distributed over a variety of shareholders. VIAG is a financial holding company, active in a number of businesses, with a total group turnover in 1997 of some DM 49.5 billion and 95,500 employees. The main business divisions are energy (Bayernwerk AG, and others); chemicals (SKW Trostberg), logistics (Klöckner & Co. AG and Kühne & Nagel), telecommunications (VIAG Interkom) and packaging (Schmalbach-Lubeca, VAW Aluminium, Gerresheimer Glas). VIAG shares are owned by the *Land* government of Bavaria (25.28 per cent), the power utility Isar-Amperwerke (15.06 per cent), and two Bavarian banks, the Bayerische Hypotheken- und Wechselbank (5.03 per cent) and the Bayerische Vereinsbank (5.3 per cent). The remainder are distributed across a number of shareholders - leaving the public sector with a blocking minority of VIAG.

VIAG itself is a decentralised group, with decision-making at Schmalbach-Lubeca constrained to only a small extent. The VIAG holding company only makes those decisions which affect the general direction of the group. The high degree of autonomy enjoyed by VIAG subsidiaries is evidenced by the fact that there is no unified strategy for or co-ordination between the companies in the packaging division. For example, VAW Aluminium is subject to the same terms as any other supplier to Schmalbach-Lubeca. VIAG does not prescribe supplier-purchaser relationships. Gerresheimer Glas (glass bottles) and Schmalbach-Lubeca (cans, PET bottles) even compete with each other. The VIAG holding company is no more concerned with such competition than it is with facilitating and developing co-operation between the two companies: Gerresheimer Glas produces milk bottles and Schmalbach-Lubeca produces caps for them.

At the time of the study, Schmalbach-Lubeca was passing through a major restructuring. Up until 1996 the company had the following business areas (with turnover): drinking cans (DM 1,363 million, 2,026 employees); PET containers

(DM 543 million, 720 employees); metal packaging (DM 1,112 million, 4,658 employees); White Cap glass stoppers (DM 711 million, 2,999 employees) and plastic packaging (DM 360, 1,700 employees). At year-end 1996, Schmalbach-Lubeca had a total of 12,351 employees, of which more than half worked in Germany.

Table 9.1 Turnover and employment at the Schmalbach-Lubeca group, 1995-97

	1995		1996		1997	
	Turnover (DM m.)	Employees	Turnover (DM m.)	Employees	Turnover (DM m.)*	Employees
Germany	1,262.90	5,715	1,226.70	5,477	21%	20%
Rest of Europe	2,483.70	5,590	2,494.29	5,455	47%	40%
North America	285.70	1,351	286.23	1,205	29%	34%
Other	91.9		81.78	214	3%	6%

*   Expected distribution of turnover and employment: 1997 total turnover was DM 4.3 billion, compared with DM 4.089 in 1996. Total employment in 1997 was 9,957 compared with 12,490 in 1996: the fall was mainly explicable by the sale of some businesses (see below).

The restructuring initiated in early-1997 was aimed at extending and developing those business areas in which the company had prospective market leadership, and disposing of those which were not regarded as being capable of development within the group. This involved not only plastic packaging but also Schmalbach-Lubeca's traditional core business, metal packaging. The metal side of the business was put into a joint venture with the French packaging manufacturer Pechiney and the British investment group Doughty Hanson & Co. Schmalbach-Lubeca and Pechiney then each owned 20 per cent of the new company, Impress Metal Packaging, with Doughty Hanson & Co holding the remaining 60 per cent. The plastic packaging division was sold to the British RPC group. This left Schmalbach-Lubeca with the PET container, drinks packaging and White Cap businesses to develop, as a result of which the PET business was expanded through the acquisition of the Plastic Container Division of Johnson Controls/USA.

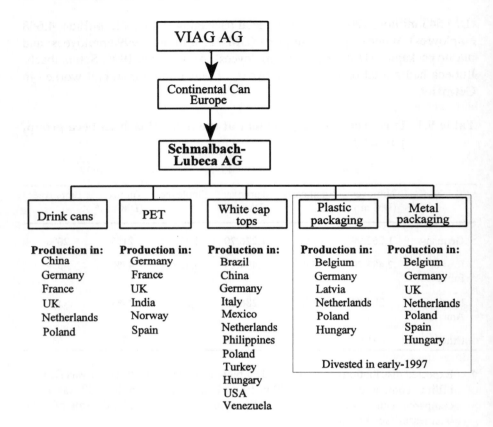

Figure 9.1   Structure of the Schmalbach-Lubeca group

The restructuring meant that within a short time Schmalbach-Lubeca had moved from being a European company to a globally active group present on both the European and American markets. The company is also now active on the Asian market and will extend its presence in the future.

The strategy calls for the remaining business areas to be either number one or two on all key markets, and if possible worldwide. Schmalbach-Lubeca already has market leadership in the glass top market, is the largest supplier in the PET area through the acquisition of the Plastic Container Division of Johnson Controls, and has also gained access through this to strategic markets in America. In the drinks can business, the company is number two in Europe.

Schmalbach-Lubeca's restructuring had a considerable impact on the EWC, in particular in Germany and the Netherlands where the production of metal packaging, which was sold, was concentrated. All the German and Dutch employee representatives on the EWC came from the metal packaging business, and these seats on the EWC had to be re-occupied. In addition, the PET companies which were bought employed some 700 employees in Europe who had to be integrated into the activities of the EWC.

Origin and Structure of the EWC

The Emergence of the EWC

The establishment of a body for European employee representation at Schmalbach-Lubeca took place in the second half of the pioneer phase. Individual pilot projects were already in operation and the trade unions had abandoned their prevarication and scepticism and had begun to actively support the establishment of EWCs. The processes of the initiation and negotiation were also supported by the institutional and material backing of the EU Commission.

In October 1991, the Schmalbach-Lubeca 'GBR/KBR' (central works council/group works council)[1] took the initiative, without consulting other European employee representatives, and wrote to the Schmalbach-Lubeca group management board calling on it to enter into negotiations on the establishment of an EWC. The management board turned down the proposal for the conclusion of a voluntary agreement, but did state that it was willing to agree to the establishment of a European Committee without a written agreement. The central works council of one of the Dutch subsidiaries was also involved in parallel activities at the same time. This body approached the Dutch and other European employee representatives outside Germany with the aim of bringing in the German employee representatives last. The Dutch representatives felt that in taking a solo initiative, the Germans had gone behind their backs. As a result, the problematic relationship between the two - who regarded themselves as competitors - came under even more strain. This conflict ran through the initial meetings of the EWC and made its internal constitution more difficult.

Supported organisationally by the European Metalworkers' Federation and financed by EU budget line 4004, workplace employee representatives from Belgium, Germany, the UK and the Netherlands met in Brussels in February 1992. The meeting was attended by a representative of the Dutch trade union confederation, the FNV, together with the General Secretary of the European chemical workers industry federation, EMCEF. No representatives of the group's management board were present. The aim of the first meeting was allow employee representatives from the various European sites to get to know each other and to discuss the aims and tasks of the European body.

In October 1992 the first joint meeting with Schmalbach-Lubeca management took place. The employee side consisted of representatives from Belgium, Germany, the UK, the Netherlands and, for the first time, France. The main point on the agenda was the discussion of the proposed standing orders. This involved the demand by British employee representatives to enshrine the involvement of full-time trade union officials at the annual meeting of the European Committee into the Committee's procedures. No agreement could be reached on this. The standing orders for the European Committee were adopted at a second meeting in May 1993. Between the meetings, the German chair of the group works council agreed an improvement in the financial provisions and facilities for the European Committee with management.

The standing orders fleshed out the correspondence - the real basis for the European Committee - in a number of important respects. The chair of the German group works council *(Konzernbetriebsrat)* was confirmed as president of the European Committee. The employee representatives on the Committee were aware that this provision breached any notion of democracy but accepted it as a condition imposed by management. The Committee elected a praesidium to support its work. The standing orders envisaged two meetings of the European Committee each year, with a report from the group's management board at at least one of them. The composition of the Committee was as follows: each 1,322 employees were entitled to one seat, with at least two seats per country irrespective of the number of employees. This yielded a total of 22 employee representatives: five from Germany, three from the Netherlands and two each from Belgium, France, Italy, Poland, Spain, Hungary and the UK. Management had originally wanted a limit of 14 but conceded on this point. The German representatives relinquished some of the seats they could have had based on the workforce size, and made up a quarter of the body - although more than half of Schmalbach-Lubeca's workforce was located in Germany at that time.

From European Committee to European Works Council

Following the adoption of the EWC Directive in September 1994, the German metalworkers' union IG Metall proposed to the members of the European Committee that negotiations should be opened with the group management board to establish a European Works Council based on a written agreement in line with the provisions of the Directive. The praesidium - basically the German chair and a full-time official of IG Metall - drafted an agreement. The draft, which was based on a number of key points set out by IG Metall and the existing practice of the European Committee, was adopted unanimously at a meeting of the Committee in May 1995 after a few small changes.

The Schmalbach-Lubeca group management board responded with a reworked draft agreement, which on some issues did not come up to the minimum standards of the Directive's subsidiary requirements. Negotiations dragged on for nine months. The text finally agreed by both parties was submitted to the European Committee, all the national trade unions represented and the EMF and EMCEF for comment. In August 1996 – with no further response from the trade union side – the agreement was signed to establish a 'European Works Council' at Schmalbach-Lubeca.

The Agreement

As with the European Committee, the EWC is installed at the level of the Schmalbach-Lubeca group. Within Germany, there is also an employee representative body at the level of the VIAG holding company in the form of a 'group working party' *(Konzernarbeitsgruppe)* composed of members of the group works councils of the individual VIAG subsidiaries. In addition, German employee representatives receive information on VIAG's group strategy via the supervisory board, on which employee representatives from the group's component companies are represented. The decision to locate the EWC at divisional rather than group level reflected the desire to establish an effective European employee representation. Since the EU Directive did not envisage the establishment of EWCs at both holding company and group level, the employee representatives on the VIAG group working party decided not to set up an EWC at the level of the holding company. And because the groups within the overall conglomerate structure each consist of a number of business divisions, locating the EWC at the level of VIAG would have meant that these divisions would have been insufficiently represented and the body would have been extremely heterogeneous. There was a worry that employee representatives from individual companies would then have brought their specific concerns to the EWC, which would have possibly restricted its effectiveness. An agreement was therefore struck with VIAG group management under which employee representatives accepted that there would not be an EWC at the level of the holding group but that existing EWCs at the level of individual companies would continue. This provision, which had the effect of cutting off the foreign employee representatives from direct contact with VIAG top management, was discussed before the Schmalbach-Lubeca EWC agreement was signed in the European Committee. The fact that the members of the European Committee agreed the provision can be seen as proof of their confidence in their German colleagues as the EWC representatives from the company's foreign subsidiaries are now reliant on the German representatives to obtain information about overall VIAG strategy.

The change in the characterisation of body from European Committee to European Works Council in itself gave a foretaste of the roles which the employee representatives envisaged for it: it is not 'just' a European information committee. The preamble is very direct on this, and refers to the fact that the body is an EWC within the meaning of the EU Directive. There is no section on corporate culture or any commitment to the interests of the company, as seen in many other voluntary agreements. Rather, cooperation between employee representatives and group management is described through incorporation of Article 9 of the Directive:

> The central management and the European Works Council shall work in a spirit of cooperation with due regard to their reciprocal rights and obligations.

The outcome of the negotiations on the EWC agreement suggest that the employee side enjoyed a fairly strong negotiating position. The agreement goes beyond the Directive in many respects. For example, the provision on costs reads as follows: 'The costs which arise as a result of the operation of the EWC will be borne by the undertaking.' In contrast, many other agreements merely require the company to cover the costs of the annual meetings.

Much of the agreement merely enshrines the practice already established in the European Committee. Over the course of time, the representatives on the European Committee extended their scope, in part through negotiations and in part tacitly. For example, the provisions on the establishment of a praesidium, on the establishment of a secretariat or on two annual meetings were all taken over into the EWC agreement. Moreover, the adoption of the EWC Directive improved the negotiating position of employee representatives, as the subsidiary requirements were available as a set of prospective minimum conditions. What was more difficult, however, was that the new negotiations were conducted with corporate management at a time when the business was not running successfully.

The central organisational powers of the EWC at Schmalbach-Lubeca are in the hands of the employee representatives. The praesidium consists solely of employee representatives. The agenda - including that of the joint meetings - is put together by the employee representatives. The EWC has its own secretariat with a part-time employee which carries out the organisational work of the EWC: that is, organising the EWC and praesidium, arranging interpreters, dealing with correspondence, answering calls and letters from other employee representatives, and much more.

The composition of the EWC is identical to that of the European Committee. According to the original draft agreement produced by management, the EWC was not to exceed 20 employee representatives. At times this figure was exceeded on the European Committee because employee representatives brought in trade union officials as 'advisers'. However, management was eager to put a stop to such 'rampant expansionism'. The text finally agreed stated: 'Efforts will be made not to allow the number of members to exceed 22'. Management was also concerned that the locations of the meetings constantly changed, raising the costs. In a minute to the agreement it was stated that the meetings would usually take place in Antwerp, with a departure from this at most once a year.

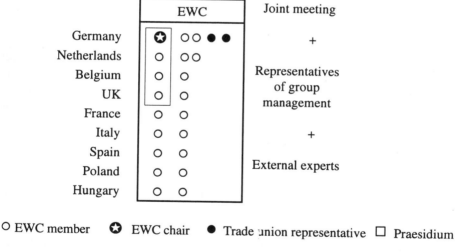

O EWC member   **✪** EWC chair   **●** Trade union representative   **☐** Praesidium

Figure 9.2 Composition of the Schmalbach-Lubeca EWC

As far as representatives from non-EU countries was concerned, the agreement lagged behind the provision in the original correspondence. In a letter from management to the group works council it had been stated: 'One indispensable precondition is that participation by representatives from all countries is secured as only through this will it be possible to secure an exchange of information which is of equal value for all'. The draft agreement proposed by the group management board only envisaged participation by representatives from those countries which were embraced by the Directive. In the agreement, a paragraph was included which created scope for the inclusion of workforce representatives from companies which had their headquarters outside the EU if both signatories to the agreement gave their consent. Evidently, management wanted to retain an option not to have to include all countries with operations in the EWC.

The agreement provided for two EWC meetings a year, of which at least one would include participation by management. Management was to inform and consult with the EWC at the joint meeting on matters 'affecting the controlling undertaking as a whole or at least two establishments in the countries represented'. The subjects embraced by the provisions on information and consultation go beyond the provisions of the subsidiary requirements. Additional issues are listed which allow a comparison to be made between labour costs at individual locations, making it more difficult for sites to be played off against each other. The following matters are listed: current position of and trends in employee skills and qualifications, training and further training, pay, working hours, developments in working conditions and the working environment, safety and environmental protection, benefits, the production and investment programme, and rationalisation proposals. The catalogue ends with a general clause guaranteeing EWC members a right to information on other developments and plans which might have a substantial impact on employee interests. Moreover, the EWC also has the right to submit its own proposals for other issues to be considered. As a result, issues which had not appeared to be significant when the agreement was signed but which could become important in the future can still be raised.

EWC members have the right to request information direct from national managements. 'The board of SLW AG and the management of CCE GmbH will ensure - if appropriate - that the members of the EWC will receive all information, data and documentation which they require for the proper exercise of their duties as EWC members direct from the responsible managements of national companies'. The passage also secures the provision of information outside annual meetings with group management, and gives the EWC scope to request information from the management of national subsidiaries which, in effect, extends German employee information rights throughout the EU. Conversely, the agreement also obliges EWC members to pass on information to national employee representatives.

The confidentiality of information is regulated in detail in the agreement. In order to count as a commercial secret, information must meet a precisely specified set of criteria. The obligation to maintain confidentiality does not apply within the EWC nor vis-à-vis national employee representatives who are covered by confidentiality provisions under their own national laws, nor towards employee representatives on the company's supervisory board and on conciliation machinery set up under the German Works Constitution Act.

The EWC has a praesidium which can consist of up to five members. Its task is to support the president of the EWC in their duties. In contrast to the European Committee, the 1996 agreement established that both the praesidium and the president are to be elected by the EWC. Up until the end of the 1996, the praesidium consisted of a German representative (the President), a Dutch representative, a Belgian and a British representative. Following the corporate restructuring in 1997, the praesidium has consisted of one representative each from the Netherlands, France, the UK and Germany.

One of the most controversial issues in the negotiations was the use of expert advisers, over which the management wanted to retain a right of veto. Finally, the relevant section of the subsidiary requirements was used, under which the EWC and praesidium can be supported by an expert adviser of their choice. Additional experts can be drawn on subject to agreement with management.

The agreement provides for the formal enshrinement of the structure which had already operated with the European Committee. The annual meeting only for EWC members, information rights between joint meetings and the establishment of a secretariat all testify to the fact that the EWC is not exclusively focused on the joint meeting with management. Rather, the agreement offers the EWC a foundation on which it can develop its own identity in the absence of management.

Fields of Interaction

EWC and Group Management

At one EWC meeting a year, group management is available for information and consultation. The management contingent also usually includes the chair of the management board, the Labour Director *(Arbeitsdirektor)*[2] and the group head of personnel. When specific problems are on the agenda, other appropriate management representatives can attend.

According to the agreement, information and consultation takes place following release of the Annual Report and Accounts, the half-yearly Interim

Reports, and Personnel and Social Reports. Any additional information required and other documentation for meetings must be made available 'in good time' in the various national languages. In practice, this has still not been fully realised. The meetings begin with a general report from the management board, usually by the board's chair, in which detailed information, sometimes on a country-by-country basis is given on the business situation, and on current projects and investments. Following this, there is scope for discussion with the board. According to one of the German EWC representatives, information is extensive, is provided at the appropriate time, and is of the same quality as the information provided to supervisory board meetings.

For most EWC members, contact with management is confined to the annual joint meeting. In contrast, the EWC praesidium has more frequent meetings with representatives of group management, especially with those responsible for personnel matters. These attend meetings of the praesidium when there is need for specific information. For the German EWC members there are also contacts as part of their activities on the joint company and group works council (the 'KBR/GBR'), as members of the company's 'economic committee' *(Wirtschaftsausschuss)*[3] and as members of the supervisory board *(Aufsichtsrat)*[4].

The Schmalbach-Lubeca EWC has succeeded in influencing management decisions on specific issues. We consider two examples. In the first, group management planned to relocate the White Cap tops division from Hanover to Italy, which would have entailed a cut of some 120 jobs in Hanover. In the Italian plant affected, the move would have led to a worsening of working conditions through the extension of three-shift working and Saturday and Sunday work since no additional capacity had been set aside to deal with the increased output and no investment was planned. The EWC was informed and established a working party with employee representatives from the plants concerned, which included non-EWC employee representatives. This group opened negotiations with group management, with the result that the impact of the planned measures could be cushioned. Production in Hanover was only reduced by 10 per cent, and weekend work was avoided in Italy. From the employee side, negotiations were helped by the fact that the relocation would have had disadvantages for the workforces at both plants – allowing a common negotiating stance to be developed. Matters might have been different had management intended to invest in the Italian plant.

The EWC was also involved in and influenced the planned introduction of a centralised logistics system. Group management had commissioned an external company, Continental-Logistik-Services-Gesellschaft (CLS), with the development of a unified pan-European logistics scheme for Schmalbach-Lubeca with the aim of ascertaining whether an external service provider, or CLS, could take on this function. Changing the internal logistics system would have had an impact on working conditions. The German and Dutch employee representatives were informed about the CLS project in the context of their national information structures, and they informed the EWC. There was a discussion within the EWC, and a common position was worked out. The EWC called on Schmalbach-Lubeca to inform employee representatives about the contracts with CLS and to consult on them before they were signed. This was acceded to. The resistance of local employee representatives to the scheme meant that CLS (which in the meantime had become 50 per cent owned by Schmalbach-Lubeca) excluded internal logistics from its brief. The scheme was then dropped altogether, probably less because of the intervention of the EWC than because it was not sufficiently developed.

The EWC's scope for influencing events has improved over time. The EWC has been able to exercise a strong degree of control over management attempts to place national sites into mutual competition because it can subject management claims to reasonably rigorous examination at the joint meetings.

The EWC has also been useful for management. Following the acquisition of Schmalbach-Lubeca by VIAG, management used the EWC as a means of welding together the individual component companies into a group with 'one' corporate tradition: initially, relations between the German and Dutch companies had been complicated by the fact that each saw the other as a competitor. Moreover, group management also sees the EWC as useful in that a large number of restructuring measures could not have been implemented as smoothly without it. This absence of conflict offered real commercial gains to the company.

Representatives of the managements of the group's foreign subsidiaries do not have any opportunity to meet which is comparable with that of the EWC. As a result, they are sometimes not as well informed as EWC members – an issue which prompted a letter from the Italian management to the group's management board. Managers from other foreign subsidiaries (especially from Spain) felt undermined by the approach to information disclosure pursued by group management. Conversely, the group head of personnel saw it as a problem that group management was open in its information disclosure at EWC meetings, but that the management of some national subsidiaries was much more restrictive in its attitude to EWC representatives locally. He is aware that the approach to information by national managements must be improved.

Overall, there is a co-operative relationship between the EWC and group management. On the one hand, the EWC has been able to develop a degree of strength vis-à-vis management, which is rooted in the cooperation between EWC members. The EWC is also beginning to develop information structures at European level in the sense that it is confident in requesting the information from management which it needs to represent employee interests. On the other hand, group management has an interest in a good working relationship with employees and has been willing to make substantial concessions to this end.

The Schmalbach-Lubeca EWC has already ventured onto the difficult terrain of sounding out the issue of pan-European regulations on working conditions in the group and discussing this with management. Talks have been held on the issue of health and safety – a subject on which improvements can be achieved for employees with broad cost-neutrality for the company. The EWC has gone a step further and formulated, albeit very tentatively, recommendations to the board to raise company social benefits in countries with a low level. There has been no response from the company. The EWC President does not regard it as possible at present to discuss such issues with the company and has also sought to avoid such discussions in the EWC as he fears that excessive expectations could be raised which will detract from its current work.

Relationships within the EWC

There are two EWC meetings each year, of which one is a pre-meeting and one a review following information and consultation with management. At the EWC meetings, EWC representatives give a brief report on current developments in their national workplaces. These country reports were initially very short and not very informative: the quality has subsequently improved considerably. Following the meeting with the group management, there is a discussion between EWC members.

In the initial phase, the meetings were characterised by a number of difficulties between EWC members. In particular, there was competition between the German and Dutch EWC representatives, which had been exacerbated by the establishment of the European Commitee on the sole initiative of the German group works council. The first meeting of the European Committee was marked by a degree of mutual mistrust which hampered the work of the Committee.

A decisive change in the quality of the relationships between EWC members took place in 1993 when the group works council acquired a new chair. This individual, acting in the traditions of IG Metall, also took over as president of the EWC. Recognising that effective representation in the long-term called for a cross-border representative body, he initially devoted some 40 per cent of his time to the EWC – a proportion which fell to around 20 per cent once the EWC had become more stable. The change of personalities also heralded a change in style. German dominance of the EWC was wound back, the interests of foreign EWC members were recognised and taken more account of, and information was more openly dealt with in the EWC. The new president made the greater amount of knowledge which he acquired by virtue of his office available to the EWC. In an effort to eliminate mutual mistrust, he initiated informal contact with the Dutch EWC representatives, which led to the establishment of the praesidium - that is, a widening of the basis of leadership within the EWC. This was also intended to reduce the dominance of the president - that is, the chair of the German group works council. One further concession to the Dutch representatives consisted in the establishment of the secretariat in the Netherlands. Since then, the former EWC secretary has left and the secretariat has been moved on organisational grounds back to the EWC president's location: however, this did not trigger any new difficulties.

The praesidium meets approximately every two months when necessary. Since the members of the praesidium meet representatives of management more frequently than other EWC members, they also have much better access to information. The flow of information between the members of the praesidium is also fairly good, based on their own frequent contacts. Communication within the praesidium is clearly more intensive than within the EWC itself. However, the praesidium has tried to include EWC members who are not represented on the praesidium in its work. For example, following joint meetings with management, there is a review meeting of the EWC with assessments, discussion and a drawing of any conclusions. Any actions deemed necessary are assigned to individuals.

Those who are not members of the praesidium are not excluded from this process. Furthermore, EWC members are sent a short note of the minutes of the praesidium meeting, together with a circular on the company's results every four to six weeks. However, the French EWC representative has complained that the members of the praesidium have access to more current information that other EWC members. Conversely, the return flow of information from EWC members to the praesidium is not well developed. The call by the praesidium for EWC members to provide it with regular reports on the situation in the individual countries has not yet met with a positive response.

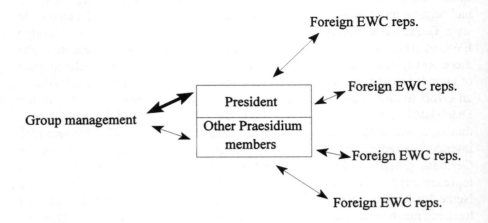

Figure 9.3 Internal communications at the Schmalbach-Lubeca EWC

According to the German EWC member, language problems have not proved to be a major impediment to communication, with interpretation available at the meetings. Informal discussions could usually be translated by company employees. The French EWC representative, however, noted that informal contacts were more difficult in the absence of a common language. In order to overcome language problems, EWC members have been offered language training tailored to their individual needs.

There is no informal contact between the EWC representatives from France and Germany. Formal contact is also not highly developed and confined to EWC meetings. Questions from the French EWC representative to the praesidium were only answered after a considerable delay, with the consequence that they no longer forward questions. The establishment of informal contacts could also prove difficult in this instance as the French representatives are not members of one of the national unions represented in the European Metalworkers' Federation (EMF) but belong to an autonomous workplace trade union. As a result, the German EWC members, who found it difficult to locate them politically, have treated the French representatives with a degree of reserve. Conversely, membership of a trade union affiliated to the EMF would certainly simplify the process of developing a relationship and reinforce the sense of a common political foundation, despite cultural and language problems.

Although it is not the aim of the EWC to take the place of local representatives, but rather to pass on information and offer assistance which might improve the prospects for solving problems locally, it will support local employee representatives if it feels this is necessary. This was illustrated in the case of a conflict in a Spanish subsidiary which manufactures PET containers. The purchaser of the containers, a drinks bottler, intended to undertake the final production of the bottles under its own management. This would have meant that a proportion of the Schmalbach-Lubeca workforce in Spain would have been transferred to the bottling company. National management refused to provide any information to the local workforce about the state of negotiations. The employee representatives brought in the EWC praesidium which asked for the relevant information from group management and made contact with the Spanish employee representatives. The praesidium then conducted negotiations with the national management which led to form of social compensation plan for those employees who were to transfer to the bottling company. Those who did not want to transfer were offered work in another nearby Schmalbach-Lubeca plant.

One example of the usefulness of a good flow of information between EWC members can be seen in the development following the group restructuring in late-1996. The German EWC representative whom we interviewed was employed in the metal packaging division and transferred to the newly-established Impress Metal Packaging. Following the takeover of the metal division, German employee representatives negotiated a social compensation plan for the event that the rationalisation might lead to plant closures. They directly informed the Dutch representatives on the course of negotiations who were also affected by the restructuring and also opened negotiations with the company. The relatively favourable German agreement, negotiated under the more stringent provisions of German law, also constituted the basis for the Dutch negotiations.

EWC and National Employee Representation

The agreement obliges EWC members to pass on information to their respective workforce. Information received at EWC meetings is communicated in Germany via the usual channels: that is, group or central works council - works council - workforce. Members of the group works council are required to report at workforce meetings on the outcomes of EWC meetings at least once a year. Moreover - in at least in one instance - opportunity has been taken to include a report on the work of the EWC in the company newspaper. However, a further planned article on the positions of the EWC in more detail failed to materialise because of organisational difficulties. There was a discussion in the EWC as to whether the outcomes of EWC meetings should be put up on the official notice board; this was rejected on the grounds, firstly, that experience had shown that hardly anyone read such notices and, secondly, that EWC members might feel themselves discharged from any further responsibility to pass on information. The scope for direct communication offered by workforce meetings was seen as being of paramount importance. Interest from the workforce is very low and is confined to situations in which they are directly affected.

The French EWC representatives pass on the minutes of the EWC meeting to the French *comité d'entreprise* with their own observations and also pin this up on the official notice board. Because there are only two manufacturing plants in France, with an EWC representative from each one, this ensures that French employees are informed about the EWC - at least in theory.

The problem of achieving effective integration between national employee representation and employees and the EWC has not yet been solved. However, there is a recognition that the EWC will forfeit legitimacy unless national structures of representation are drawn in and employees convinced of the need for interest representation at European level.

EWC and Trade Unions

The question of the participation of full-time trade union officials has been a subject of repeated conflict and discussion. During the negotiations on the agreement, group management wanted to exclude the possibility of full-time officials participating in EWC meetings. But there were also differing opinions within the EWC itself. The trade unions had put the demand for greater involvement both to the EWC and its predecessor, the European Committee. In May 1993, the European Committee issued the following opinion.

> This Committee regards the participation of external trade union officials as not being necessary within the context of dealing with corporate issues. There is a need for cooperation with full-time trade union officials at European level. The Committee can approach full-time trade union officials or others in connection with specific matters, if it regards this as necessary.

This negative stance towards the trade unions led the EMF to call a European conference on its own initiative to which were invited - in addition to EWC representatives - full-time trade union officials. One aim of the conference, which took place in Amsterdam in February 1994, was to develop a joint structure for trade union coordination. Neither the German EWC representatives nor representatives of IG Metall considered there was any need to take action. The participants eventually agreed that a Dutch-German trade union delegation should negotiate with group management on trade union inclusion. These negotiations proved unsuccessful. As a consequence, the final outcome of the efforts to achieve greater trade union involvement was initially simply a commitment on the part of the members of the European Committee that they would work closely with the trade unions in the future and inform national unions about the course of meetings. However, the final written agreement did include a provision which allowed full-time trade union representatives to attend EWC meetings as experts - an option which has not yet been exercised.

However, full-time trade union officials - an IG Metall official and up until the 1997 group restructuring an official of the German chemical union - are represented as full members of the EWC. This special status was accorded to the German trade union representatives under the Committee's standing orders because of their role as members of the company's supervisory board. Trade unions from other countries and the EMF are regularly informed about the EWC's activities by being sent the agenda and minutes of the meetings.

In practice, the large French national unions are barely involved in the work of the EWC, a fact attributable to their low level of membership in the French Schmalbach plants. However, the level of trade union membership in these plants is astoundingly high by French standards: around two-thirds of the workforce - including the two French EWC representatives - are members of an autonomous enterprise-based trade union. In the view of the French EWC representatives interviewed for this study, the organisation of this union can be explained by the fact that the 'mostly young and professionally inexperienced employees at the plant were not interested in joining one of the large national unions which, in their eyes, were too political and too conflictual - yet at the same time insufficiently knowledgable about local [employee] needs'. Initially, the German EWC representatives were very wary about the fact that neither of the two French representatives belonged to a national union. The chair of the German group works council saw it as a 'fundamental problem'. He himself derives his legitimacy from the 75 per cent unionisation rate at Schmalbach-Lubeca and is committed to the standpoint and policies of IG Metall. As a result, he is very cautious about any union which is not a member of the EMF.

Overall Assessment

The initial motive for the establishment of an EWC at Schmalbach-Lubeca lay in a desire to extend the well-tried practice of employee representation in the home country to the European level. The German chair of the groups works council and the first EWC president was not willing to consider the interests of the group's foreign workforce. Rather, existing German practice was to be transferred to the new institution. The change in the chair of the group works council initiated a major transformation in the EWC's development. The new chair and EWC president attempted to put the strength of German workplace employee representative arrangements at the service of the EWC rather than using this strength to dominate it. This led to greater concern for the interests of non-German EWC representatives and enhanced scope for their inclusion in the operational and leadership structures of the EWC: in other words, the EWC was simultaneously democratised and Europeanised.

One of the key dynamic forces in the development of the EWC has been the 'relationship of tension' between two strong national groups of employee representatives - the German and the Dutch. Although the power struggle between the two for primacy within the EWC initially served to obstruct development, via the change in the EWC leadership it has subsequently become a factor driving forward the democratisation and Europeanisation of the EWC. For example, the need to offer more scope for participation by the Dutch representatives led to the establishment of a praesidium in which employee representatives from other countries were included.

The effectiveness of the EWC has been promoted by the fact that genuinely 'opponent-free' EWC meetings occupy a substantial place. The construction of an autonomous structure for obtaining and communicating information between EWC members has also contributed to the EWC's strength. The significance of the EWC is not in the joint meetings with management and the information obtained in that forum. In the final analysis the success of the Schmalbach-Lubeca EWC is also crucially dependent on the individual currently occupying the position of EWC president who consciously wound back the domination exercised by EWC representatives at the parent company and improved the position of the foreign representatives.

The EWC has been exposed to its first big test since mid-1997 as a result of a restructuring of the group which has resulted in virtually the whole praesidium having to be re-appointed. Further developments will show whether the structures which have been established are sufficiently robust to allow the EWC to continue its work despite this turnover of personnel.

Notes

1. 'Gesamtbetriebsrat/Konzernbetriebsrat'.
2. Under the 1976 Codetermination Act *(Mitbestimmungsgesetz)*, which covers companies with more than 2,000 employees, the supervisory board - on which employees have 50/50 representation but not a casting vote - elects a Labour Director who sits on the management board. This individual has special responsibility for personnel and social matters: although employees cannot veto the appointment, Labour Directors are expected to enjoy the confidence of employee members.
3. The 1972 Works Constitution Act *(Betriebsverfassungsgesetz)* provides for the setting up of an 'Economic Committee' in all companies with more than 100 employees: this is a sub-committee of the works council and has the specific role of being the recipient of information from the employer on commercial and financial state of the business.
4. Large German enterprises have a two-tier board structure, with a supervisory board, responsible for general oversight, and a management board responsible for the day-to-day running of the business. The supervisory board appoints the management board.

10 Hoechst:
The EWC as the 'Fourth Tier of Codetermination'

The Hoechst group, with 100,000 employees and an annual turnover of DM 50 billion, is one of the 'big three' German chemical companies. In 1995 the group embraced a total of 406 companies worldwide. There were significant foreign subsidiaries in France, the UK, Italy, Austria, Spain and the Netherlands, in Brazil and the USA, Japan, South Africa and Australia.

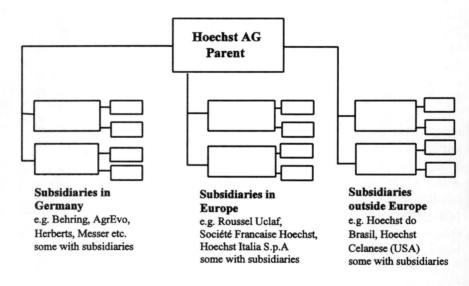

Subsidiaries in Germany
e.g. Behring, AgrEvo, Herberts, Messer etc.
some with subsidiaries

Subsidiaries in Europe
e.g. Roussel Uclaf, Société Francaise Hoechst, Hoechst Italia S.p.A
some with subsidiaries

Subsidiaries outside Europe
e.g. Hoechst do Brasil, Hoechst Celanese (USA)
some with subsidiaries

Figure 10.1 Hoechst group structure before restructuring

Group figures for employment reveal the European and particularly the German focus of the company's activities: some 60 per cent of the group's employees work in Europe (40 per cent Germany, 20 per cent the rest of Europe), around 30 per cent in America (20 per cent North, 10 per cent Latin

America) and around 10 per cent in Africa, Asia and Oceania. In 1995 Europe accounted for some 60 per cent of total group turnover and nearly 70 per cent of the group's investments.

Following a major management overhaul in 1994, the group has been radically restructured. In the past, Hoechst AG operated as a centralised headquarters with strategic and operational responsibility for the group's divisions: chemicals and textiles, paints, fibres, polymers, health, technology and agriculture. Since mid-1997 the group has been managed by a strategic management holding company with decentralised business area organisation: management at holding company level is now responsible only for strategy, with operational management conducted within each of the business divisions which are also under an injunction to develop a more global orientation. All operational activities have been removed from Hoechst AG. The new core businesses have been identified as health, agriculture and industrial chemicals. The 'core core-business' is the pharmaceuticals division. This restructuring has given the group a new more horizontal character. Previous units in the group have been broken up and the new companies allotted to the business divisions: for example, the site at Frankfurt/Main has been sub-divided into 20 individual businesses. Non-core activities have been sold off: since 1995 a large number of disposals has been carried out including Schwarzkopf (4,200 employees), Uhde (3,370 employees), Ceramtec (1,900 employees), SGL Carbon (5,300 employees) and most spectacularly in 1997 the demerger of the speciality chemicals division with 16,000 employees which was sold to Clariant, a company spun-off from the Swiss Sandoz corporation, in which Hoechst is the biggest single shareholder with 45 per cent of the equity. Conversely the core business areas were strengthened with a series of acquisitions (including Roussel Uclaf, Marion Merrell Dow), joint ventures and co-operation agreements (for example, in the sphere of biotechnology) and their global orientation was increased. The core business areas are now managed as single global units.

Whereas in the past, the foreign subsidiaries reported directly to the group parent company in Frankfurt, the restructuring has seen the creation of a new intermediate level of management, with foreign subsidiaries now reporting on operational matters to the core business area level.

Following the restructuring, the holding company exercises strategic management of the following groups: Hoechst Marion Roussel (pharmaceuticals), AgrEvo (joint venture with Schering in agricultural chemicals), Hoechst Roussel Vet (animal health), Celanese (chemicals), Trevira (PET, fibres), Ticona (technical synthetic materials), Messer (industrial gases) and Herberts (paints). Operational management is located exclusively in Germany and the USA. Although Hoechst is now an undertaking with a global focus it is still nevertheless highly nationally centred. The homebase is Germany, not Europe.

Origin and Structure of the EWC

The Hoechst European Information Meeting (HEIM)

In 1991 group management and the chair of the Hoechst AG central works council *(Gesamtbetriebsrat)* decided to establish a European information body, the Hoechst European Information Meeting - abbreviated to HEIM. The chemical workers union in Germany (IG Chemie, Papier, Keramik - later IG BCE) can lay claim to responsibility for much of this initiative. In the late-1980s it adopted a strategy of seeking to establish EWCs in the three main chemical concerns, Bayer, BASF and Hoechst because of the influence of the 'big three' on the rest of the industry. The tyre manufacturer Continental was also chosen because of the good contacts maintained with the company. Discussions between the union and the chair of the central works council at Hoechst on the possible establishment of an employee representation body at European level were well received as there was an evident need for more cross-border exchange within the group, with employee representatives from the company's foreign subsidiaries increasingly seeking to establish contact with the central works council at Hoechst AG.

At about the same time the chemical workers union had negotiated an agreement with the German chemical employers association, BAVC, setting out a series of basic principles to guide the establishment of European employee/employer contacts. Although the agreement, which was accepted in August 1990, was non-binding - dubbed a voluntary 'social partnership accord' rather than a collective agreement - it did have a practical political effect and gave further impetus to the decision by Hoechst management to take up the union's and works council's proposal. Hoechst group management was also favourably disposed to the proposal as the traditionally co-operative relationships between employee representatives and management at group level had demonstrated their value over many years. Management hoped that European dialogue would serve as a 'confidence building measure' and offer a forum in which the parties 'could become better acquainted, enabling each side to locate the other's "pain threshold", and work out how far the other side would go without anyone losing face' (statement from Hoechst group personnel manager).

Based on the tradition of social partnership between the two sides, fairly swift agreement was reached on a common set of principles. What proved much more difficult was convincing the management of the foreign subsidiaries of the value of such a body. 'The foreign subsidiaries had to be introduced gently to the idea of employee representation'.

The basis of HEIM was a verbal agreement between group management and the chair of the Hoechst AG central works council. A written agreement was not regarded as necessary. The main points of the agreement were:

- All the main foreign subsidiaries in the European community were to be included; however, there was no obligation to join.
- HEIM would as a rule consist of two employee representatives (a blue collar and a salaried employee) as well as a management representative from each foreign subsidiary.
- One meeting a year. Information exchange would take place on European matters. There would be no right to information and consultation.
- The agenda would be set in agreement with the central works council.

In practice, representatives from Spain, Italy, France, The Netherlands, Germany and Portugal (but only on the third meeting) attended the HEIM meetings. No employee representatives were elected for the British subsidiary. In all there were three HEIM meetings. The meetings included discussion on the interrelationships between Hoechst companies in Europe, the Hoechst group philosophy, health and safety and environmental protection, and arrangements for employee representation in the countries involved.

The 'Committee for European Dialogue' (CED)

When it became apparent in late-1993 that the EWC Directive would be adopted, the German chemical workers union urged the Hoechst group works council *(Konzernbetriebsrat)* to conclude a written agreement. (A group works council had been established in 1994). Although the union had been primarily concerned simply to conclude agreements in the early-1990s, in order to create precedents, this had not ruled out the possibility of being able to improve these in subsequent negotiations. The chair of the group works council approached personnel management and negotiated an agreement which was also checked over by the trade union. Foreign employee representatives were not involved in the negotiations, and nor was the draft agreement discussed at a HEIM meeting. On the management side the foreign subsidiaries were involved inasmuch as group personnel management sought to win acceptance for the agreement by the management of the subsidiaries before the provision was finally agreed.

In the view of personnel management at group level, the conclusion of a voluntary written agreement rested on a commonality of interest. Hoechst management wanted a company specific solution. And the employees' side – the union and group works council – had an interest in not having to seek agreement with trade unions and employee representatives from other countries prior to establishment of an EWC. The agreement was concluded in September 1994 and subsequently accepted at the first meeting of EWC representatives in February 1995. The forum was given the name 'Committee for European Dialogue', abbreviated to CED. Three meetings had taken place by May 1997.

The CED Agreement

The CED agreement defines information and consultation in a non-binding manner as a joint exchange of views and dialogue. Employee representatives committed themselves to a business objective, although the employers have not been obliged to meet any social objectives. Co-operation and a spirit of mutual trust were strongly emphasised as characterising the relationship between the two sides within the CED.

CED is a joint body of employer and employee representatives with the employee side having almost twice as many representatives as the employers and also occupying the posts of chair and deputy chair. All countries within the EU with more than 500 employees are included. Each country can send two employee representatives and one employer representative, with the exception of France, which had four employee and two employer representatives, and Germany, with seven employee and four employer representatives.

Initially the representatives attended from Germany, France, Italy, The Netherlands, Portugal and Spain. Subsequently the body has grown to encompass Belgium and Greece (although these subsidiaries employ fewer than 500 employees), the UK, Austria and a contingent from the Nordic countries. In arranging the distribution of seats between countries priority was given to ensuring representation for all countries on the CED if possible ('representativeness'). However, places are not allotted in accordance with the number of employees in the countries concerned ('proportionality'). Notably the German employee representatives are underrepresented in relation to the number of employees they represent: two-thirds of Hoechst employees in Europe work in Germany and they have seven seats out of a total of 29. In contrast, in the event of any votes being taken on the employee side, votes will be weighted in accordance with the number of employees per country, enabling the German employee representatives to command a clear majority. Full-time trade union representatives can be invited as guests. There is no provision in the agreement on the invitation of experts.

The CED meets once a year. Employee representatives have a right to a pre-meeting without the presence of the employers. Matters for discussion at the CED are meant to be of transnational significance affecting the Hoechst group as a whole. This includes: corporate structure and business situation of the group, group finance and investment policy, the employment situation in the group, important changes in the organisation, the relocation, reduction or closure of companies, establishments or key parts of such units which have a substantial impact on employee interests, training, health and safety, environmental issues. The last three points, which identify qualitative subjects on which a consensus might be achieved, go beyond the provisions of the Directive's subsidiary requirements and indicate that the CED is not merely an information body.

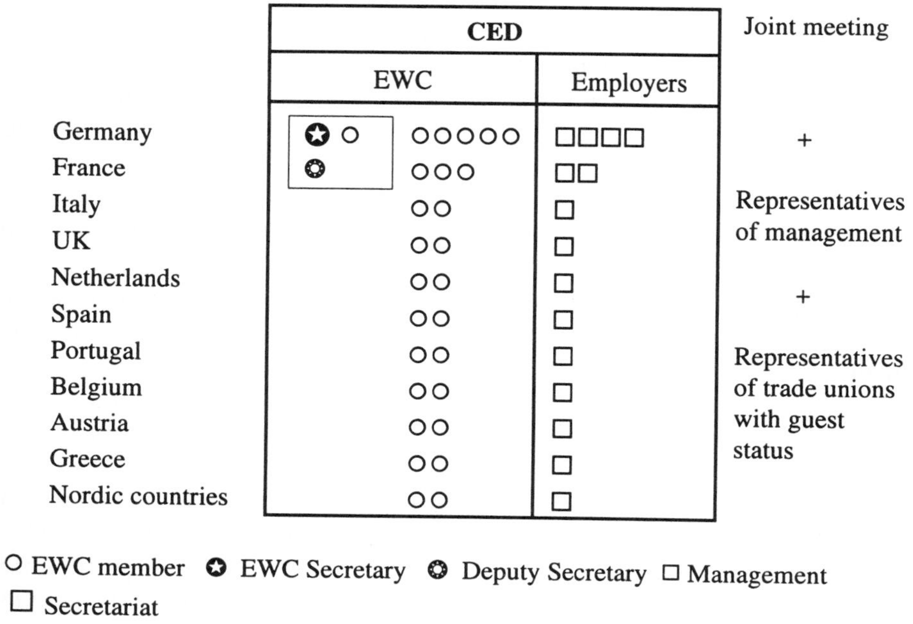

	CED		Joint meeting
	EWC	Employers	
Germany	✪ ○ ○○○○○	☐☐☐☐	+
France	◉ ○○○	☐☐	
Italy	○○	☐	Representatives
UK	○○	☐	of management
Netherlands	○○	☐	
Spain	○○	☐	+
Portugal	○○	☐	Representatives
Belgium	○○	☐	of trade unions
Austria	○○	☐	with guest
Greece	○○	☐	status
Nordic countries	○○	☐	

○ EWC member ✪ EWC Secretary ◉ Deputy Secretary ☐ Management
☐ Secretariat

Figure 10.2 Composition of Hoechst CED

The agreement provides for a strong role for the CED chair. He or she is responsible for the preparation and organisation of the meeting, is the central contact person for corporate management and responsible for agreeing with them the agenda, the date and invitations to the meeting, agreement on any extraordinary meetings, and the invitation of guests. All this bears the imprint of the chair of the group works council who very consciously shaped the office to suit their needs.

HEIM, the predecessor to the EWC, was established during the pioneer phase of the development of European works councils in 1990. Two factors played a role in this; firstly, the decision by the German chemical workers' union to begin EWC work in the late-1980s and the agreement which followed from this between the German chemical employers and the union; and secondly the traditionally co-operative relationships between management and workplace employee representatives at the parent company which have demonstrated, from the management standpoint, the value of dialogue between management and employee representatives.

The verbal agreement which underpinned HEIM was set out in writing and given more specific content during the phase of 'enforced voluntarism' in 1994. The prospective directive gave employee representatives a much better negotiating position to pursue the greater degree of formalisation seen in the agreement, and the chemical workers' union urged them to use this negotiating position to the full. The decision to opt for voluntary agreement left scope to both parties to shape the institution to its needs. There was no right to information and consultation as such, but the chair of the EWC was given a strong position, with *de facto* dominance exercised by the German employee representatives.

The EWC at Hoechst is in a process of change in two respects. On the one hand, the body has embarked on the step-by-step path to constituting itself as an institution, and functioning structures are gradually emerging from within. On the other hand, the composition of the EWC has already been put in question. The current restructuring of the group into a management holding company with decentralised business divisions has meant that the CED, although only two years old, is already lagging behind the development of the group and no longer fits adequately with the new structures. The CED has been destabilised and in some respects is no longer capable of functioning properly because of the transitional state in which it now finds itself. Whilst continuing to exist with its old composition (less the CED representatives who switched to Clariant), despite the fact that no longer corresponds to underlying representational arrangements, it is awaiting new divisionally-based structures. It is uncertain whether the EWC will continue to exist at holding company level.

Fields of Interaction

EWC and Group Management

Communication between EWC members and group management is confined for the vast majority of employee representatives to the annual EWC meeting. In addition, German EWC members have scope for discussions with representatives of group management within the framework of the supervisory board, group works council and economic committee, where they can obtain information. There are especially intensive contacts between the chair of the EWC and group management as the former simultaneously occupies a number of key functions in the German structure of workplace employee representation. He is chair of the works council of the largest plant, the chair of the central works council of the parent company and member of its economic committee, chair of the group works council and a member of the company's supervisory board. Moreover, in his function as EWC chair he also serves as the official contact person for group management between annual meetings.

The CED is primarily an information body. Consultation is understood merely as the possibility for employee representatives to question management immediately after their presentations or to offer their own opinion. Employee representatives are allotted no time to come to a common position as there is no provision for decisions to be delayed following such consultation.

The CED meeting is usually structured as follows. Representatives of group management give oral reports on a number of subjects lasting about 45 minutes followed by a discussion of about the same amount of time in which EWC members have an opportunity to put questions and state their own opinions. Complementary to the presentations, all members of the EWC are given written material (copies of transparencies, appendices) in their own national language. EWC meetings are simultaneously interpreted so that participants can communicate during the official part of the meeting in their own mother tongue.

Group management gives information during the meetings on the economic and business situation of Hoechst in Europe and globally as well as global group strategy. Evidently the restructuring which has been taking place in the group has been at the centre of discussions in meetings so far.

For foreign employee representatives, the CED meetings are especially important as this is their only contact with group management and the information which they obtain has great value in their local work. As a consequence they expressed a need for at least one more meeting per year. The

Italian representative judged the information from the CED as very useful for his work as a good deal of information was not passed on within the context of national information and consultation processes and on some issues was not available locally as Italian management did not have access to it.

In contrast, the fact that the German CED members do not discover anything which is essentially new means they place less value on the joint meetings. In the view of the chair of the EWC, management is just as open in its disclosure of information in the EWC as it is to the economic committee and at meetings of the supervisory board. As a consequence the EWC chair does not see it as a priority to argue for and organise an additional meeting and was hoping to avoid this.

As far as management is concerned the CED offers a number of benefits. It promotes a greater willingness to co-operate on the part of employee representatives since the presentations given at CED meetings serve to improve understanding of the strategy and structure of the group, leading to dialogue which strengthens mutual trust. It also raises management's confidence in its own approach by facilitating feedback on the impact of policy on information disclosure and allowing it to come to a better informed judgement on the behaviour and response of the employee side.

Group management also uses the mixed composition of the CED as a forum for internal communication and a management instrument in the relationship between parent company and subsidiary. Its concern here is to extend to the European level the approach to conflict and inclusion of employee representatives which characterises the German parent company. At the same time, it is concerned to prevent foreign EWC representatives establishing direct contact with group management by bypassing their own managements. Where this happens, it refers EWC representatives back to their own national management with a request for them to achieve a resolution at local level.

In the future, the CED could move beyond the purely informational role and allow agreements to be concluded on precisely defined issues on which a consensus can be achieved. Such a development has been considered by both employer and employee representatives. The EWC chair, for example, has considered the conclusion of a common European workplace agreement on employment security. And a representative of group management has toyed with the idea of a joint initiative on issues where there are at least common interests and the possibility of consensus, such as training. The chair of the group management board also considers that group-wide agreements at company level will be necessary in the future, as reported in an interview in *Zeit-magazin* on 6 December 1996.

I need to find an approach to managing the group, and this must embrace our employees abroad....I would venture the proposition that I need a solution at company level which extends across the entire group, but I am enough of a realist [to know] that, for the German employees and in recognition of the current legal and collective bargaining position, I have to integrate the other players.

Relationships Within the EWC

The communications structure is radial. The central figure is the EWC chair. All threads of communication run through him. This central position is explained by the fact that he is the main contact to group management, with the 'shortest path' (EWC chair) to the management board and access to information from the supervisory board which can be passed on to employee representatives from the foreign subsidiaries. The management representative from the Italian subsidiary cited one reason for the strong position of the EWC chair as being not only his proximity to group management but also his know-how in employee representation, nourished by practical experience in the German culture of codetermination: he also referred to the fact that the EWC chair had the necessary skills and competencies to exercise this central function. Although there is a praesidium, it does not have a role in the management of the EWC - a task divided between the EWC chair and group personnel management. The praesidium consists of three people: the EWC chair and secretary, both from Germany, and the deputy EWC chair from France. There are no regular meetings and praesidium members contact each other when necessary. Many issues are resolved over the telephone.

There is no secretariat. The tasks of a secretariat, such as translation, preparation and organisation of CED meetings, are carried out by personnel management, which also distributes written information to employee representatives from the foreign subsidiaries. Discussions with representatives of the personnel department revealed that they were the best informed about the internal structures of the EWC.

The desire for communication with the EWC chair on the part of employee representatives from the subsidiaries is primarily rooted in the fact that they can use him as a conduit for obtaining information from group management which they need for their local work. This was very clearly expressed by the Italian employee representative who regarded one EWC meeting a year as far short of sufficient, and argued that this necessitated maintaining contact with the EWC chair between meetings. In contrast he had no contact with other EWC representatives. He did not advocate a dissolution of the radial structure of communication, but rather more effective use of it. In terms of internal communication he saw one key problem as lying in the fact that the German EWC representatives sometimes had difficulty in obtaining information because of the speed with which changes happened and the delays in the flow of information caused by their excessive workload. As a consequence, he argued that the German EWC representatives should be enabled to operate with greater efficiency in order to be able to respond more quickly to questions put by their foreign colleagues. Although the Italian employee representative was aware that the EWC chair could use his central position to push for his own sectional interests (dominance of the parent company), he did not regard this an acute problem because of the personal integrity of the individual concerned whom he described as highly co-operative and in a good position to take up and resolve problems raised by employee representatives in the group's foreign subsidiaries. There had been no conflicts in the EWC between employee representatives from the various national locations.

The internal communications structure can be depicted as follows.

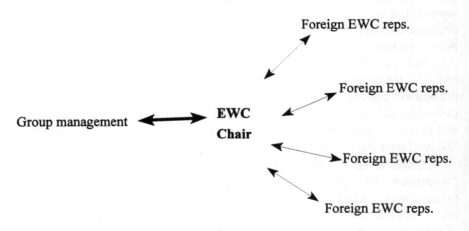

Figure 10.3   Internal communication structure at the Hoechst CED

Closer informal contacts only emerge when the foreign employee representatives press for them. EWC members from Portugal, France, the Netherlands, Austria and Italy also contact the EWC chair between EWC meetings. The main means are telephone, fax and conventional post. There is an especially close contact to the French EWC members who also supply the deputy chair. For example, the EWC chair participated in a French group works committee meeting and has also discussed organising a joint protest demonstration by French and German employees. Employee representatives from the foreign subsidiaries contact the EWC chair to obtain information from group management or help or enlist their help in resolving local problems. Information can also flow in the opposite direction, with employee representatives from the foreign subsidiaries passing information to the EWC chair. In one instance, he was told by a French colleague about the demerger of the speciality chemicals division, and an Italian colleague sent him the trade union claim for workplace negotiations.

Employee representatives have access to the beginnings of their own information structure, enabling them to be more independent of management and force management to disclose more information. For example, EWC members have brought information to the EWC chair which he should have been able to obtain through national procedures. In one case the Italian EWC representative knew more than their own local management and provided them with documentation which they did not have.

The language problem experienced in maintaining informal contacts between meetings has been eased in the case of Italian employee representatives by the fact that two RSU colleagues are able to take on the tasks of interpretation and translation. However, since translation during an individual's free time can take up a substantial amount of time, the flow of information can be delayed. In addition the French deputy chair of the EWC speaks German.

The EWC chair sets considerable store on the maintenance of informal contacts between members, ensuring that interpreters are present during the informal part of EWC meetings in the evening and seating them so that discussions can take place in small groups. On their birthday each EWC member also receives congratulations as well as a personal assessment on the part of the EWC chair on the prospective problems and developments within the group. At New Year the EWC chair puts together a package of information and sends this – with best wishes for the coming year – to all EWC members. As well as information on the development of the concern, this 'gift' also contained the text of a social compensation plan which the EWC chair wanted to show to foreign colleagues as an example of good practice in the field of employee representation.

EWC and National Employee Representation

The EWC is based on a differentiated formal structure which allows information to pass through to local employee representatives and workforces. For the

German part of the group there is – reflecting the group structure – a complex pattern of institutions for employee representation. Since 1994 the Hoechst site has been divided into 20 companies. The only organisation on the employee side which now has access to the top level of group management is the group works council. In theory, the vertical flow of information should cascade via the group works council to the central works councils of the German subsidiary companies, and via the works councils of the individual plants to the employees and back. In practice, employees have very little information about the work of the EWC. The flow of information tends to get thinner and thinner the lower it goes. The EWC chair reports on the results of the meeting to the group works council and the central works council, but only very selectively to lower level works councils. EWC activity is not raised in staff meetings. Although the company newspaper does contain articles on the CED these reflect the views of management: there is no independent comment by employee representatives.

This thinning out of the flow of information can be explained by the low status accorded to EWC work by German employee representatives. They see the CED as a fourth tier of co-determination which is unsatisfactory because it lacks the rights afforded to other institutions in the national German system of co-determination. The CED is an information body. It offers means for foreign employee representatives to have access to information from group management. As far as German EWC representatives are concerned it has a relatively low significance since it does not provide anything which is not already available via their national institutions. Its greatest use consists in the fact that they can get tips from their EWC colleagues about information which they do not already have and which they can then request via their national bodies. As far as the German EWC members are concerned the EWC is an additional institution with a low current significance and uncertain prospects. As a result German EWC representatives see no particular reason to inform local employee representatives and workforces about its work.

The European level of work place industrial relations at Hoechst has been conceived as an extension of the workplace industrial relations of the central location of the group, Hoechst AG. The structure of interest representation built around the chair of the group works council continues in the EWC. From his viewpoint it represents an additional labour intensive sphere of activity which raises his workload and stress. He is both the driving force of the EWC and also the central link between the national structure of interest representation and the EWC. There is no organisational link for example via an EWC committee within the group works council. This accumulation of functions is seen as necessary in order to forestall the emergence of any disputes as to competencies between the

EWC and the group works council. In the case of the Italian subsidiary the EWC representative, the RSU representative and also employees, have argued that the EWC should be more closely integrated with national structures of employee representation, based on the assumption that the restructuring of the group will give the EWC a central role in the future as employees become more dependent on decisions made at group level. The group's plans have prompted concern amongst employees who are worried about job security and as result they have followed the activity of the CED with great interest because of their need for information about the company's group strategy.

However, so far the formal structure has not been able to ensure that information has flowed downwards to the lower levels of representation. Although there are other RSU bodies in addition to the RSU to which the EWC representative belongs, there is no organisation linking all RSUs which could serve as a link between the European and the workplace levels.[1] And although all RSU members meet once a year in the context of agreed consultation and information procedures, the long gap between these meetings mean that they do not lend themselves to the task of passing CED information on to RSU representatives. The EWC representative informs 'his' RSU and via this the staff meeting and workforce. However, he has omitted to inform other RSU bodies on a systematic basis and has left this to the Italian management representative in the EWC with whom he has a very co-operative relationship. The fact that the management representative informs the RSU does not seem to bother the employee representatives overmuch. Following the EWC sittings the management representative holds a special meeting in every company in which there is an RSU in order to report the outcome.

Italian employee representatives have recognised the problems with this formal position and wish to set up a communications structure specifically to deal with it. They plan to have one individual within each RSU to be responsible for the EWC: they will be given information by an Italian EWC representative, and in turn their task will be to inform other RSU members and the workforce. All those undertaking EWC-related activities will constitute a committee which is intended to link the EWC, national representative arrangements and EWC representatives. The fact that a specific national structure will be created is illustrative of the importance of the CED to Italian employee representatives.

EWC and Trade Unions

Under the CED agreement only employees of the Hoechst group may be members of the CED. With the agreement of management the CED chair can invite full-time trade union officials to attend as guests but not as expert consultants. At all previous meetings a representative of EMCEF was present as an observer. In contrast, representatives of national trade unions have been deliberately not invited in order to ensure that conflicts which exist on account of and between political trade unions are kept out of the meetings.

The German EWC members, who dominate the politics of the EWC, have marginalised the trade unions and allotted them a subordinate role within the EWC. EMCEF was invited as a symbol that the EWC did have a relationship to the trade unions, but without running the risk that the exclusive focus on group-related issues would be impinged upon. Although the German chemical workers' union was behind the initiative to establish the EWC at Hoechst and was involved at crucial turning points in its establishment, its participation in the regular activities of the EWC has been marginal. There is no framework for an exchange of information, and nor does the union offer ongoing support for the EWC, which the German works councils do not regard as necessary. There is integration between the union and the EWC inasmuch as German EWC members are also union members and have been socialised as such: nevertheless, they are also sufficiently self-confident to act as experts in their own cause and to be able to decide when they need trade union support. The trade union is seen as a service organisation which can support their work. However, workplace representation within company-based institutions takes priority in the event of doubt.

In the case of the Italian subsidiary, however, it was the Italian chemical workers' union which – despite the manifest need – has shown very little interest in the activity of the EWC and in supporting the Italian EWC representative. The Italian EWC representative was particularly interested in opportunities for further training; in language training in order to be able to exchange views without the need for an interpreter, for information on the various national systems of industrial relations, and in exchanging experiences with the other EWCs in Italy. The Italian EWC representative informs 'his' trade union, the FILCEA/CGIL, at regional and provincial level, which in turn is supposed to pass on the information to the higher structures. As yet he has had no contact with the national EWC representative for FULC, the confederation of the three chemical workers' unions, and did not even know that FULC had appointed such an official. The reason for the lack of interest on the part of the Italian unions in the Hoechst EWC may well lie in the fact that they see Gruppo Hoechst Italia as too insignificant.

Overall Assessment

The establishment of the Hoechst CED meant an extension of the industrial relations which characterised the company's central location to the European level of the group. The main features of these industrial relations are:

1) The structure of representation is built around one individual who has accumulated a number of central functions and the power and resources associated with them, a fact virtually built into the construction of the German system of codetermination. This is all the more the case when – as in the case of Hoechst – a group has grown up from a central location and a central core business. Votes on both the central works council and group works council are weighted according to the number of employees, so that the chair of a works council representing a large plant can exercise a substantial number of votes on the group works council.

2) Because of the status of Hoechst as one of the 'big three' in the German chemical industry, the industry trade union is in a somewhat weak position vis-à-vis company-level employee representatives. The German chemical workers' union is more dependent on support from the Hoechst works council than vice versa. Company-level issues tend to take precedence over trade union aims and objectives.

3) Co-operation between group management and senior employee rests on a long-established practice of compromise. The works council has proved to be a reliable partner, acknowledging and supporting the need for rationalisation and cost-cutting, provided employee representatives are properly consulted and consideration given to employees' social concerns.

The German works councils view the CED as the 'fourth tier' of codetermination, following on logically from the establishment of a group works council (as the third level). This view, and the straight-line extension of national industrial relations, is reflected in fact that CED came about through a process in which foreign employee representatives had no involvement. It is also reflected in the substance of the agreement in which the parties commit themselves to social partnership, in which votes are weighted in accordance with number of employees represented, and in which the strong position of the EWC chair is enshrined. The influence of national industrial relations is also mirrored in the processes of communication and the development of the CED, in the central position of the EWC chair, in the marginalisation of the trade unions, and in the sterility of the meetings, which – despite massive retrenchments and uncertainties – has restrained overt conflict.

Those responsible for the CED within group management and the group works council chair are the real power centre in the development of European-level employee representation at Hoechst. The direction has been set by the arrangement described above, in which each has their own distinct motives for establishing and developing a European body. German employee representatives, and especially the chair of the group works council, have assumed the role of guaranteeing order at European level in order to raise their significance for group management. They assume an internal control function for management and also allow themselves to be controlled by it.[2]

In view of the speed and scale of the restructuring of the group, employee representatives in Hoechst's foreign subsidiaries have a particular interest in obtaining information from group management. One meeting a year was seen as by no means sufficient to satisfy this need. Employee representatives of the foreign subsidiaries rely on the intermediation of the EWC chair who is the main contact person to group management. This places the EWC chair at the hub of a radial structure of communication and hence in an ideal position to control the flow of information. And because he is the main interface in the exchange of information, he exercises a key role in determining the internal coherence and capability of the EWC. He wields power in terms of information and control and can advance or delay development. As such, he carries great responsibility for how the EWC will develop in the future. His 'pluralistic' role is both the precondition for his prominent position vis-à-vis management yet also highly problematic in that he is required to be no less committed to his colleagues on other bodies as to those on the EWC. In the first instance, this is a problem of how best to allocate time and resources to the plurality of bodies on which he serves, but it can also lead to conflicts of interest.[3]

Notes

1. In all, there are two members from Italy, representing two separately operating subsidiaries and with barely any contact between themselves. The line of communication in which the second EWC representative is involved was not the subject of this study.
2. The EWC chair reported to us how he had blocked an effort by Italian employee representatives to organise protest strikes at the factory gates and diverted them to the EMCEF.

3. On the EWC chair's own estimate, his time is broken down as follows: 60 per cent local work, 25 per cent group works council, 10 per cent central works council, with 5 per cent left for the EWC.

11 The EWC at Bull: Tackling the 'Long Haul'

Bull: From French Nationalised Undertaking to European Group

The French information technology group Bull operates in some 85 countries. The holding company is divided into three regional divisions: France and Europe, Asia and Africa, and North and South America. Vertically, the group consists of three businesses (enterprise information systems, personal computers and Bull electronics and personal transaction systems), together with three service divisions (systems integration and services, systems operations, and customer services). These units have both strategic and operational responsibility for their region and for their product and service offer. Foreign subsidiaries in the group – mostly distribution and maintenance companies – are tightly controlled by central management, except in the social field, in which they enjoy a reasonable degree of autonomy. This policy is aimed at ensuring that the relatively favourable terms and conditions which prevail at the parent company are not diffused to the subsidiaries.

In 1996 Bull had a turnover of FF 24.05 billion, a decline from the 1990 figure of FF 34.58 billion. Turnover was still being sustained at FF 30.18 billion in 1992. After seven years of losses Bull managed a net profit of FF 300 million in 1995, following the injection of several billion Francs of public subsidy and a rigorous restructuring programme which included halving employment in the group since the early-1990s. The group earned 85 per cent of its turnover in Europe, of which nearly a half was obtained in France; 12 per cent was accounted for by North and South America and 3 per cent for Asia, Africa and other regions. The distribution of turnover mirrors the geographical distribution of the 21,700 employees in the group. In all, 88 per cent of the workforce are located in Europe, of which 58 per cent work in France. North and South America have 8 per cent with the rest of the world accounting for just 4 per cent. The development of the group since the early-1990s has been shaped by three key factors: privatisation, the establishment of strategic alliances, and the strengthening of the service division. Nationalised in 1981, Bull was subsequently privatised in two stages. In 1995 the French state reduced its share in the group from 79.6 per cent to 36.4 per cent. Its place was taken by the

Japanese group NEC, which had worked with Bull for more than two decades, DAI Nippon Printing, which had co-operated with Bull since 1989, IBM (co-operation since 1992), and Motorola (co-operation since 1994). In a second stage of privatisation undertaken in early-1997, the state-owned France Telecom, NEC and Motorola raised their shares in the Bull group to 18.7 per cent each. Smaller shares went to DAI Nippon Printing (5.8 per cent) and IBM (0.7 per cent). Private and institutional investors hold 3.4 per cent of the company and employees of the Bull group 3.5 per cent. The French state retains a share of 30.5 per cent. This transfer of ownership marked the end of efforts by the French government to find a European industrial investor for the group. For many years the French state had regarded the company, which was founded in 1931, as a strategically important industry and had sought to shelter it from foreign influence. The lack of interest on the part of industrial investors led Bull to toy with the idea of issuing shares to its workforce in order to achieve a majority privatisation of the group.

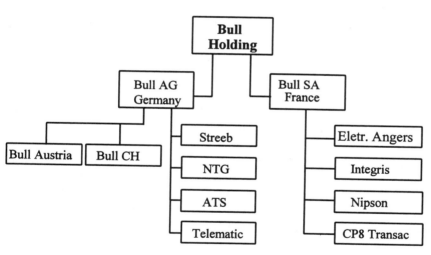

Figure 11.1 Group structure of Bull in France and Germany

In the PC area Bull is in an alliance with NEC and Packard Bell, the largest PC manufacturer after Compaq, IBM and Apple. In early-1996 Bull put its loss-making Zenith Data Systems PC manufacturing business into Packard Bell, following the increase by NEC and Bull of their stake in the company to 19.9 per cent each. In the early-1990s Bull's acquisition of the computer division of the US electronic company Zenith created the sixth largest PC manufacturer in the world. However, the expectations associated with the investment were not met. Bull is now hoping that its alliance with NEC and Packard Bell will lead to a strengthening of their joint position in the growth markets of computers and multimedia.

In addition to mainframe computers, multimedia PCs, small network computers and on-line services the Bull group also offers information system projects, outsourcing services, and system maintenance. The main growth area for the Bull group is in the service field, with the manufacture of IT equipment steadily losing in importance. With a market share of 7.9 per cent in Europe, Bull is one of the leading providers of systems integration, trailing IBM (21 per cent) and Andersen Consulting (9.5 per cent). In accordance with its greater focus on services, Bull now sees the swift response and problem-solving capabilities of its employees as critical success factors for its businesses. Flexible and team-based structures are to be given priority over traditional hierarchical arrangements.

The Bull holding company owns Bull SA in France and Bull AG in Germany. The subsidiaries Bull Electronique Angers, Intergris, Nipson and CP8 Transac all report to Bull SA. Following massive workforce reductions Bull now employs 11,000 people in France. With the exception of the manufacturing plant at Angers these employees are mostly administrative staff, technicians and managers.

Bull Germany (Bull AG) was established in Cologne in 1960 and has management responsibility for Central Europe (Germany, Austria and Switzerland). The Austrian Bull subsidiary has been wholly-owned by Bull Germany since 1992, although the share capital of the Swiss Bull subsidiary is held by the French parent. In Germany, Bull AG in Cologne is reported to by the subsidiaries Steeb Software Service GmbH, the MTG Network, Telematic GmbH and Advanced Technology Services für Informationsysteme GmbH. Bull AG also has a 40 per cent share in W. Schraml Softwarehaus GmbH. The 1,400 employees of Bull Central Europe contribute some DM 4 billion to the group's total turnover.

Origin and Structure of the EWC

The Experimental Phase: The Bull European Information Committee

In March 1988, following several years of negotiation, the workplace co-ordination committee of the CFDT trade union and Bull group management –

then a nationalised concern – concluded an agreement on the establishment of a European Information Committee (CIEB - 'Comité Information Européen Bull'). The CIEB was the third such group-level committee to be set up in a French undertaking, and also the third in Europe, following the agreements on transnational information and consultation bodies at Thompson Multimedia – then Thompson Grand Public - and BSN (Rehfeldt, 1998, pp. 208-9). The agreement was also signed by the union FO and later by all the other unions represented at Bull SA with the exception of the CGT. As with all other large French companies in France following the establishment of the mandatory group committee *(comité de groupe)* in 1983, Bull was already well-acquainted with information and consultation mechanisms at national level.

During negotiations the CFDT co-ordination committee at Bull was given support by the European Metalworkers Federation (EMF). This ranged from the provision of conference rooms and interpreters to making contacts with workplace employee representatives in Bull subsidiaries elsewhere in Europe – a process which would have been difficult without the intervention of European and national trade union bodies, not only because of the difficulties of dealing with language differences but also because of the diverse systems of employee representation involved. The EMF was also helpful in overcoming the reservations about such a European forum expressed by trade unions in other countries with Bull establishments: these had feared that they would be forced to surrender their national monopoly on information to foreign employee representatives. For these trade unions the establishment of the CIEB was regarded as experimental in nature.

Group management at Bull, which acknowledged the trade unions represented at the company as established partners for consultation and negotiation and which was predisposed to support the initiatives of the Socialist government on the creation of European information bodies, met with a negative response and no support from the metalworking employers association, UIMM. UIMM, which was criticised for its conservatism by Bull management, opposed the establishment of European-level committees up until the adoption of the Directive in 1994 and as a result tended to treat Bull as errant because of its more welcoming attitude and willingness to negotiate on this issue.

The CIEB consisted of 23 employee representatives. As is common in French works and group committees, the chair is occupied by a representative of group management. Of the employee representatives 10 were from France, two from Germany, and one each from The Netherlands, Belgium, Denmark, Spain, Greece, Norway, Portugal, Sweden and Switzerland. Representatives from the UK and Italy only received a permanent seat following the CIEB's second meeting. A praesidium, which consisted of representatives of several countries, prepared the joint meetings with management and had the right to hold preparatory meetings. At the joint meetings group management gave a presentation on economic, financial and social developments in the group as a whole. The cost of the meetings, travel and accommodation were all met by the company. In accordance with the experimental character of the CIEB, the agreement provided for negotiations on revising the arrangements to begin at the end of 1991.

'In the Shadow of the Directive': The 1992 Agreement

A reworked agreement was passed in September 1992 'in the shadow' of the draft Directive on European Works Councils. The CIEB was renamed the 'Bull European Committee' (CEB - 'Comité Européen Bull). The preamble to the new agreement referred to the Community Charter of the Fundamental Rights of Workers (the 'Social Charter') which envisaged the establishment of bodies and procedures for information and consultation in European undertakings. This positive relationship to European integration was paralleled by a demarcation of the agreement from the European legislative process in that the negotiating parties 'immunised' their agreed provision against any possible higher or lower standards. Article 8 of the agreement stated that 'the agreed regulations will prevail via-à-vis any changes which could occur within European legislation'. At the same time both sides announced their willingness 'to continue and develop this forum'. The agreement was to run for two years, to be automatically extended by a further two years provided none of the signatories indicated that they wished to terminate it within three months of its expiry date.

Although the renegotiations were formally conducted between the president of the previous forum, the CIEB, and group management, in practice it was the same group of workplace CFDT representatives who had been involved in the first set of negotiations. The new agreement required ratification by managements and workforce representatives from the individual countries. This was intended to ensure that local management assumed some responsibility for the outcome, and would give the delegation from their plant the required time off. In the UK and Spain there had been difficulties with obtaining release for employee representatives. Amongst other things, local managements were anxious that employee representatives might acquire more information about the group at central level than they had access to themselves.

Twenty-nine employee representatives, elected in accordance with national procedures, sit on the CEB: ten from France, three from Italy, and two each from

Germany and the UK, together with one from The Netherlands, Belgium, Austria, Switzerland, Greece, Portugal, Sweden, Norway, Denmark and Hungary. In addition, a representative from Zenith Data Systems also attended up until the company's disposal.

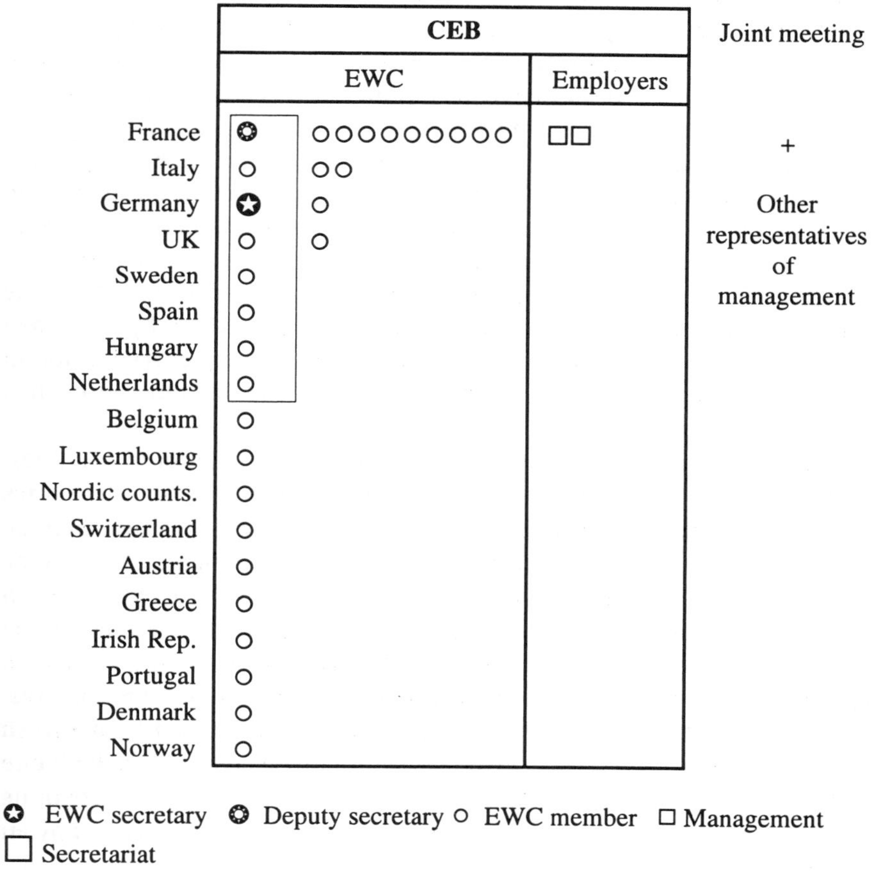

	CEB		Joint meeting
	EWC	Employers	
France	✪ ○○○○○○○○○	□□	+
Italy	○ ○○		
Germany	✪ ○		Other
UK	○ ○		representatives
Sweden	○		of
Spain	○		management
Hungary	○		
Netherlands	○		
Belgium	○		
Luxembourg	○		
Nordic counts.	○		
Switzerland	○		
Austria	○		
Greece	○		
Irish Rep.	○		
Portugal	○		
Denmark	○		
Norway	○		

✪ EWC secretary ✪ Deputy secretary ○ EWC member □ Management
□ Secretariat

Figure 11.2 Composition of Bull European Committee

This assignment of seats reflects the relative size of the workforces in each country. However, the French delegates relinquished their right to full proportional representation and have limited their share to just one third although they accounted for some two thirds of all European employees in the group in

1992. Group management is represented on the CEB by the general director - that is, the chief executive - of the Bull group, who is also the chair of the committee. The agreement allows group management to be represented and also to draw on additional management representatives for support. However, such management representatives must have an operational responsibility for the agenda items for which they attend. Managements of individual plants or regional subdivisions of the group do not participate in EWC meetings.

The committee meets twice a year in France for a two-day plenary session. One day of the plenary is dedicated to the meeting with group management, and one day set aside for an internal EWC representative meeting. The meeting with group management is prepared by a secretariat elected by employee representatives: this consists of a secretary, their deputy and representatives from five other countries. The secretary's task is to maintain links with group management between plenary sessions. The secretariat also serves as the link for EWC members. Following a long period when the function of the secretary was exercised by a French EWC representative it is now carried out by a German representative. The secretariat meets one month before the plenary session in order to prepare the agenda and agree it with management, but otherwise when required.

The representatives in the secretariat each represent a cluster of countries. The Central European cluster consists of representatives from Bull subsidiaries in Germany, Austria and Switzerland. Representation is carried out by a German works council member who is also a member of the German metalworkers' union IG Metall. The Iberian cluster is currently represented by a Spanish representative. Belgian and Dutch representatives alternately represent the Benelux cluster. The Nordic cluster (Sweden/Norway/Denmark) has a Swedish representative, and the Eastern European cluster a Hungarian representative. Representation of the British/Irish cluster is currently exercised by a British employee representative who may be replaced by an Irish colleague in the future as Bull has acquired an additional undertaking in Ireland, boosting the size of its Irish workforce. Representation of the Greek/Italian cluster is carried out by an Italian employee representative.

The agreement provides for information to be provided on economic, social and financial questions which affect the entire Bull group with the CED regarded as a 'body for exchange and dialogue' (Bonneton et.al., 1995, p. 59). It was agreed that information would be provided on the economic and financial position of the company together with the production and sales situation, research and development strategies, production programmes and investment, rationalisation and restructuring of the group, changes in methods of manufacture and work organisation, the closure or relocation of activities and closures of plants, and the acquisition, disposal or merger of companies. Furthermore, in a step which goes beyond the subsidiary requirements of the Directive, there should be an exchange of views, based on information presented, on decisions which have an impact on the employment, skills and vocational training and working conditions of employees.

Group management assumes responsibility for all costs arising out of the CEB. The secretariat has its own budget and has to submit accounts at the end of each year; there is also a separate budget for translation which has to be renegotiated annually with group management. Cost issues have proved to be not entirely uncontroversial. At the end of 1996 group management decided to exercise its right to terminate the agreement on the grounds that it wanted to reduce the size of the EWC, as well as the number of workplace representatives in general, on cost grounds given the reduction in the headcount of the group.

Fields of Interaction of the EWC

EWC and Group Management

The two meetings held annually in France are the fulcrum of the CEB's activities. These meetings are accorded a high importance, even by French and German EWC representatives who can also obtain additional information via their direct access to the management of their respective national Bull companies. For the majority of EWC representatives these meetings offer the only possibility for a joint exchange of information and views with group management. Whereas the meetings were originally chaired by the general director of the group, the group head of personnel management now attends for management. This is seen by EWC representatives as a sign of declining interest by group management in the committee, as well as a reaction to the – at times very severe – criticisms of the group's policies and strategies expressed at CEB meetings. The fact that the non-French members of the EWC feel themselves demoted by the demonstrative absence of the chief executive of the group is evidently accepted by management, as long this can be passed off as a reaction to the often confrontational style of the French EWC members.

The joint meeting with group management follows an established course. At the spring meeting the CEB focuses on an analysis of the company's annual reports and accounts. The autumn meeting is dedicated to forecasts of developments in the individual business divisions. As yet there have been no extraordinary meetings. The EWC representatives can issue opinions and recommendations both during the plenary meetings and in the two weeks following; these must be responded to by management within 15 days in writing. The second half of each of the joint meetings is used for a discussion of the situation of the subsidiaries in the individual countries. The agenda is put together by the secretariat and agreed with group management. During meetings there is simultaneous translation between French and English as well as – depending on needs – a further language.

After some initial difficulties the EWC representatives now view the information provided by group management, which is set out in French and English at the beginning of the plenary sessions, as 'significant in terms of quantity'. It is accepted and conceded that management's attitude has improved over the years. However, the quality of information has not yet reached the standard which would be expected in a German company economic committee *(Wirtschaftsausschuss)*. One major difficulty is that written information is only provided at the beginning of the plenary sessions, leaving insufficient time for a thorough analysis. And important points are often wrapped around with less important issues. Group management takes minutes of the meeting which are passed to the secretariat. A summary of this is then forwarded to EWC representatives.

There has been dissatisfaction on the part of EWC representatives with the chairing of the committee, with too much time – it is claimed – spent on secondary aspects, with important problems not being dealt with on grounds of time. This has had an impact on the mood of the meetings. Whereas initially discussions were very formal – questions to management had to be submitted in writing in advance – oral interventions and questions are now permitted. In practice, this has meant that the style of discussion has become more aggressive.

Despite complaints about shortcomings as far as the quality of information and the management of meetings is concerned, the non-French EWC representatives have seen considerable value in the opportunity for direct contact and unfiltered exchange of information with group management. They can discuss their local situations and draw attention to problems. This also prevents local management avoiding responsibility for making a response to employee calls for local measures by blaming group management for not having a policy.

Information which has been categorised as confidential is only passed to EWC representatives in the CEB to a limited degree. There are evident national differences amongst EWC representatives in how they deal with confidentiality. Whereas the German representatives accept confidentiality of information and 'react but do not publish', the French representatives want to see confidentiality restricted to only very few areas and do not accord much importance to the confidentiality clause in the EWC agreement.

The issue of consultation has also proved to be highly controversial, more even than the issue of information. Group management has been very negative in this area and regards 'consultation' as opening the floodgates to forms of co-decision making which could impinge on managerial prerogatives. Although the concept 'consultation' was cited in the 1992 draft agreement, it was removed from the final text at the instigation of group management as the term, as understood in France, refers to a highly-formalised procedure for including employee representatives in company decision-making, with the implication that decisions cannot be taken until consultation is complete. Consultation within the context of the CEB is understood by management as meaning obtaining the views of the workforce via employee representatives. However, the German EWC representatives in particular want to develop the consultation procedure as the first step in negotiations with group management. The EWC has been seeking to establish a pilot project on cross-border transfers.

External trade union representatives, for example from the EMF, are not permitted to attend the plenary meetings. This is justified by group management by the need to confine meetings to specifically corporate matters and to ensure confidentiality, both of which – in their view – would be prejudiced by the presence of external representatives. It also views the demand for external participation, especially from the CFDT, as a sign of the weakness of the French trade unions. According to one management representative they first need to 'demonstrate their internal strength and one could then talk about this with them'. In his judgement, companies which have accepted the participation of external representatives at their meetings can only allow such a 'social showcase' in view of their exceptionally good business position.

The question of recourse to experts has also been controversial. The CFDT favours drawing on the experts who already analyse the annual accounts or evaluate new technologies for the company's group committee (*comité de groupe*). Group management has indicated that it would not be opposed to this, but has refused to cover the costs. As yet EWC representatives have not succeeded in their demand for a translation of the French expert report which is put together for the group committee or for an extension of the mandate of the expert to analyse the economic situation of the European subsidiaries. Although the expert concerned, who is close to the CFDT, is seen by the management as being entirely competent, the employee representatives in the *comité de groupe* do not always accept their conclusions – a contradiction which management exploits. These expert reports also contain direct criticisms of the strategy of the

Bull group. In the view of management, such criticism compromises the legitimacy of the strategy, and leads to uncertainty on the part of employees. As a result it has rejected any extension of such expert consultation to the European Committee.

The absence of precisely specified legal rights has meant that the conduct of group management on the issue of information disclosure is more relaxed with the EWC than with French representative bodies: it does not have to fear that it might be breaching union rights or statutory consultation procedures. As a result the CEB offers group management a stage for the realisation of its own objective – that of ensuring that the strategy of all the units in the group is present at all levels in order achieve greater coherence ('common rationality') of personnel management at group level. One aspect of this is 'resource allocation sharing' – that is the group wide use of local human resources, to be translated into a group-wide mobility programme. One aim of the dialogue within the CEB is to help transcend national cultural boundaries.

As far as group personnel management is concerned, the importance accorded to communication within Bull is a function of the especially crucial role of the human factor in the IT industry, and in particular by the fact that for the customer a company is embodied in its employees. Moreover management regards its – often graduate – employee representatives as a useful touchstone for the acceptance of its actions by employees. This strategy is intended to provide a support mechanism for the restructuring of the group. Above and beyond this group management also has an interest in using the CEB to obtain direct information on the situation in the constituent companies and foreign subsidiaries, given the fact that lower management levels either do not forward information upwards or often embellish it. Management at individual locations or regional divisions of the company are informed about the agenda before each meeting of the committee. In general there is no additional information after the meeting. However, if the committee discusses the problem of a local operation, the relevant local management is subsequently informed. Group personnel management also has regular meeting with local personnel managers from the subsidiaries. Some local managers have resisted the activities of the CEB. In Britain, for example, the CEB has exacerbated the rivalry between local trade unions over the two seats allocated to it.

Management style towards the EWC has changed in recent years. What were paternalistic relationships have now become more hardened. Conduct on both sides has become more conflictual within an environment characterised by the insecurity triggered by job losses and restructuring. Group management senses that some EWC representatives would like to use the CEB to bring forward their own demands and go beyond the information function, and fears losing control over the forum. Group management has now used the shrinkage of the French share of employment in the overall concern and its restructuring as an opportunity to begin negotiations on redrafting the agreement on the CEB, including its size. The demand to reduce the size of the body has also been justified by management because of the absence of some French EWC representatives from the plenary sessions. The demand to cut the CEB has gone hand in hand with an offer to provide an additional seat for representatives from the Irish Republic and Russia.

Management's desire to reduce the number of French and Italian seats – in the former by two and in the latter by one – has been seen by one French EWC representative as a management attempt 'to get a grip on the EWC'. In his view, the most conflictual representatives are to be traded in for more co-operative members, and moreover those who are either not members of trade unions or are protegés of local management. However, the driving force behind the conflict is the view of management that the approximately 150 employee representatives in the French Bull group and the duplication of information and consultation bodies no longer fits with the smaller scale of the business. In its eyes employee representation must represent an organisational value-added proposition for the company.

Internal Interaction Within the EWC

At the heart of the internal communication structure of the Bull EWC is the CEB secretariat. In addition to organising the four or five meetings held a year it also organises the flow of information between EWC sittings. The most important means of communication are the telephone and fax which will also be supplemented by e-mail. Some EWC representatives feel that the meetings of the secretariat are of more strategic importance than the plenary meetings. As a rule only the members of the secretariat, plus the French representatives, make interventions in the joint meetings with management. Problems originating in local operations and workplaces can also be worked into agenda items by the secretariat, possibly as problems relevant to the group as a whole.

Initially the first day of the plenary session was reserved for the meeting of the EWC. In some respects, these are the most interesting parts of the meeting as the non-French EWC representatives express themselves with less reserve. The reserve expressed during the joint plenary meetings also reflected the fact that for the one to two person national delegations, the priority is to ensure that they have registered the information provided by management, which makes intervention more difficult. Conducting a review meeting also gives the EWC scope to evaluate the information it has received and where appropriate to respond with its own opinion. However, in contrast to the situation in French law this opinion does not serve to delay any managerial decisions. As a consequence, the direct influence of the EWC on group management decisions is meagre.

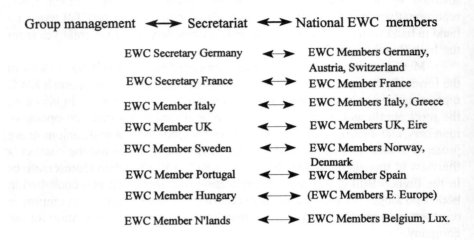

Figure 11.3 Internal communication structure of the Bull EWC

Despite several years of working together on the EWC, representatives have not found it easy to develop the cohesion of the institution. Four basic features of the underlying structure of the Bull EWC, which in turn shapes the process of communication, serve as barriers to these efforts. Firstly, the committee is characterised by the quantitative dominance of the French delegates and the fact that they enjoy a 'home advantage'. Secondly the French delegation is not a unified force, but one plagued by inter-union competition and political differences. Thirdly, there is a clash between more conflictual and more co-operative representative styles in the EWC – styles which are rooted in differing national systems of industrial relations. Finally, the large number of one or two person national representations and their scattering geographically make it difficult to establish a unified position within the EWC.

Although the French employees have decided not to pick up their full weight of delegates within the EWC and despite having passed on the function of secretary, the 'home advantage' of the French EWC representatives is hard to eliminate completely. Their close contact with group management at national level and the familiarity which this creates with the procedures and positions of group management flows more or less directly into their work in the EWC and strengthens their role. This is difficult to avoid even if there is a certain degree of conscious restraint on their part in order – as one French EWC representative put it – 'to avoid creating the impression that one knows the answer to everything'.

The agreement for Bull SA in France states that the five trade unions represented at Bull and recognised as representative each receive one seat on the EWC: these are the CFDT, CGC, FO, CFTC and CGT. The remaining five seats are allocated on the basis of the result of elections to works committees in which the trade unions compete for workforce votes. Corresponding to the results of the most recent elections, the CFDT has four seats, the CGC and FO two each, and the CGT and CFTC one seat each on the CEB. The CGT, which initially was opposed to the establishment of an EWC, has now taken up its place following a lost court case in which it objected to the under-representation of the French employees (Rehfeldt, 1998, pp. 210 and 217-8). In fact, the accumulation of representative functions by some of the French EWC members has meant that several of them have been unable to participate in the CEB plenary meetings.

Despite several years of building up knowledge of each others' systems of industrial relations, the conflictual and co-operative cultures represented on the EWC still clash quite directly and offer repeated opportunities to group management to play such differences off against each other. These differences became very evident when the agreement was being renegotiated. Whereas the French representatives initially wanted to mobilise the workforce, the German representatives favoured reaching an agreement via informal talks. Differing national traditions and practices have also prevented the EWC from putting forward a common set of demands. Differences in trade union culture – in addition to language affinities – have also influenced the intensity of communication between EWC representatives both at and between the plenary meetings. The French EWC members have closer contacts with the Italian representatives, those of Switzerland and the Benelux countries whose trade union cultures are closer to the French than to the Nordic trade union culture.

Nonetheless, the EWC does view itself as representing the Bull group at all locations in all countries. Each vote in the EWC has the same weight: and there is a genuine effort to listen to each other and to develop an understanding for the positions of other representatives. This has enabled the EWC to achieve some results. For example, in one instance a proposed relocation of production could be prevented after management had wanted an order which had been won by the British Bull local subsidiary to be executed in France. After seeking the intervention of the French representatives the EWC took the view that 'whoever wins the order makes the goods'. The business stayed in the UK.

The fact that the information disclosed by group management at the meetings of the CEB is in all essentials the same as that provided by management at the works committee *(comité d'entreprise)*, the French members often discovered only little that was new for them at the joint plenary sessions. Moreover, the French representatives also considered that the information which emerged in the second part of the joint meeting, dedicated to discussions of the situation of the subsidiaries in the other 14 countries, was only of marginal importance for their national representational work. This view of the function of the EWC as being focused on Bull SA suggests that merely improving the technical means of communication between scattered EWC members would not automatically lead to a more cohesive position. There would also be grounds for doubting the hopes attached to a more networked structure of electronic communication to replace the current radial pattern centred on the secretariat.

Although the 1992 agreement gave the EWC a firm foundation within the group, with information now disclosed by management after some initial problems, EWC representatives have the feeling that the EWC has possibly begun to stagnate or even enter into a crisis. Behind this is the more fundamental problem that, having successfully translated the agreement into practice and constituted the EWC, the forum now lacks concrete tasks. The EWC is seeking to combat this stagnation with the establishment of working groups which are intended to improve the flow of information between EWC representatives.

EWC and National Employee Interest Representation

Information destined to pass to national employee representative bodies is dealt with differently by different EWC representatives. In some cases, as in the case of the CGT representative, extensive handwritten notes with personal marginal comments on the information received are prepared and passed on to workplace representatives – who usually accord them a lower priority than more pressing subjects such as restructuring and job cuts. CFDT representatives also pass on information to trade union members on employee representative bodies. Other trade unions behave in a comparable way. However, information is only rarely passed on to workforces locally in full and sometimes does not take place at all. The lack of information has meant that there is barely any interest on the part of workforces in the work and activities of the EWC.

Because of the low value accorded to the EWC in workplace trade union strategies, there are also problems in recruiting people to attend the EWC. Whilst there are always enough candidates for work on the French group committee it has proved consistently difficult to find volunteers for the EWC. This personnel problem is also connected with the fact that the concrete value of the EWC for CFDT trade unionists at Bull has so far not been self-evident.

In Germany the flow of information takes place via the group works council or central works council and then via the individual works councils into local workplaces. Employees can also use an internal database to download references to the information which can be obtained from EWC representatives. However this opportunity is not greatly used.

EWC and Trade Unions

Integration between French and German EWC members and their trade unions remains only poorly developed. The German EWC representatives worked closely with their trade union during the period in which the EWC was being established, and trade union representatives also participated in the early meetings. Since then contacts have become more sporadic and are not especially sought by the trade union members on the EWC. In fact they now help out the trade union by giving presentations, and offering advice and training. The French CFDT's workplace trade union organisation at Bull also has little contact with the CFDT's head office. This also reflects the autonomous nature of workplace activity within the CFDT at Bull which has led to a very 'introverted' method of working. Contacts were only intensified after the appointment of a CFDT member employed at Bull to a full-time official position at the union.

In contrast, the CGT representative, who passes on EWC information not only to the workplace trade union section but also to the branch trade union, has recently been involved in a CGT European Works Council working party which meets two or three times a year. This close contact between EWC representatives and the trade union is due both to the tighter organisation of the CGT but also its minority position at Bull. The CGT sees its role within the Bull EWC as putting pressure on management to respond to workforce interests. However, the CGT lacks the support of other EWC representatives in pursuing this approach.

The CGT's minority status on the CEB is underlined by the fact that it is represented neither on the secretariat, although invited to attend meetings, nor on the negotiating commission established to redraft the agreement. Despite not having signed the Bull agreement, the fact that the CGT actively exercises its mandate is an indication that it will not accept second-class membership for much longer, and would hope to be able to use its full enfranchisement as a springboard for a more aggressive position on the committee.

Overall Assessment

The Bull EWC has successfully tackled its initial challenges. The body is firmly established, even though its recognition has sometimes been put in question by group management. And despite a number of persisting problems, the EWC has also managed to develop a degree of cohesion in its operation which rests on the common understanding that the EWC is an autonomous institution for the representation of employee interests at European level within the group. However, the Bull EWC is still some way off being a 'true collective', capable of aggregating local and national interests and offering strategic direction to national and local representative bodies. Moreover the EWC has not yet found an answer to the fundamental changes under way at Bull. The obstacles to this are not only attributable to problems of language, time or national differences in trade union and representative cultures and the lack of powers on the part of the EWC, but also to the inability of the trade union representatives in the Bull group to give the necessary impulse and make greater personnel resources available.

Workplace arrangements for employee representation are also being confronted with new challenges within the Bull group. In 1996 management established a 'Committee for Progress' *(comité de progrès)* which consists of representatives of management and employee representatives from the main component parts of the group, domestic and foreign. For management this involves the participation of the general director, his deputy and other top managers. Employee representatives consist of the three French trade unions plus one representative each from Germany, the UK, Italy, and Spain. Three or four of these individuals also sit on the CEB. The choice of employee representative takes place in agreement with the secretariat of the committee. The 'Committee for Progress' meets every three months. The future division of labour between this committee and the European committee remains entirely unclear, even to management.

The notice to terminate the CEB agreement issued by management in late-1996 in order to reduce the size of the body marked the beginning of a new phase of development for the EWC. For a long period the relationship between employee representation and management was shaped by the fact that the company was in state ownership. A paternalistic management style was compensated for by the relatively secure environment offered by a nationalised concern. The development of the company and its privatisation have changed both management style and the environment. Declining sales have led to large job losses, and privatisation has pitched the company into more severe international competition. The restructuring of the Bull group has been accompanied by new methods of personnel management which have entailed an active policy of incorporating employee representative bodies into corporate strategy.

With its institutional investors from the USA and Japan, and the business relationships which these imply, together with its first forays into global sourcing, Bull has now become an international concern. Nevertheless, it is still some distance away from being a truly global player. Turnover and employment remain concentrated in Europe; the European single market has now become its home market. A national undertaking has been turned into a European group, and is developing a European corporate identity in which employees are expected to participate in cross-border co-operation and be internationally mobile. Initially group management saw no difficulty in integrating the EWC into its corporate strategy as an instrument of managerial communication. It was only when the EWC proved to be a little less 'amenable' and began to develop its own approach to representing employee interests that group management began to lose interest. The establishment of the 'Committee for Progress' shows that management has now started the search for alternatives.

The early phase of EWC activity at Bull was characterised by striving to ensure that the agreement was properly implemented. This initial impulse has now faded. For EWC representatives the central problem lies in raising the quality of work carried out by the EWC and of sustaining the initial dynamic, otherwise – according to one EWC representative – the EWC is in danger of running into the sand. Given a management which has as yet shown no interest in negotiating at group level, the EWC must now prepare itself for a long haul before it is in a position to negotiate with, and prevail over, group management. Although trade union support will be vital in this, the EWC must also develop its own culture of representation which is able to transcend approaches rooted in the categories and experience of national workplace representation.

12 The EWC at Rhône Poulenc: The Politics of Incrementalism

Rhône Poulenc: from European Chemical Undertaking to Global Pharmaceutical Group

The chemical and pharmaceutical group Rhône Poulenc is represented in more than 160 countries. It has four main business divisions: agro-chemicals, chemicals, synthetic fibres and pharmaceuticals. The divisions are organised as business units and have management responsibility for their worldwide activities. A group-level executive committee makes all strategic decisions and maintains the cohesion of the group. Individual subsidiaries are subject to rigorous performance scrutiny by group management.

In 1990 Rhône Poulenc and the US pharmaceutical concern Rorer Group Inc placed their pharmaceutical activities into a joint venture in which Rhône Poulenc holds a 60 per cent stake. In 1997 Rhône Poulenc spent FF 27 billion buying the outstanding shares in the company to take full control, making it the second largest pharmaceutical company in the world.

At times this expansive loan-financed acquisitions strategy, combined with weak results in the chemicals, fibres and polymers sphere, has led Rhône Poulenc itself to be seen as a candidate for takeover. Although the market value of the company rose by 30 per cent in early-1996, the break-up value was rated as being slightly higher. However, the fears of a hostile takeover and break-up of the group were not realised. In early-1997 Rhône Poulenc restructured its health and agrochemical divisions by merging parts of the pharmaceutical business with those of agro-chemicals. The new pharmaceuticals division will consist of Rhône-Poulenc Rorer and another subsidiary Pasteur Mérieux Connaught. Animal feeds, animal medicine and agro-chemicals were brought together in one organisation. This paved the way for the division of the group into two companies, one for pharmaceuticals and one for chemicals. In mid-1996 group management decided to concentrate on the pharmaceuticals business and to spin off the chemical division and float it in 1998 – a step which led to an immediate 16 per cent increase in the company's share price on the Paris Bourse. The new company, Rhodia, became operational on 1 January 1998.

Rhône Poulenc's turnover rose from FF 65.3 billion in 1988 to FF 86.3 billion in 1996. Of this 36.3 per cent was accounted for by the pharmaceuticals division, 28 per cent by chemicals, 22.5 per cent by agrochemicals, and 12.5 per cent by fibres and polymers. Profits did not rise proportionately to turnover. Operating profits rose from FF 5.9 billion (9 per cent of turnover) to FF 6.9 billion (8 per cent of turnover) in 1996. 80 per cent of turnover is earned outside France. This share has risen continuously in recent years and reflects the globalisation of the group. Some 50.6 per cent of turnover is accounted for by Western Europe (including France), 24 per cent by North America, 9.6 per cent by South America, and 2.2 per cent by Eastern Europe and Russia: 1.0 per cent is accounted for by the Near East and 9.7 per cent in Asia. Turnover grew most rapidly in Asia, where it increased by 24 per cent compared with the previous year.

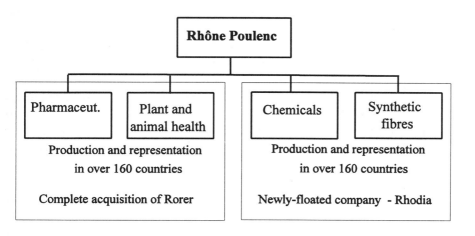

Figure 12.1 Structure of Rhône Poulenc group

In 1996 the group employed 75,250 employees worldwide (compared with 91,500 in 1990) of which 33,430 – 45 per cent of the total – were employed in France. Excluding France 17 per cent of the group's workforce were employed in Europe, 18 per cent in North America, 9 per cent in Brazil and 11 per cent in the remaining regions of the world. The fall in the number of employees of 'some 10,000 employees between 1990 and 1994 can be explained by the withdrawal of the company from non-core spheres' (Koubek et.al., 1996, p. 167). This development has since continued, without effecting any substantial change in the proportions employed in the individual divisions. In 1996 50 per cent of employees worked in the pharmaceutical division, 28 per cent in chemicals, 11 per cent in fibres and polymers and 9 per cent in agrochemicals.

In 1969 Rhône Poulenc was France's largest undertaking. After a series of severe setbacks in the 1970s it was nationalised by the Socialist-Communist coalition government in 1982. Since the mid-1980s group management has pursued three objectives intended to bring about fundamental change in the organisation: acquisition, internationalisation and privatisation. These have allowed the group to catch up with its international competitors, which had already created internationally-oriented structures.

By the mid-1990s Rhône Poulenc had been privatised through the sale of the majority of its shares. In parallel the company also embarked on an acquisition spree, spending more than FF 50 billion buying companies and research laboratories, either wholly or through acquisition of a majority stake. At the same time around 60 companies were sold or closed. Some FF 40 billion were invested in the pharmaceutical sphere alone, where turnover rose from FF 5 billion to FF 40 billion over the course of a decade. This increase in turnover also led to a shift in the relative weight of the group's divisions. When the textile crisis erupted in 1967 the company had two thirds of its business in synthetic fibres. By 1990 the share of turnover accounted for by fibres and polymers accounted for only 17.5 per cent, and by 1996 had fallen to 12.5 per cent. Instead the pharmaceuticals division emerged as the largest sector within the group. These ambitious acquisitions have also created a high level of debt, which stood at FF 34 billion net in 1996.

The aim of achieving critical mass in pharmaceuticals worldwide and being in the first ten companies in the field, and in the first five in the other core areas, had almost been attained by 1991. Rhône Poulenc ranked seventh amongst the largest chemical concerns. The group regards itself as a world market leader in vaccination materials, painkillers, vanillins and rare earths, as number two in animal feed supplements, number three in veterinary products and number four in agricultural chemicals. However, the chemicals business and the fibres and polymers divisions have lagged behind the rest of the development of the group. Although they contributed 41 per cent of overall turnover in the mid-1990s, they accounted for only 18 per cent of operating profit.

Rhône Poulenc intends to continue its policy of concentrating on a few business areas and clearly defined product groups. The last ten years have seen strong external growth via acquisition and the extension of the company's geographical presence. In the future, growth is intended to be more endogenous, especially through the sale of internally-developed products. Research and development has been strengthened since the mid-1990s and expenditure in this area rose from FF 1.4 billion in 1994 to FF 8.1 billion in 1996. The sale of further companies – so-called non-core holdings – is also to be continued in order to reduce indebtedness which serves to depress earnings. Concentration on the pharmaceuticals business and withdrawal from chemicals is one of the consequences of this strategy. During 1997, Rhône Poulenc brought its chemical business and fibres and polymers divisions into an independent company, Rhodia. Despite the flotation of the new undertaking Rhône Poulenc will retain a clear majority in the company.

Origin and Structure of the EWC

An Evolutionary Approach: The 'Forum for European Dialogue'

After several months of discussions with the chemical section of the CFDT (FUC-CFDT) and EMCEF, in November 1990 Rhône Poulenc's group management invited workplace representatives from the company's most important plants to an initial information meeting: this was attended by 15 representatives from France, four each from the UK, Italy, and Germany, three from Spain, and one from The Netherlands. The aim was to establish and inaugurate an 'Instance de Dialogue Européene' (IDE, or 'Forum for European Dialogue'). The employee representatives on IDE represented a total of 18 trade union organisations. Group management, which set the agenda, provided information about the group's general strategy and development, financial results, the acquisitions strategy, restructuring and employment in the group. The first meeting was regarded as 'useful' by employee representatives, although they criticised the lack of scope for them to influence the agenda and the insufficient time allowed for discussion. Workplace and trade union representatives had an opportunity to meet beforehand. Agreement was reached to hold a subsequent meeting in November 1991, again with a pre-meeting of employee representatives. For this meeting, trade unions represented in the company at national level put forward the names of employee representatives who were then invited by group management.

The selection of employee representatives was the trigger for the first conflict within the IDE. In the UK the number of trade unions represented in Rhône Poulenc subsidiaries is much greater than the number of seats available on the IDE. And since French group management did not have any precise information about the representativeness of the trade unions in the companies concerned they left the choice of which unions which would be delegated to local management, subject to the condition that they had to be *bona fide* trade unions. After protests from a British trade union that it was unable to exercise any control over the selection procedure for representatives of the British subsidiaries, EMCEF threatened to boycott the next IDE meeting; as a consequence, the meeting had to be postponed. Although the selection criteria have now been set out in writing the problem of the status of the British representatives has not been conclusively resolved and doubts as to the trade union legitimacy of one of the four British representatives has been raised in the EWC. The establishment of a European forum was also disputed within group management. The president of the group supported the initiative, which was actively promoted by personnel management; however, other managers at group level and in some of the subsidiaries viewed the process with feelings ranging from indifference to hostility. One further problem was that the national industry employers' association UIC, as well as most of members of the European chemical employers association CEFIC, were opposed to EWCs. Group management therefore initially dispensed with formalising the joint committee in an agreement, but did agree to assess the situation annually and to propose improvements. Only when it became apparent that the Directive, which would require a written agreement, would be adopted and transposed into national law, did group management move towards institutionalising the joint committee. The proposal to examine the procedure every year and where necessary to change it was retained in the 1994 agreement as well as in a codicil added in 1996.

Under the Impact of the Directive: The 1994 Agreement

In November 1994 a written agreement on an 'Instance de Dialogue Européene' (European Social Dialogue Forum) was signed: it was only with the adoption of the Directive that Rhône Poulenc's group management speeded up its incrementalist approach. The title 'IDE' was insisted on by group management and reflects their refusal to use the term 'committee'. This was intended to demarcate the European body from the *comité d'entreprise* and *comité de groupe* and to underline the independent European character of the IDE. Group management thus made it clear that in their view the powers of the IDE were not comparable with those of French representative bodies. The agreement was improved on in 1996 and adjusted to the legal position following transposition of the Directive into French law. The current agreement runs until 1999.

The agreement is characterised by the evolutionary approach which group management pursued in view of the opposition within other layers of management to any information and consultation body. In the preamble, group management announces its intention 'to continue the tradition and practice of dialogue with trade union organisations at a European level'. They state that they are prepared 'to develop a regular dialogue with employee representatives' and 'to listen to their responses, proposals, and opinions on the strategy implemented by central management'. This definition of information and consultation, which follows that of the Directive, includes a readiness to examine the provisions for implementing the agreement once a year 'especially if the transposition of the European Directive on works councils into French law offers more favourable provisions'. In the view of group management 'the success of social dialogue at European level' requires 'a procedure which is both dynamic and capable of development' and which will take place 'within the context of the social cultures, legislation, and traditions of the respective country'.

The representation of group management in the FED is not set out in the agreement. In contrast, the representation of the 36 employee representatives is very precisely regulated: 15 employee representatives come from France, four each come from the UK, Italy, Belgium, Germany, and Spain, and one from The Netherlands. The composition of the committee is aimed at *not* pursuing proportionality in three respects. In the first place it is intended to ensure that each of the French trade unions represented in the group has a sufficient and equal representation. This means that the largest trade union, the CGT, and the almost equally large CFDT had to give up some seats in favour of the CGC, FO, and CFTC. The French trade unions have accepted this allocation of seats. Secondly, the ratio of 15 French to 21 non-French employee representatives is intended to ensure that foreign employee representatives account for the majority. And finally, the allocation of four seats per country is intended to ensure that there is a national representative for each of the four business divisions of the company.

The procedure for establishing national delegates is set out in detail in an appendix to the agreement. The criteria for delegation is a production facility with more than 150 employees. In view of the significance of the Dutch distribution company they have one seat on the IDE. In Belgium there is one seat for the plants in Wallonia (plastics) and in Flanders (chemicals). They are appointed by the FGTB in co-operation with the local works council. In addition there is a seat for white collar workers and for senior managers, determined by the joint works council of Rhône Poulenc Belgique and Rhône-Poulenc Rorer. In Spain employee representatives are elected by the group and workplace-level works committees. Since there are more than four such committees, delegation operates on an annual rotational basis. The Spanish delegates meet once a year for an annual preparatory meeting. The German delegation consists of the chairs of the works councils of the four largest business divisions.

In Italy EWC representatives are determined by the elected joint trade union representation – the RSU – from four plants deemed to be representative of the four production divisions. In contrast, the system of representation in the UK is fairly complex. The four EWC representatives each represent one production division. As a rule they are determined by the existing joint or consultative committees. In the chemical sector there is an annual rotation between two plants. The four largest trade unions represented at Rhône Poulenc's UK plants (AEEU, GMB, MSF, and TGWU) are each informed about the outcome of the electoral procedure. They participate in the preparatory meetings at which the newly-designated EWC representatives, representatives from the previous year, representatives of other plants and of local management all meet.

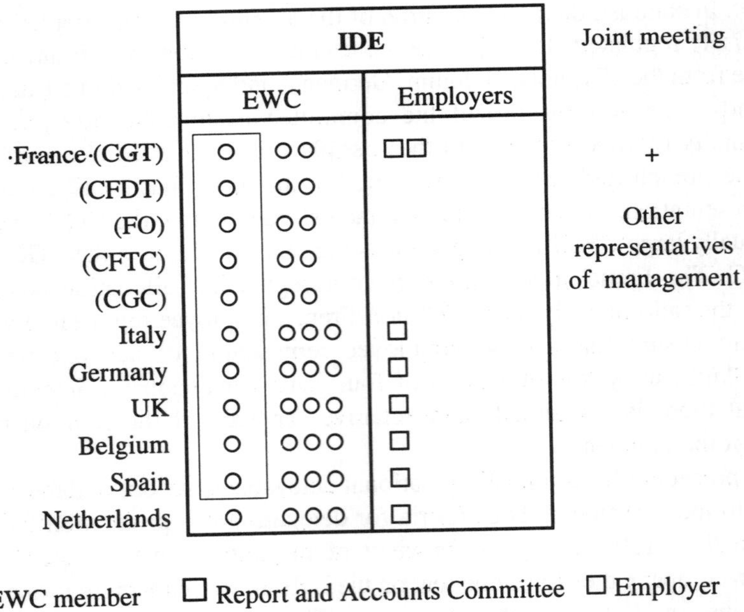

o EWC member   ☐ Report and Accounts Committee   ☐ Employer

Figure 12.2 Rhône Poulenc Forum for European Dialogue (IDE)

The FED meets once a year in France for a one-day meeting, with the company covering all associated costs. Before lunch there is a pre-meeting of employee representatives. If they wish, EWC members can also meet for an additional session three months before each meeting. Full-time trade union officials and officials representing EMCEF can also be invited to the meetings of the EWC. Their number is not limited but group management will not cover the costs for travel and accommodation of any more than five trade union representatives. In the codicil to the agreement signed in February 1997 there was an additional provision according to which there could be an annual meeting of a more restricted committee consisting of one representative from each of the French trade unions and one representative from each of the countries. The aim of this meeting, which is attended for part of the time by group management, is to assess the annual report and accounts. Because the EWC representatives meet during the first part of the meeting without group management, the committee *de facto* has assumed the role of a steering committee, the formal establishment of which was rejected by group management. Employee representatives may submit proposals for the IDE agenda, which will have been agreed by group management in discussions with all those involved three months before the date of the meeting. Topical issues can be placed on the agenda of the joint meeting up to four weeks beforehand. Minutes of the meeting are taken by the group management in French and passed on to the local management which is responsible for translation into local languages and distribution to EWC representatives. Trade unions represented at Rhône Poulenc are informed about the agenda and also receive a copy of the minutes.

Provisions on the subject matter of information and consultation are kept fairly general in the agreement and are tailored to the requirements of group management. The agreement provides for the annual meeting of the IDE to give group management an opportunity to present the commercial results for the entire group as well as setting out group strategy and 'opening a dialogue with the participants on the developmental objectives which have been decided'. Moreover 'joint consideration' should be developed 'which can assist in making a contribution to the progress and development of all the business units in the group'.

Fields of Interaction of the EWC

EWC and Group Management

It is the aim of group management to deal with one specific issue per meeting. The first subjects covered were continuing training, occupational safety, and industrial relations in the group. The issue of industrial relations also offered scope for discussing group strategy in this area with local managements, illustrating how the IDE is used by group management as an opportunity to align personnel policies within the company – an approach opposed by employee representatives.[1] The subjects which are of interest to them are the social and economic situation of the company, safety, and product development; they also wanted to present a report to group management about the problems encountered in the company's foreign subsidiaries. However, group management rejected a discussion of these reports by noting that local problems were to be discussed with local management, whereas the IDE was intended only to discuss problems affecting the group as a whole. Nonetheless, group management also refused to discuss the consequences of group strategy for individual manufacturing sites. In early-1996 this generated a conflict at the joint meeting when the EWC representatives left the meeting early in protest at management's refusal to discuss the effects of an announced overall cut of 3,000 jobs on individual sites in the group.

Discontent within the EWC, especially on the part of the French EWC representatives, with the approach to information taken by management and the use of the IDE as a tool for corporate dialogue, led to discussions between group management and the EWC on steps to improve information and consultation procedures. The EWC representatives called for more written information to be provided and for information generally to be supplied on a greater scale. A supplement to the 1994 agreement was eventually concluded which was intended to improve procedures. Under this agreement EWC representatives will receive all the quarterly reports of the company, all press reports, and all other information 'which facilitates dialogue with the presidency of the group'. In preparation for the IDE meeting, documents, usually the annual report and accounts, are sent to the EWC representatives in French, English and often also in German.

After these initial problems had been overcome the quality and volume of the information provided by group management was rated by one EWC representative as 'very good' with information provided 'very openly'. However, problems did crop up when more specific questions were put in response to the information supplied. Whereas not enough questions were put to group management at the IDE's first meetings, with the meetings cut short early, EWC representatives now see themselves confronted by the problem of formulating their questions so that management will respond to them. According to the supplementary agreement, the summary of the meetings, often not obtained until several months later, should be prepared more quickly. The quality of translation of these summaries by local management was also an issue for further criticism on the part of EWC representatives.

The EWC receives strategic information on the group's development plans from group management – material which local management only receives later. However, group management does not disclose confidential information, which would include, for example, any proposed acquisitions or disposals. Despite the greater openness of group management, there is still a structural problem which affects the provision of information. Whereas EWC representatives lack the competencies needed to come to a judgement on the primarily financial aspects of the group's overall strategy, group management, for its part, is not in a position to discuss how this strategy will be translated into production and technical issues at individual companies. Only time will tell whether future meetings of group management and EWC representatives within the context of the annual report and accounts meeting, as provided for in the supplementary agreement, will be able to overcome this difficulty.

Consultation, in the sense of a regulated and agreed exercise of influence on the part of the EWC on corporate policy, has been rejected by group management on the grounds that 'the business is much too complicated at a European level to allow such a procedure'. It plays no role in the practice of the IDE. As a rule EWC representatives on the IDE are only informed once a management decision has already been made. Direct influence over group management decision-making exists, in the words of one EWC representative, 'only as a possibility'. However, the EWC is able to influence corporate management decisions indirectly by indicating how decisions will be viewed locally by employees and what their reactions might be.

Those attending the joint meetings from group management are usually top management and the head of personnel. Depending on the agenda item other management representatives can be included. Representatives of local management, a 'national delegate' per country, participate in IDE meetings as observers. These are often personnel managers and usually a representative of the largest subsidiary. The meetings also provide one of the rare opportunities for national managements to be informed about corporate strategy directly by group management. However, they do not have speaking rights – a provision which management would like to change by allowing them to participate in discussions on specific subjects. There has also been consideration as to whether national representatives of the four product divisions should also attend the IDE meetings – although this may prove to be superfluous in the wake of the proposed division of the company. External advisers to central personnel management also participate in the IDE sittings as 'silent' observers: these consultants prepare the meetings and organise them on behalf of group management.

By setting up the IDE Rhône Poulenc wanted to conform with its image of being a company which 'cares about' industrial relations. The voluntary anticipation of statutory regulation already had a long tradition at Rhône Poulenc. For example, the company had established a group works council before the Auroux laws of the early-1980s required it. However, this policy of drawing in trade unions and their workplace representatives often met with a lack of unanimous support from management in the foreign subsidiaries. According to one group personnel manager 'trade unions are our business partners' and they have a right 'to be involved in all key decisions'. This was rejected by the management of the British Rhône-Poulenc Rorer subsidiary ('keep the EWC without influence'), especially after having been confronted with the criticism from the British trade unions that it had not kept to the rules of the game as set out by group personnel management.

In addition to this the forum is also intended to promote a sense of group involvement on the part of the European subsidiaries. In the view of group personnel management this has not only been achieved as far as the EWC representatives are concerned, but there is also a greater degree of identification with the group on the part of local management. The joint meetings also give group management an opportunity to learn more about local developments direct from workplace representatives.

Internal EWC Relationships

The Rhône Poulenc EWC is marked by the competitive relationship between the main French unions represented in the parent company, the CGT and CFDT – a competition which is only gradually abating. Although the CFDT, in particular, was eager to establish an information and consultation body at European level, the two unions nevertheless acted separately. The CGT, the majority union in the French company, saw itself placed in a minority position vis-à-vis the 19 European trade unions affiliated to EMCEF represented in the group. The CGT and CGC were initially excluded from the two annual meetings of the EWC at the instigation of the CFDT, FO and CFTC, despite the fact that EMCEF had argued for more openness. Joint meetings of all employee representatives have only begun to take place following the signing of a written agreement with management.

The practice of exclusion pursued by the French trade unions meant that the CGT was better able to accept the informal and evolutionary approach of group management towards the establishment of the IDE since any formalisation of the joint committee and EWC could have led to a formal enshrinement of its minority position within these bodies. In contrast to the CFDT, the CGT was therefore more reserved in its calls for a greater formal institutionalisation of the IDE and EWC. However, the CGT did in fact sign the agreement establishing the information and consultation body at Rhône Poulenc, adding in an accompanying declaration to the agreement that it would 'take its rightful place' on the forum 'as the most important trade union in France and within Rhône Poulenc' in order to 'promote the creation of a workers' Europe'. Specifically, the CGT called for the possibility for a preliminary meeting for the IDE to be held in each country and criticised the restriction of the IDE to representatives from the Member States of the European Union.

The participation of the CGT in EWC meetings did not eliminate the rivalry with the CFDT: in fact, it elevated it to a new level. This was crystallised in the issue of the establishment of a secretariat, which the CGT had called for but which had been rejected by group management. The proposal made by the German EWC members not to wait for the agreement of group management but rather to organise one on their own was supported by the CGT. The CGT and the German EWC representatives had repeatedly expressed their dissatisfaction with the preparation for and course of the EWC meetings. In contrast the CFDT wanted to stay with solutions which had been negotiated with group management because, as the largest French member union of EMCEF, it would automatically obtain the chair of this secretariat.

Since it is the customary practice of group management to come to an agreement wherever possible with all the French trade unions represented within the company, the disagreement between the CGT and CFDT on the appointment to this post made it easy for management to refuse to set up a secretariat. Only during the course of negotiating amendments to the agreement, following the transposition of the Directive into national law, was a body created to assess the annual report and accounts which also functioned as a steering committee. One representative of each of the French trade unions and one non-French country representative sit on it. They are also responsible for informing all EWC representatives. At the same time, the representatives agreed that EWC meetings would in future have a rotating chair from a French and two non-French EWC representatives. The French chair would also rotate with a non-French member; up to then the chair of the EWC had consisted of a representative of the CFDT.

The protracted conflict over composition and procedures has been more of a hindrance to the establishment of a coherent EWC at Rhône Poulenc than language problems, which can be resolved with trade union support even outside the official part of the meeting. EWC representatives have quite soberly referred

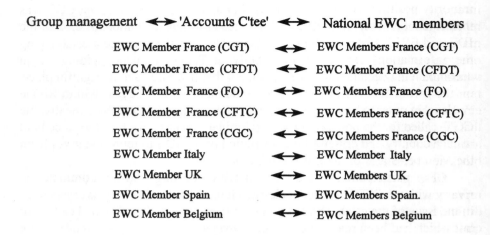

Figure 12.3 Internal communications in the Rhône Poulenc EWC

to the lack of mutual trust and openly expressed their dissatisfaction with how the EWC has worked. For example, EWC representatives only found out on the fringe of the meetings that redundancies were threatened in the UK and that local management had put pressure on EWC representatives in Belgium and Spain to act with more restraint at IDE meetings. And despite the range of technical possibilities (telephone, fax, e-mail), communication has been slow to build up between meetings of the EWC as not all representatives have made use of the means of communication available to all EWC representatives via EMCEF or bilateral trade union contacts. Communication may improve with the establishment of a steering committee, especially as national delegates are now expected to ensure that information flows to EWC representatives in parallel to the disclosure and distribution of information via local management. The first steps towards using the steering committee as an organisational pole for the EWC have already been taken in that it has assumed the task of drawing up lists of questions for group management and with this of seeking to build a degree of co-ordination and consultation within the EWC.

The information gap between the French and non-French EWC representatives has also hindered the establishment of effective representation at European level. The information which the French representatives obtain in the IDE is no more than they have already received via the *comité de groupe*, although the IDE may contribute to clarifying some issues. Their main interest is in establishing contact with non-French EWC representatives. In contrast, the information role of the IDE is much greater for the non-French EWC representatives, especially where, as in the British case, information from local management is extremely sparse. This 'information gap' has handicapped the operation of the EWC in its relationship with group management, especially where crucial employee interests are concerned. For example, although EWC representatives responded to a refusal by management to provide information on employment development with a joint withdrawal from the IDE, the supposition that the French EWC representatives had had access to more specific information about job cuts within the group via their national information channels served to block any further action by EWC representatives.

Despite these criticisms the establishment of a European level of representation has been warmly welcomed by EWC representatives. Those difficulties which have arisen have not been seen as fundamental obstacles to cross border co-operation but rather as surmountable problems in what is, as yet, the largely unmapped terrain of transnational employee representation. Nonetheless, the prospective capacities of the body are adjudged very differently. Views range from wanting an extension of consultative powers to seeking to influence top management decisions through to procedures for genuine codetermination. The developmental potential of the EWC, and its capacity to negotiate with and prevail over management, is not least dependent on the extent to which it is firmly rooted in the employees of the group and integrated with the activities of national trade unions.

EWC and National Employee Representation

Although integrating the EWC with national structures of employee representation and workplace trade union organisation will ensure that information received at the IDE will be passed on, it does not guarantee that any real discussion of its strategic implications will take place. The EWC occupies a low rung in the hierarchy of interest representation behind that of national arrangements. For example, the CGT representatives on the EWC prepare a report on the outcome of the meetings which they pass on to CGT bodies at workplace level. However, this is accorded a low importance because it contains very little new information. The CFDT representatives in the EWC also pass information on to their workplace organisations, although this is more on a case-by-case basis and tends to focus on the issues covered. There is no systematic practice of informing the workforce. The British representatives who pass on their report to local shop stewards have also met with little response. The work of the EWC is almost unknown amongst employees of the British subsidiaries.

Despite the low practical relevance of the EWC for workplace employee representation, there is pressure for change at the national level as a result of the existence of a European level of representation. For example, the FUC-CFDT regards the proposal of group management to abolish the national group committee *(comité de groupe)* and replace it with the IDE as an attainable objective in the longer term. In contrast, the EWC has revitalised the meetings of national employee representatives in Rhône Poulenc's British subsidiaries, although these are viewed as national preparation for the EWC by the management of Rhône-Poulenc Rorer and hence impermissible. The British MSF union also sought to establish a forum for all the companies in the Rhône Poulenc group in the UK, including participation by full-time officials: however, this proposal was rejected by the British management.

EWC and Trade Unions

In contrast to this, the relationship between the EWC and national trade unions is more intense, simply by virtue of the fact that EWC representatives are active members of their trade unions. Some are directly responsible for 'their' company at executive level, or report direct to a full-time trade union official. In addition the French trade unions hold meetings with all EWC representatives in their organisational sphere, although this is on an irregular basis. In France and the UK, EWC representatives see the trade unions as a link between the EWC and workforces which serves to legitimate the EWC. In contrast to Germany, EWC representatives in France and the UK derive their legitimacy more via their respective trade unions than via workplace elections. However, procedures for maintaining contact and providing support have not been definitively decided in the case of all trade unions. In addition EMCF also offers support to the EWC and its representatives participate in EWC meetings.

That trade unions' support structures for EWCs are not necessarily aimed solely at raising their effectiveness can be seen in the ways in which EWCs have been used as a means to promote national trade union organisational goals. Although the CFDT is no longer the majority union at Rhône Poulenc, its membership of EMCEF allowed it to establish itself as the negotiating partner for management on the agreement to establish the IDE. As far as the CFDT was concerned this was viewed as shifting the balance of power towards those unions represented in the company which were affiliated to EMCEF and was justified by the fact that there a greater degree of trade union agreement at European than at national level.

Overall Assessment

Rhône Poulenc's group management responded to the initiative made by the French unions to set up a body for information and consultation and pursued it successfully, in the face of resistance on the part of their own management, through a strategy of 'incrementalism'. The French trade unions supported this approach and initially dispensed with having a written agreement. Acceptance of the policy pursued by group management has been eased through the promise of annual improvements. At the same time the acceptance of an evolutionary approach was also a manifestation of inter-trade union competition in the French parent company which has obstructed the formulation of a common strategy by employee representatives and characterised the subsequent development of the EWC. Employee representatives' ability to prevail over group management had less to do with trade union strength at the workplace and more to do with the advancing discussion on, and adoption and transposition of, the EWC Directive. The Directive also made it easier for group management to prevail over criticism within its own ranks.

However, management and employee representatives do have the same views on the role of the IDE. Whereas group management sees the IDE as a platform for setting out its approaches to personnel management, non-French employee representatives in particular are eager for information about the group's employment policies. The right to information from management was won, and linked with an extension of structures of communication – with the whole mechanism secured by means of an agreement. At the same time the EWC succeeded in reducing the domination of the French trade unions, enabling them to free themselves a little from national inter-trade union competition. Despite the success in institutionalising the EWC, a systematic approach to information extending beyond individual issues is still in its infancy. In formulating their demands for information EWC representatives remain highly dependent on their own resources, given the fact that the limited support and service capacities of the trade unions, based on their low strategic evaluation of EWCs, is overstretched.

These divergent conceptions as to the function of the EWC and its prospective importance in workplace employee representation also make it more difficult for the body to raise its effectiveness and legitimacy. The CGT, in particular, has been hesitant to boost the profile of the forum. Although it has acknowledged its minority status within the group of EMCEF trade unions by signing the agreement, allowing it to widen its scope for activity within the Rhône Poulenc EWC and making possible a greater range of alliances apart from those aligned simply with membership of CGT or EMCEF unions , the CGT's rejection of the EWC as a negotiating body and its emphasis on the national level as the proper locus of negotiations has drawn a boundary between the national and European levels of interest representation. However, in doing this, the CGT has run into the dilemma of having to deny the EWC the right to negotiate with group management in its own cause. And because the EWC has gained a new profile following the break up of the company the CGT must find a solution to this dilemma. Excluding non-French employee representatives from negotiations with group management can only lead to the re-isolation of the CGT – reversing a process which it has only just passed through.

Against the background of the restructuring of the group and its focus on the pharmaceutical sector, the stagnation of the EWC represents a step backwards in terms of interest representation. Although in the view of one French EWC representative the trade unions are still far removed from representing a 'genuine intervention force' within the group, able to use the EWC as an instrument for their power, any such development would not necessarily depart from the national framework but would certainly have to be supplemented by a European level. The globalisation of the group means that employee representatives are likely to be confronted by a diminishing interest on the part of group management in European information and consultation structures. Rhône Poulenc has already succeeded 'in internationalising itself on a large scale both in terms of production and sales' in its pharmaceutical business (Koubek et.al. p. 166). Further internationalisation will lead to greater loosening of the ties to its French and European roots. This alone is sufficient reason for the EWC to direct its focus more on the company's strategic development.

Note

1. The decision to focus the meetings around specific themes was inspired by the model adopted at BSN-Gervais-Danone, where there were negotiations on a corresponding agreement at European level. Matters have not developed in this direction at Rhône Poulenc.

13   The EWC at GKN: Still Searching for Independence

The British engineering group GKN plc has its origins in the merger in 1900 of the iron and steel company Guest & Co with the family-owned nut and bolt makers Keen. Following their merger with the screw manufacturer Nettlefolds in 1902 the company has been known as Guest, Keen and Nettlefolds Ltd (GKN). Ownership of the group is dispersed with most shares held by institutional investors.

GKN underwent a wave of major restructuring during the 1980s in which it disposed of all its large-scale steel operations, creating a group primarily focused on manufacturing technically demanding products. In 1994 GKN took over the British helicopter manufacturer Westland and divided the group into three business divisions: automotive and agritechnical products, aerospace and special vehicles, and industrial services.

GKN has a marked European focus. Some 79 per cent of production takes place in Europe, of which 43 per cent is in the UK. In 1996 of the c. 30,000 employees, 27,000 were in Europe – of which 14,000 worked in the UK.

Table 13.1   Turnover and employment in the GKN group

	1995		1996	
	Turnover (£ m.)	Employment	Turnover (£ m.)	Employment
UK	1,201	13,900	1,440	14,100
Mainland Europe	1,177	11,900	1,206	12,300
America	467	4,000	518	2,250
Other	169	1,300	162	1,350

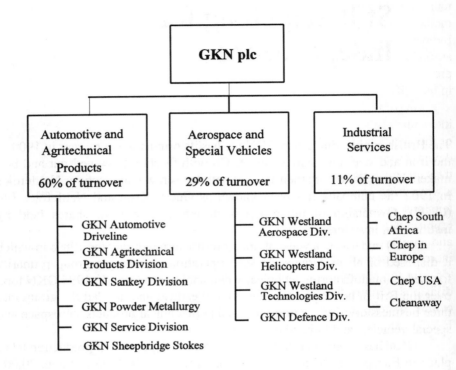

Figure 13.1 Group structure of GKN

However differences do emerge when one looks at the individual divisions. The automotive and agritechnical division is highly focused on the European market. Almost 75 per cent of production is conducted in Europe, and almost 20 per cent in the UK, with sales showing a similar distribution. The company's activities have extended beyond Europe towards the American market, with strategic alliances with globally active companies adding a global orientation to these divisions. In contrast the aerospace and special vehicles division is nationally focused, with 95 per cent of production carried out in the UK and exported worldwide. The third sphere, industrial services, is globally orientated with regional concentrations in Europe and America.

The bulk of GKN's shares are held by institutional investors whose main interested is in obtaining short-term profits. Group strategy has been dictated by a shareholder value approach. In recent years this has led to growing pressures on the management of the company's subsidiaries, with tighter control by group management over their scope for independent decision-making. The subsidiaries, including their personnel policies, are managed via a range of prescribed indicators. Group management allows the management at subsidiary level autonomy on deciding investments only up to a level of some £ 70,000. These pressures on costs have also put pressure on working conditions in GKN's plants in the UK.

In parallel to this group management has sought to introduce team working into some plants. In the British companies included in the study, which were part of the Westland group, more than 30,000 working hours of training have been devoted to manufacturing one particular model of helicopter via teamwork. At the same time the group has been divided into profit centres, a step which has not always been readily accepted by the workforce and which has engendered tensions between group management, employees and their trade union representatives. The German plants included in the study, in which teamwork and employee motivation are also accorded considerable importance, has seen increasing pressure put on national management since the late-1980s.

In the past, different corporate cultures have co-existed in the individual divisions. Group management is now keen to develop a uniform corporate culture at group level - although this initiative is still in its early stages - and the EWC is seen as one instrument through which this can be achieved.

Origin and Structure of the EWC

Origin of the GKN European Forum

Talks on establishing an EWC at GKN took place as early as 1986 between the group works council of the German subsidiary and the German metalworkers' union IG Metall. Negotiations with group management on the establishment of an EWC began in the early-1990s. The fact that the European Metalworkers Federation (EMF) became involved in subsequent negotiations on the establishment of an EWC can be explained by the coincidence that a former GKN employee was then working at the EMF.

An initial meeting for GKN employees was organised by the EMF and financed via EU budget line 4004. The EMF's aim was to conclude a pioneer EWC agreement in the UK engineering industry.

At that time group management had rejected the proposal: the company had had no experience in operating group-wide consultation machinery, and there was no immediate prospect of the EWC Directive being adopted. It was only when the adoption of the Directive was imminent that group management changed their approach. Initially, they would have preferred to set up an EWC at the German subsidiary, which would have excluded British and Spanish employee representatives. However, during negotiations the view that an EWC had to be established at holding-company level and not at divisional level prevailed. The EMF was also keen to locate the EWC at parent-company level in order to be able to hold up an example of a voluntary agreement in a UK engineering company. In addition, the management of the German subsidiary was also strongly in favour of an EWC at holding-company level.

Based on the procedures set out in the Directive, negotiations were carried out in a type of special negotiating body, with representation of two workplace employee representatives each from Germany, the UK, France, Italy and Spain, and one each from Sweden and Denmark, together with full-time officials of the AEEU, IG Metall, an Italian trade union and the EMF. Management was represented in negotiations by the board member for human resources, personnel managers from each of the countries listed above, and the German general manager – the latter because of his specific know-how in working within the framework of German codetermination.

The EWC agreement was finally signed by the EMF and group management in November 1995 and ratified at a constitutive meeting by the EWC members in March 1996. The body was dubbed the GKN European Forum.

The Agreement

The extent of management's obligation to inform and consult is very broadly defined in the agreement. Group management must disclose information on the business activities of the group, and specifically on production, finance, sales and employment. In addition, it is also expected to indicate in which direction the group is moving and offer its assessment of market developments. There is no provision for information on social and employment issues. A joint meeting with management is intended to provide an opportunity to discuss the information which has been disclosed and to facilitate a constructive exchange of views, which is interpreted as 'consultation'. Questions which fall under the scope of national codetermination regulations or which only affect one country are not dealt with.

Group management can disclose certain information subject to a requirement of confidentiality. The agreement provides for serious sanctions against EWC representatives who breach the confidentiality provisions, ranging from exclusion from EWC meetings to disciplinary procedures in accordance with the national law of the representative's country of origin.

The EWC consists of 30 employee representatives, of which 13 come from the UK, six from Germany, three from Italy and two each from France, Spain and Denmark with a single representative from Sweden. One seat remains unoccupied. The distribution of places reflects the fact that each country in which there are at least 100 employees can send a delegate to the EWC with the remaining seats divided in accordance with the number of employees.

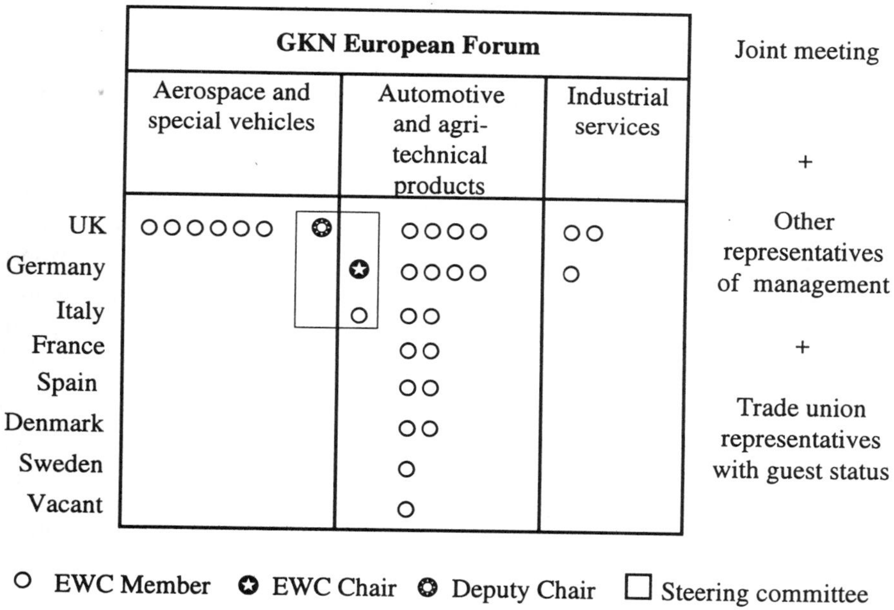

GKN European Forum			Joint meeting
Aerospace and special vehicles	Automotive and agri-technical products	Industrial services	
UK ○○○○○○ ☻	○○○○	○○	Other representatives of management
Germany ☻	○○○○	○	
Italy ○	○○		+
France	○○		
Spain	○○		Trade union representatives with guest status
Denmark	○○		
Sweden	○		
Vacant	○		

○ EWC Member   ☻ EWC Chair   ☻ Deputy Chair   □ Steering committee

Figure 13.2 Composition of GKN European Forum

The agreement provides for one joint meeting with management annually. As a rule this is supposed to take place shortly after publication of the annual report and accounts. In extraordinary instances, for example where there are events or developments of major significance for the European workforce, an additional meeting can be called. This takes place via group management, either on its own initiative or after a request from one or more EWC members or the steering committee. Prior to the joint meeting the EWC can get together for a preparatory meeting. The agenda is distributed two weeks beforehand.

The EWC members have elected a steering committee which consists of a maximum of three employee representatives and at most one from each country. Moreover, there is a wider steering committee which consists of four additional employee representatives from countries which are not represented in the smaller steering committee. The steering committee has the following tasks:

a)   Together with representatives of group management, it organises the annual joint meeting and the EWC preparatory meeting.

b)   It sets the agenda jointly with representatives of group management: individual EWC members can submit proposals up until four weeks before the meeting.

c)   It chooses the experts to be invited to the meeting and informs management.

d)   It informs management as to the outcome of the preparatory meeting, and in particular passes on questions raised by EWC members for the joint meeting, in order to 'fine tune' the subsequent joint meeting.

e)   Finally, the broader steering committee puts together a communiqué with representatives of group management, which sets out the results of the meeting of the joint committee. The communiqué is sent to all EWC members and the management of domestic and foreign subsidiaries, who are responsible for making it available at plant level.

These tasks clearly indicate that the steering committee is formally a purely employee body. In practice, however, the steering committee always meets with representatives of group management and is viewed by the latter as a joint body.

The agreement also provides for the establishment of a secretariat within the group personnel department which is responsible for the ongoing work of the EWC and in particular for co-ordination between EWC representatives and management.

Group management was only willing to make small concessions during negotiations on the agreement. As a result the French employee representatives and IG Metall were both unhappy with the course of the talks, and IG Metall even considered breaking off negotiations as it felt that the information rights on offer were too weak. It was eventually persuaded to continue by German group works council representatives as they were keen to achieve a quick agreement in order to set contacts in train with employee representatives from other countries as swiftly as possible. This position coincided with that of the British trade unions who were eager to come to some kind of agreement and remedy any shortcomings in subsequent negotiations.

Fields of Interaction of the EWC

EWC and Group Management

The GKN EWC meets once a year with group management. On the day before the joint meeting employee representatives hold a preparatory meeting. Whilst the time available at the first meeting was relatively short, the second meeting lasted six hours. The first meeting in spring 1996 mainly served to allow EWC members to become mutually acquainted and to hold elections for the steering committee. The EWC agreement was also signed by EWC representatives.

The joint meeting with management included members of the group personnel department, the personnel manager at group level responsible for co-ordinating the EWC, the head of the automotive and agritechnical products division, the head of Westland Aerospace, the group finance director and the head of corporate planning. Personnel managers from foreign subsidiaries and the managing director of the German subsidiary also attended.

EWC representatives received written documentation one week before the meeting. At the meeting itself management provided an overview of each of the production divisions, a specific presentation on the automotive and agritechnical products division, discussed the development of the aerospace industry, and set out financial developments within the group, which included a short introduction on how to read the profit and loss account and balance sheet.

Those participants spoken to in course of this study regarded the quantity of these presentations as generally very good, but had differing views as to the quality of the information. The British EWC representatives, who receive no information at national level from group management, gave the information a relatively high ranking. In contrast this information was not new for the German EWC representative who already had access to information on group strategy in his capacities as chair of the group works council and a member of the supervisory board of the German subsidiary. One member of group management also sits on the German supervisory board.

Following these presentations there was a discussion with management at which the prospect of redundancies in a British plant was discussed. The discussion had no impact on the ultimate decision made by group management.

In accordance with the British tradition in which employee workplace representative bodies also serve as forums for negotiation on terms and condition, British employee representatives proposed to the steering committee that there should be a discussion at the joint meeting on wages in the various countries represented: this was turned down. Nonetheless, the British EWC member used the joint meeting for an informal discussion on pay issues, conducted on the fringe of the meeting with group management and the relevant personnel managers. For him this represented the most useful element of the joint meeting.

In the view of the German EWC member the key role of the EWC, which still remains to be developed, consists in the fact that employee representatives from different locations can be safeguarded against the provision of inaccurate information by management. In his view the main task of the EWC should not be directed towards obtaining better information at the joint meetings but in building high-trust relationships between employee representatives. This would allow the creation of an alternative channel of information and with this a mechanism for cross-checking information provided by management.

Group management had agreed to the establishment of an EWC given the imminent prospect of the Directive, but saw little use in it and had few expectations. At best it hoped that in the long term it would contribute towards the development of a European corporate culture. The managing director of the German subsidiary saw the future benefit of the EWC for management primarily in the fact that the joint committee offered a forum at which employees could be convinced of the necessity of corporate restructuring, thus avoiding conflicts. In this respect the EWC could represent a value-added proposition for management. He also felt that the EWC would lead to a convergence of industrial relations as provisions in one jurisdiction were applied to other countries. For example, he regarded it as conceivable that the successful system of rewards for employee suggestions for production improvements which operated in Germany could be extended to the European level.

Following dissatisfaction with the first two meetings, which members of the steering committee said had left too little time for informal discussion, a meeting with representatives of group management was held in mid-1997. The steering committee was given an undertaking that this point would be taken account of in future meetings. There was also criticism that, although the agenda had allotted two-thirds of the joint meeting for questions from employee representatives, poor preparation had meant that this time had not been fully used. In future, the steering committee will meet well before the meeting, discuss possible questions, and send them to EWC members for comment.

Relationships Within the EWC

Communication between EWC members is essentially confined to the annual meetings. As yet there have been no informal contacts based on mutual EWC membership. EWC members elected the chair of the German group works council as chair of the EWC. A number of reasons were decisive in this: experience of German employee representatives with representation at group level, German labour law, which provided for time-off and financial resources, employment in the automotive and agritechnical products division which was both the largest division overall and the biggest GKN division in Germany; and finally participation in the EWC negotiations from the beginning – combined with the fact of the important role which participants from Germany played in the negotiations as a whole.

In addition to the EWC chair the steering committee consists of a British and an Italian EWC representative. Neither was involved in the EWC negotiations as they were employed in companies which were taken over by GKN after the agreement had been concluded. Representatives from group management still participate in meetings of the steering committee. As yet the meetings of the steering committee and the extended steering committee have not gone beyond the tasks set out in the agreement, the most central of which is setting the agenda prior to the annual meeting and drawing up the minutes afterwards. Although the agreement states that the steering committee is a purely employee body, EWC representatives view it as a joint body and have not tried to press for more frequent meetings.

However, the steering committee is aware of the need for more autonomy on the part of the EWC and has decided to focus on particular issues for mutual discussion at the EWC preparatory meetings. Over the longer term this is intended to allow the EWC to develop its own identity. The second EWC preparatory meeting in spring 1997 was dedicated to safety provisions in the individual countries. The next meeting was planned to deal with the subject of pensions. Environmental protection is another possible subject. Reviewing the current situation in each of these different fields is also intended to forestall workforces at different sites being played off against each other. If it is thought useful the personnel manager responsible for the EWC can also be included. According to the EWC chair such issues could become the subject of negotiation with group management, as they might also have an interest in a Europe-wide regulation of such areas.

EWC and National Employee Representation

Following the meeting of the joint committee the extended steering committee draws up a communiqué with group management on the main aspects of the joint meeting. The communiqué which followed the first meeting was only two pages long and simply reproduced the main points of the meeting. It very much reflected the views of group management, with little scope for criticism or for the positions adopted by employee representatives. It was sent to all EWC members by the secretariat of the personnel department.

The agreement provides that information for the workforce about the outcome of the meetings is not passed on through existing structures of employee representation but rather via management: the secretariat sends the communiqué to management at subsidiary level which then makes it available to employees. The British EWC representative took the view that this is not always displayed in every plant and is only looked at by a small proportion of the workforce.

However, the UK structure of employee representation is poorly disposed to facilitating the flow of information between the EWC and employees as there are no company-level employee representation arrangements. Employees in subsidiaries which are not represented by their own EWC member are reliant on information being passed onto them by management. In Germany the flow of information is guaranteed through the overlapping memberships of the various representative bodies such as the works council, central works council, group works council, and European works council. The EWC representative interviewed in the course of this study gave his reports within the context of national bodies and at staff meetings *(Betriebsversammlungen)*. However, in his view workforce interest was very low, one indication of which is the fact that very few questions were asked. Only threats to relocate production were seen as sufficient to generate an interest in the EWC.

EWCs and Trade Unions

Representatives both of national unions and the EMF were involved in the negotiations to establish the EWC. One contentious issue during the negotiations was that of the participation of full-time officials in EWC meetings and the joint committee. A compromise was agreed under which full-time officials could be invited to the meetings as experts but would not have voting rights. The EWC members agreed amongst themselves to invite full-time officials depending on their potential contribution to the subjects being discussed and rejected the principle that national trade union representatives should be invited on a rotating basis. However, problems could arise in the future on reaching agreement on precisely which full-time officials are most appropriate for which topics.

A representative of the UK engineering union, AEEU, who had conducted the negotiations with the company in the context of his activities at the EMF, was invited to the first two meetings. However, he was unable to attend so that no full time official attended the first meeting; and although he did attend the second meeting he exercised no influence over its course. This disappointed the EWC representatives to some extent as they had hoped that he would have been more involved.

In the UK, the EWCs and trade unions are linked through the fact that most British EWC representatives are also trade union members and the trade unions have the right to nominate at least some of the EWC representatives. However, the flow of information between trade-union organised EWC representatives and full-time officials is very sparse on issues related to EWCs. The union cannot be said to have provided an effective service to the GKN EWC.

IG Metall also withdrew from servicing the EWC once the agreement had been concluded. There are service and support structures at national level – an IG Metall official is responsible for employee representatives at GKN in Germany. However, the EWC has played no role in this and there has been no exchange of information about the work of the EWC. This lack of support has been criticised by EWC representatives who expected IG Metall to provide more back up in the establishment of a functioning EWC.

Overall Assessment

The EWC at GKN is still relatively new. Only two meetings had taken place at the time of writing. Group management is not especially interested in the EWC and sees no particular value in it at present. The fact that the company is concerned to establish a corporate culture at group level means the EWC could become more important for it in the future.

Group management – probably because of its uncertainty – has displayed a high level of need to control the EWC and wishes to be involved in all its activities: meetings of the steering committee, preparing the agenda, and drawing up the minutes following the meetings. Reflecting this, the central focus for the EWC members is the joint meeting with group management. As yet the EWC has not emerged as an independent body for employee representation. However, the focus on concrete themes at preparatory meetings represents the first step in this direction.

The differing levels of international orientation of GKN's business divisions could prove a problem for the work of the EWC in the future. Employee representatives in the aerospace and special vehicles divisions might have a relatively low interest in a European information body as this is mainly a nationally-focused business. As yet interest has been confined to obtaining information of significance for the regional locations and to using meetings to negotiate with regional management representatives on the fringes of meetings, or of communicating with EWC colleagues from the same division. As such the EWC serves to replace the lack of any national structure of consultation.

In contrast, the automotive and agritechnical products division is extremely European in its strategic orientation. The domestic and foreign subsidiaries are in supply and purchaser relationships, and in some cases in competition with each other. EWC representatives from this division therefore have a substantial interest in a European body. Their interest is primarily that of establishing an alternative channel of information to prevent different sites being played off against each other by group management.

The German EWC representatives, who represent the largest national contingent in this business area and supply the EWC chair, have been especially active in promoting this approach. Their aim is to build up a structure of information at European level which parallels that of the group works council, and to make the EWC into an alternative information forum in which the prime role is occupied not by information passed on by group management but by information exchanged between EWC members.

Trade unions, as yet, are not integrated in a formal sense into the ongoing work of the EWC. As with many other agreements, their involvement has been restricted to participation in the negotiations. Once negotiations have been concluded their service and support has primarily taken the form of attending meetings.

14 ICI: The Untypical Briton

Imperial Chemical Industries (ICI) was formed in 1926 out of a merger of the four largest British chemical companies with the aim of mounting an effective response to the creation of the German group IG Farben.[1] Up until the 1980s the degree of internationalisation was low, with production concentrated in the UK.

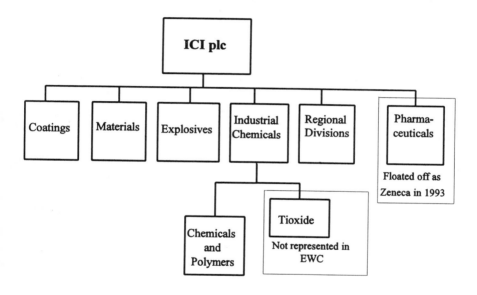

Figure 14.1 Group structure of ICI - as of 1996

The group was substantially restructured in early-1993 through a break-up into two companies: the pharmaceuticals business was demerged and listed separately as a new company, Zeneca, with ICI retaining the chemicals business. ICI held on to only a small stake in Zeneca. There were three reasons behind the break-up: firstly, there was a desire to achieve greater flexibility through a reduction in the size of the organisation; secondly, the sale of the company's pharmaceutical activities was needed to raise the resources to finance the global expansion of the chemicals business; and thirdly, ICI was worried that it might

169

itself be acquired and broken up by an outsider. The flotation of Zeneca led to a substantial rise in ICI's share price, thwarting the threat of a hostile takeover. In 1993 ICI sold all its nylon businesses to Dupont, in exchange taking on the latter's acrylic activities.

With a total turnover of £10.52 billion ICI is the sixth largest chemical company in the world and by far the largest in the UK. ICI also exercises a substantial influence within the British chemical employers association, the CIA. In 1996 the group employed 64,000 people worldwide, of which 17,700 worked in the UK, 6,100 in the other European countries, 16,600 in America, 14,200 in Asia, and 9,400 in other countries.

Table 14.1 Turnover and employment at ICI, 1994-96

	1994		1995		1996	
	Turnover (£ million)	Employees	Turnover (£ million)	Employees	Turnover (£ million)	Employees
Coatings	1,712	15,400	2,003	17,300	2,437	19,600
Materials	1,748	8,400	2,067	7,400	1,991	7,000
Explosives	786	13,700	778	12,600	808	10,700
Industrial chemicals	3,881	17,800	4,250	16,100	4,045	15,000
Regional divisions	1,477	10,900	1,604	9,800	1,682	10,000
Corporate	415	1,300	433	1,600	443	1,700

Based on the locations of its production facilities ICI is now a global group, with operations not only in the major regions of Europe, the USA and East Asia but also on a considerable scale in Africa. The group's strategy is to extend its activities in the South East Asian and American regions, with more limited investment at its existing chemical plants in Europe. The mid-1990s also saw a large number of disposals and acquisitions of companies, accompanied by a programme of radical cost-cutting and productivity increases as well as restructuring programmes to improve efficiency and productivity.

One of the most recent large-scale restructuring operations took place in 1997. The Tioxide division, which had previously been granted a degree of independence in the group and which did not send employee representatives to the EWC, was floated separately. In May 1997 the company also bought the special chemicals division of Unilever. This included the National Starch and Chemical Co., a supplier of plastics and industrial adhesives, Quest international, a producer of aromatic and food components, Unichema International, a supplier of oil chemical products, and Crosfield, a manufacturer of inorganic chemicals. In order to finance these acquisitions ICI sold the bulk of its basic chemicals divisions to Dupont. These included the polyester and polymers divisions, titan dioxide (outside the US) and the polyester film business. These disposals had a particular impact on employment in the UK. The regional division ICI Australia Ltd was also floated separately. The underlying strategy has been to withdraw from the low margin and highly cyclical basic chemicals business and concentrate on speciality chemicals. Ultimately, the group intends that 80 per cent of the business should be in the higher value consumer side of chemical production.

These restructuring measures have had substantial effects on the number of employees in the group, with the global workforce falling from some 96,000 in 1968, primarily in the UK, to 64,000 by 1996. These changes have also affected the European Works Council at ICI, which has found it difficult to establish and sustain itself as a functioning body because of the disruption caused by frequent restructuring.

The group remains dominated by corporate head office and efforts to decentralise decision-making to the subsidiaries have so far been not proved to be successful. For example, an attempt to give subsidiary companies more autonomy in their personnel policies failed and total headcounts continue to be controlled by group headquarters. There are supplier-purchaser relationships between subsidiaries. The Italian subsidiary, which was visited in the course of this case-study, was supplied by other non-UK businesses within the group. However, national managements have only a very limited scope for independent action.

Origin and Structure of the EWC

The British trade unions had established contact with ICI management with the aim of establishing an EWC at ICI as early as 1990. Negotiations then dragged on for over four years. This extended period is attributable to the fact that no British company wanted to be the first to conclude an EWC agreement in the UK in order to avoid being seen as running counter to the European social policy of the Conservative government. In contrast the British trade unions – the main participants were representatives of the TGWU – pursued precisely the opposite objective. They were eager to conclude voluntary agreements in the UK in order to show the then-Conservative British government that their opt out from EU social policy was misplaced. The choice fell on ICI as, in contrast to many other British companies, it had a long tradition of information and consultation with employee representatives. Relations between the trade unions and management were also very good. Moreover, ICI commended itself because of its influential role within the British chemical employers association. The trade unions assumed that any agreement at ICI would make EWCs more readily acceptable to other firms in the chemical industry. However, group management was initially unwilling to set up an EWC as it felt that there were good reasons for not having an information and consultation body at European level at all, citing language difficulties and diverging cultures. Their main argument was that ICI was a global undertaking and that there was no rationale in a merely European body. Management also considered that the costs of running such an institution were too high – with few discernible or quantifiable offsetting benefits.

As a consequence, the first European meetings of employee representatives from the group were organised by the TGWU, the largest union represented at ICI, using EU budget line 4004. In all, three such meetings were held in Brussels. Management representatives were also present. At the first meeting there was merely a brief exchange of information between trade unions and management. At the second meeting there was joint dinner and at the third meeting there were some additional informal discussions. Following this, more frequent meetings were held between group management and the British trade unions, primarily the TGWU, to discuss how an EWC might operate. Workplace employee representatives, and in particular those from abroad, were drawn into negotiations via the 4004 meetings as this allowed them to discuss the key points of any proposed agreement.

For a while group management toyed with the idea of establishing an EWC only for the European workforce outside the UK. Eventually, they agreed to the establishment of an EWC in order to use the option of concluding a voluntary agreement under Article 13 of the Directive: they included UK employee representatives simply because they expected the government in the UK to change and the opt-out to be ended. This change of heart was also influenced by the German chemical employers association BAVC which had advocated the conclusion of such agreements based on its own experience with voluntary EWC agreements. The British chemical employers CIA was also not rigorously opposed to the conclusion of voluntary EWC agreements. Although it did not call upon its members to conclude them, it provided assistance and training once any company interested in such a body turned to it for help.

The Agreement

The agreement establishing a European consultative forum was signed in November 1995 by representatives of the British trade unions TGWU, GMB, AEEU, MSF, AMPS, EESA, and a representative of the European chemical workers association EMCEF. The EWC members subsequently signed the agreement at the constitutive meeting in December 1995. The agreement was the first at a British chemical company and one of the first British agreements overall. It was concluded during the period of 'enforced voluntarism' and would not have come about without the pressure exerted by the prospect of the Directive. The agreement also had a specific impact within the British context as every agreement concluded in the UK lowered the threshold of resistance of other British companies.

The agreement is based on the existing national mechanism for information and consultation at ICI, the Business and General Committee (BGC) which has operated for many years. The task of the EWC is seen as that of facilitating a discussion with employee representatives on strategic decisions affecting the whole group. Information provided by management is restricted to economic and business data, with no reference to employment and social issues. Existing information and consultation bodies at national or workplace level will not be replaced by the EWC. Any issues which concern only one country must be discussed at national level.

The agreement provides for an annual meeting of the EWC. The joint meeting with corporate management takes place under the chairmanship of a representative of group management. The body consists of both employer and employee representatives, with fewer management representatives – although there is no provision on exactly how many management representatives may attend. Additional meetings can take place if either management or employee representatives deem this necessary. There is a prior preparatory meeting solely for employee representatives. Employee representatives also elect their own executive body, which organises the preparatory meeting and co-ordinates the contributions made by employee representatives at the joint meeting.

The agenda is established by the 'Agenda Forming Committee' which meets one or two months before the joint meeting. The agreement itself does not specify whether this committee should be a purely employee body or a joint forum. In practice it has proved to be purely employee body. The number and allocation of employee representatives on the Agenda Forming Committee is not regulated in the agreement. Initially it consisted of two representatives from the UK and one from France. Later it was extended to embrace a German and a

Dutch representative, with five representatives in all. The committee meets for one day and makes proposals for the agenda at the joint meeting. On the following day the committee meets with a representative of group management, the group personnel director, to discuss the agenda. The administration of the EWC is handled by the group personnel department.

The agreement makes very detailed provisions on the election of EWC representatives. Employees from the Tioxide division were excluded from the outset and instead were offered their own European consultation body, reflecting the fact that it was already clear when the agreement was signed that this division would not be in the group for much longer. In spring 1997 the Tioxide division was floated separately.

In general, the agreement provides that EWC representatives should be appointed by means of existing national arrangements for employee representation. The exceptions to this are the UK, where EWC representatives consist of the national Business and General Committee, and Germany, where there is an agreement between the group works council and management on the election of EWC representatives which provides for delegation from the group works council.

As far as the distribution of seats in the EWC is concerned, the national shares of employment in the group as a whole are taken into account through a series of stages. Each country with at least 150 employees in an ICI subsidiary has one EWC representative. Additional seats are then allocated on the basis of one extra representative for each additional 1,000 employees.

This formula yields 18 representatives from the UK, two from France and Germany and one each from The Netherlands, Belgium, Spain and the Irish Republic. In addition, one EWC member each is delegated from the two countries which have the most employees out of all those countries which only send one employee representative. At present these extra delegates come from Belgium and The Netherlands. Overall, British EWC members have the absolute majority.

Employee representatives can invite full-time union officials and other experts to both the preparatory and joint meetings. As a rule there are no more than three such individuals present. External members have no voting rights. The company pays for overnight accommodation but not travel. This could operate in practice to enable the company to influence the selection of experts, and might adversely affect relationships between the trade unions.

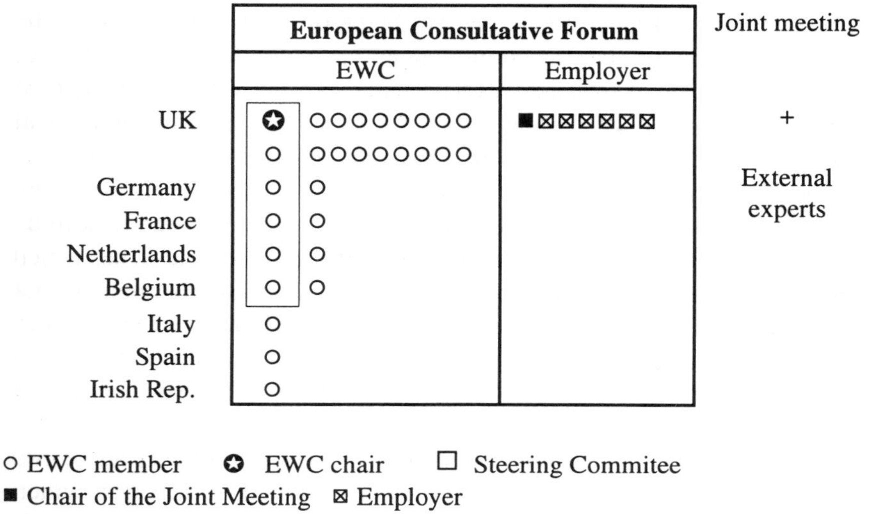

	European Consultative Forum		Joint meeting
	EWC	Employer	
UK	✪ ○○○○○○○○ ○ ○○○○○○○○	■ ⊠⊠⊠⊠⊠⊠	+
Germany	○ ○		External
France	○ ○		experts
Netherlands	○ ○		
Belgium	○ ○		
Italy	○		
Spain	○		
Irish Rep.	○		

○ EWC member　　✪ EWC chair　　□ Steering Commitee
■ Chair of the Joint Meeting　⊠ Employer

Figure 14.2 Composition of the ICI European Consultative Forum (ECF)

Fields of interaction

Fields of Interaction between EWC and Group Management

The steering committee and standing orders were agreed at the constitutive meeting held in December 1995. Following this EWC representatives gave an overview of their trade union organisations and national systems of collective bargaining. Finally, management representatives provided some very general information on the position of the group.

The first official meeting took place in March 1996 and the second in March 1997. In addition in 1997 there were two extraordinary meetings. In late-1996 there was a meeting with the group management at a joint training session attended by both management and trade unions.

From the employers' side the meetings were attended by board members, the group personnel director, the British personnel manager and the relevant executives from the individual business streams. All the management representatives came from the UK. The presence of board members signalled the fact that the EWC was seen as a top management issue. A further indication of this was that the British group headquarters put pressure on national managements to ensure that their EWC members attended the meetings.

The first part of the joint meeting was taken up with a discussion of the questions prepared by the steering committee agreed with management. So far, employer and employee representatives have had divergent views on the choice of subjects. For example, group management felt that one issue was a national matter and should not be discussed at the EWC, although it finally conceded that it could be dealt with at the EWC meeting. The fact that there are very few conflicts over the selection of topics is primarily due to the co-operative attitude of the British employee representatives who are concerned to avoid issues which could prompt conflicts, in one instance convincing a Spanish EWC member not to address a difficult and potentially controversial matter at the joint meeting. For its part, group management is also concerned to avoid a conflictual style emerging during the joint committee – one reason behind their desire not to have a French EWC member as EWC chair.

As yet the questions put to management have overwhelmingly addressed national matters, with the main intention being to obtain information which would could be used for national employee representation. The first step towards putting material demands on group management were planned for the 1998 meetings. For example, the German EWC representative has asked that there should be negotiations on measures to compensate homeworkers for expenses. Because this demand could not be won at national level the subject will now be brought up at the European level with the aim of a uniform European solution.

The time allowed for replies to questions was regarded as sufficient by the EWC members interviewed for this study. The answers provided by management were also regarded as sufficient and satisfactory. However, on looking at the minutes EWC members often noted that management replies contained little new information – something which had escaped their attention during the meetings.

The second part of the joint meeting featured presentations by group management. In the meetings held so far information was disclosed on business issues and investment plans, product planning, and disposals. The 1997 meeting also had a report from the group health and safety manager. In the view of the EWC members this was mainly a presentation of the good practice followed by the company in this sphere. However, alongside this official agenda there is also an unofficial agenda for the British employee representatives – that is, discussions on wages and working conditions which are conducted on the fringes of the joint meeting.

Management does not disclose confidential information to the EWC. The British EWC representative interviewed for this study said that such disclosures were not wanted by employee representatives. For example, group management did not inform the national consultative body, the BGC, about the flotation of Zeneca. Similarly the EWC was only informed about the restructuring plan after the acquisition of the special chemical division of Unilever and the sale of the basic chemicals division to Dupont. Group management justified this with the argument that the decision was subject to very rigorous confidentiality requirements. However, employee representatives often obtained information before national management representatives. At two subsequent extraordinary meetings the EWC was informed two weeks after the acquisition and one week after the sale and given information on the effects of the restructuring, with an attempt to convince them of the necessity of these measures.

In addition group management has also been very active in its approach to information. There is an ICI internal e-mail network offering up-to-date information on the group's development to which most employees have access. Group management have also introduced a new forum for the disclosure of information called 'The Way Forward'. This was a CCT satellite transmission in which ICI's chief executive set out the situation of the group and its global strategy. Because the transmission had an interactive dimension, there was also scope for employees to put questions.

An evaluation of the first meeting took place at a training event held in Eastbourne in late-1996. This was organised jointly by the TGWU, which had proposed the event, and group management, which had initially felt that training was not necessary but which acceded after the trade union indicated that it would proceed on its own. The decision by management to work with the union can be seen as an indication of its concern that it might have lost control over the EWC had it failed to participate. In addition to evaluating the first meeting the event also included a presentation of the various systems of employee relations in Europe, organised by the trade unions, together with an information pack on the ICI group provided by management. The TGWU is aware that financial information should not be obtained solely from group management, but given the lack of resources it is grateful that management assumes this task. Following the assessment of the EWC meeting, it was possible to win an additional meeting of the steering committee. However, as yet, the steering committee has not yet met twice-yearly as two extraordinary meetings took place in 1997 in addition to the regular meetings. No changes had been implemented in the EWC as a result of the training event at the time this study was completed.

The EWC was accorded only a very limited value by employee representatives. The main focus was the joint meeting with management, where the information provided was not regarded as especially important – and with nothing resembling consultation.

Group management initially had low expectations of the EWC and thought that such an institution made little sense, given the global character of the group. However, following the decision to proceed with establishing the EWC in the light of the Directive, it then sought to ensure that it also met its concerns. In the view of the group personnel director, management did not obtain any new information from employee representatives, but was better placed to judge the situation at individual sites and the views of the workforce on particular problems. As a consequence, the EWC offered management a further instrument and layer of corporate control. This is especially important for group management as the highly-centralised structure requires considerable investment in control mechanisms. One further use of the EWC for management consists in the fact that employee representatives can be convinced of the necessity of restructuring measures and pass on these arguments to national employee representatives, allowing restructuring to be carried out with much reduced 'frictional losses'. The two extraordinary meetings testify to the validity of this presumption. Moreover, one EWC member suspected that the EWC had also been established for grounds of corporate image – although creating a European corporate culture is felt to be a second-order issue for management.

Regional personnel managers have a bi-annual meeting with the group personnel director at which a discussion of the EWC takes place – although there is no systematic evaluation of EWC meetings by management. Regional personnel managers are sent all the papers and minutes from the joint meetings. This explains why the Italian personnel manager was reasonably well-informed about the EWC although he had never attended a meeting.

Interaction Within the EWC

UK representatives dominate the meetings in sheer quantitative terms, with almost two-thirds of the seats. They also appoint the chair of the employee side and two of out five seats on the steering committee. So far, all the meetings have taken place in the UK – an issue discussed at the training meeting at which the employee side decided that meetings also ought to be held outside the UK to offset the British 'home advantage'. However, this was rejected by management on cost grounds.

The EWC meeting on the morning of the meeting of the joint committee is taken up with preparation for the session. Discussion of other issues or an internal exchange of information only take place on the margins. Although the TGWU representative, which also took part in the preparatory meetings, noted that it was union policy to try and convince EWC members to use the preparatory meetings primarily for information exchange, he had not been able to succeed in this. Relations between EWC members at the members were described as open and trustful. Evidence for the gradual emergence of a European perspective could be seen in the fact that national sites no longer competed between themselves but perceived a common interest in the promotion of Europe as a whole as a manufacturing location. A mutual exchange of information between EWC members only took place after the joint meeting at a final meal, at which interpreters were present to allow communication between different nationalities.

There is no contact between members between meetings. Nor has the steering committee been able to establish itself as a clearing-house for information exchange between meetings; rather it has confined itself to preparation for the joint meeting. However, there is no reason why EWC members should not communicate between meetings, and the company's internal networks - including fax and e-mail - could be used for this. Some first steps towards an exchange of information can be seen in the fact that the minutes of the national consultation committee, the BGC, are sent to all EWC members by the EWC chair, who is also chair of the national body.

Overall, language was seen as a major problem in communication between EWC members. This issue was raised at the EWC training meeting, and management was called on to finance training. However, there are no plans to provide language training specifically for EWC members, although the company does finance further language training as part of its overall training strategy. A number of members are currently learning English on this scheme.

EWC and National Employee Representation

Contact between UK employees and the EWC is provided for through the fact that all the British representatives sit on the national consultative committee and can pass on the information they receive in the EWC to workforces through national structures. There are plans to inform employees about the work of the EWC through company publications and other media, such as e-mail. The EWC chair also stressed that including the workforce in the work of the EWC was necessary in order to prevent it sliding into an elite forum lacking in legitimacy. However, feedback from the workforce has been non-existent.

In theory, employees at the Italian subsidiary could also be informed using national structures. The fact that the Italian EWC representative does not do so is probably atttributable to the low importance accorded to the body. This is understandable, given the fact that the Italian representative has only recently become a trade union member and was chosen to carry out the task mainly because of their knowledge of English and willingness to travel. At the same time, it is an indicator of the lack of interest on the part of Italian employee representatives and trade unions, for whom skill and experience in workplace representation were evidently not the main criterion for appointment to the role.

EWC and Trade Unions

All the British unions represented at ICI together with EMCEF were involved in the negotiations to establish the EWC. The trade unions are also represented at the meetings. Only full-time officials of the TGWU attend the preparatory meetings, although EMCEF representatives and full-time officials of other national unions attend the joint meetings. The trade unions also initiated the training event for EWC members.

In Italy, the unions are not involved in the work of the EWC – probably because of the fairly minor economic importance of the Italian operation which has only 200 employees. In contrast, the British unions are heavily involved through a variety of mechanisms. In the first place, UK EWC representatives are nominated by the national unions and maintain contact through the ICI national consultative committee. And secondly, the unions – principally the TGWU – provide support for EWC meetings. Both group management and the trade unions view the EWC as a positive example of co-operation.

The TGWU is very involved in support for the EWC and has been the driving force behind its development from the outset, but has not appropriated it. It regards the EWC as a body for employee representation within the group as a whole and does not wish to direct it externally. As with most other British unions, its prime aim has been to conclude as many agreements as possible as quickly as possible. In doing so, there has been some neglect of the task of elaborating an overall approach to the role and future development of EWCs.

Overall Assessment

The EWC at ICI is characterised by the long-standing experience of the national consultative body, the business and general committee, and the – for British circumstances – co-operative relationship between employee representatives and management which this reflects. Equally untypical for the UK is the systematic use of an employee representative body as an instrument of human resource management.

Internally, the EWC is marked by the dominance of the UK employee representatives. As yet, this has been accepted as being entirely natural, given the fact that the UK has by far the biggest concentration of ICI facilities. However, the need to reduce this degree of dominance has already been acknowledged and some tentative steps taken in this direction. The EWC is still in a phase in which it remains highly focused on the joint meeting with management. Preparatory and steering committee meetings are taken up with preparations for the joint meeting. This is viewed as an information meeting for national employee representation – although there have been some attempts to negotiate on European issues.

Management continues to exercise a major influence on the EWC, although it is beginning to show signs of independence. For example, there are plans for the steering committee to meet more often and hold exchanges of information between EWC meetings.

The creation of the EWC is due to the efforts of the British trade unions. However, their involvement has not been confined to negotiating its initial establishment and they have continued to support it. The ways in which the trade unions seek to move management in their direction follows a repeated pattern. Their readiness to organise and finance European employee meetings and training has put management under pressure since they are eager to present an image of co-operative relationships with the unions. The trade unions support the EWCs without dominating it, and without stifling independent activity by employee representatives.

The establishment of the EWC at ICI can build on foundations which are more favourable than at many other UK groups as the existence of long-standing consultative machinery means that the EWC does not have to act as substitute for this, as it does in many other organisations. The development of the ICI EWC may also be favoured by the fact that European employee representatives have a common interest within ICI as a *global* business in that they all want to retain investment in Europe. On the other hand, the pursuit of a global strategy could make life difficult for the EWC as an institution, as the constant selling and acquiring of businesses, with its impact on the composition of the EWC, hinders the development of continuity, and through this, of a capacity to act cohesively.

Note

1. IG Farben had been created in 1925 out of a combination of BASF, Bayer AG and Farbwerke Hoechst.

15   The EWC at Merloni: 'Left in the Lurch'

Merloni was founded as a family undertaking in 1930. Merloni Elettrodomestici SA was established when the main family group was broken up in 1975. The president since its foundation has been Vittorio Merloni, son of the company's founder. With some 8,200 employees, Merloni is the smallest of the groups in this study. Despite rapid growth it has never entirely lost its provincial character. The group headquarters is in Fabriano, a small town in central Italy. The group began to internationalise in the late-1970s, and now has subsidiaries in Portugal (1980 Fri-Sado), France (1989, Scholte), Turkey (1994, Pekel As) and the UK (1995, New World). Outside Europe, Merloni established a joint venture in China in 1995 and in 1996 bought a company in Argentina. The company's domestic strategy has also been one of growth via acquisition; in 1987 the company bought Indesit (1987-90 Indesit, 1995 Philco and Star).

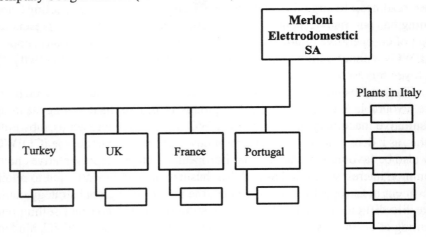

Figure 15.1 Structure of Merloni Group in Europe

External expansion has also corresponded with a period of organic growth. Over the last 10 years output has multiplied sevenfold and foreign turnover fifteenfold. Merloni is paramountly a producer of white goods (washing and washing-up machines, fridges, freezers and cookers). In all, the company has 11 plants in Europe of which six are in Italy, two in Portugal and one each in France, the UK and Turkey. With a market share of 26 per cent Merloni is the market leader in Italy, and with a market share of around 10 per cent the fourth largest manufacturer in Europe.

In recent years the company's strategy has been aimed at raising its market share in Italy, but especially in Europe, through the acquisition of brands. Its sales strategy remains clearly focused on the European market, where its 10 per cent market share has given the group 'sufficient critical mass to sustain itself against its European competitors'. However, given declining sales volumes and increased competition in western Europe, Merloni has decided to look towards less developed markets in Eastern Europe, South America and South East Asia. Merloni is on the cusp of switching from a European to a global sales strategy.

In contrast, production is still highly nationally concentrated and export-oriented, as can be seen from a comparison between turnover and employment in the group. Whereas 74 per cent of group turnover is earned abroad, 60 per cent of the workforce continues to be located in Italy. This national production strategy is also manifested in the relationship between the parent company and its subsidiaries. The group is tightly managed from the centre. Subsidiaries are closely integrated with the parent company, and group-wide functions, such as distribution, are organised centrally rather than by each subsidiary individually.

In 1995 Merloni bought the British company New World and integrated the business into the group. A large proportion of the activities previously carried out within New World were then outsourced in line with the group's strategic objective of lowering the degree of vertical integration in its manufacturing operations. Some components are now sourced from Italy or from British companies with contacts to the Italian group. There were five waves of redundancies following the acquisition during which the New World workforce was reduced from some 700 to 270 employees, leading to fears on the part of employees and their representatives that the plant might be closed entirely.

Origin and Structure of the EWC

The Origin of the Merloni EWC

Merloni became the first Italian group to establish an EWC in September 1993, following the conclusion of a collective agreement for the group, one element of which was a decision to establish a 'European Committee' *(comitato europeo)*. The agreement was concluded by workplace employee representatives at the company's six sites in Italy, together with the trade union secretaries of the three engineering unions FIM, FIOM and UILM and in the presence of the trade union secretaries of regional trade union organisations. The Italian engineering trade unions had included the demand for the establishment of an EWC in their claim for the 1993 company-level bargaining round, in doing so also implementing the EMF's strategy of gaining an EWC foothold in Italy. The inclusion of provisions for a European information procedure in a collective agreement was in line with the customary process for establishing and extending workplace information and consultation procedures in Italy. Information and consultation procedures already existed at company level in the Merloni group in Italy (with an annual meeting in accordance with the national sectoral collective agreement) and at workplace level (meetings held every four months in accordance with the local agreement). Management viewed the experience gained with these information and consultation procedures at national level in a very positive light. In their view, it had demonstrated that employees who were better informed were inclined to be less adversarial and combative in the conduct of industrial relations. As a result, management was already well-disposed to the idea of establishing an information body at European-level.

The collective agreement simply set out the aim of the Committee (information and discussion body for the situation and prospects of the company), the composition of the body (18 employee representatives from the group distributed over the various European plants in proportion to their workforce, as well as company representatives), the frequency and duration of the meetings (once a year for a maximum of two days) and the date of the inaugural meeting (during the first four months of 1994).

In order to give some additional impulse to the EWC, in April 1994 the Italian engineering unions organised a '4004 meeting' in conjunction with the EMF which was attended by trade union delegates from France, Portugal and Turkey. The meeting included a session with group management which was used to clarify the subsequent steps for negotiation and explore how an EWC could be formally established.

The trade union delegates in attendance gave the Italian trade unions a mandate to proceed with negotiations and present a text for an agreement. The aim was that the draft agreement was to be ratified by all the trade unions involved and the EMF. For its part, group management indicated its willingness to put forward the text of an agreement later in 1994 and call a meeting. However, it was opposed to inviting employee representatives from the Turkish plant as it was eager to avoid introducing the conflict between two of the trade unions represented at the Turkish plant into the European Committee. By September 1994 the initial draft agreement had been worked out and – in view of the adoption of the Directive – was then reworked.

During the course of company-level bargaining in 1995, the group head of personnel and a representative of the executive committee of FIM, negotiating on behalf of all three union confederations, reached a definitive agreement on the introduction of an EWC. Both sides based their positions on the provisions of the EWC Directive. Negotiations were conducted for the most part without controversy and also without the attendance either of any workplace employee representatives, representatives of foreign trade unions or the EMF. The agreed draft was subsequently sent to employee representatives in the company's foreign subsidiaries – some workplace, some trade union – and to the EMF for approval; this process was completed by December 1995. The final signing of the agreement took place in July 1996 at the first official meeting. The body was dubbed the European Group Committee.

Almost three years had passed between the decision to establish an EWC in September 1993 and the first official meeting and signing of the agreement in July 1996. According to the head of the international department at FIOM this delay was attributable to the fact that neither group management nor the trade unions were prepared for the establishment of an EWC. This led to both sides underestimating the amount of time involved in organising and coordinating the procedure. For example, the Italian engineering unions had to obtain a guarantee from the British TUC for those trade unions which were represented at the British Merloni subsidiaries but which were not members of the EMF. Several other factors also dragged out the introductory phase of the EWC: for example, the adoption of the EWC Directive in September 1994, the consequences of which had to be assessed for the Merloni agreement; the first elections of RSU representatives at Merloni in 1995, representatives of which were to appoint the EWC delegates; the bi-annual rhythm for company bargaining within the Italian system, during which in 1995 the draft agreement was negotiated; and finally the acquisition of New World in 1995 which increased the number of EWC members.

The establishment of the EWC at Merloni took place during the phase of 'enforced voluntarism'. Even at the moment when the collective agreement was first concluded in 1993, the adoption of the Directive was already in prospect. And after its adoption both sides expressly readjusted the agreement to the Directive's provisions.

The Agreement

The preamble to the agreement defined the 'European Group Committee' as 'an institution for the exchange of information and for discussion'. In contrast, there was no mention of consultation. Indeed, there was an explicit reference to the fact that the EWC was not intended to replace existing national information and consultation machinery.

The agreement also contained a passage which expressly defined it as an agreement concluded voluntarily under Article 13 of the Directive. However, following the transposition of the Directive into Italian law a meeting was to take place between representatives of the employee side and management in order to examine whether any further adjustment of the voluntary agreement was needed to bring it into line with the statutory provision. The agreement was concluded for three years.

The EWC consists of 18 employee representatives allocated according to the following formula. Every country in which Merloni has a plant can send one employee representative. The remaining seats are allocated in proportion to workforce size. Each EWC member also has a deputy. Based on this formula there are at present nine members from Italy and three each from Portugal, France and the UK. At the meetings the EWC members can draw on up to seven experts. However, only representatives of trade unions which are represented within the group and recognised by the company are allowed to act as experts.

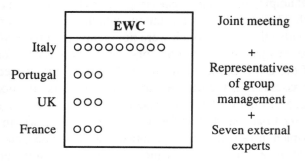

O EWC member

Figure 15.2 Composition of Merloni EWC

The EWC meets once a year for two days. On the first day the EWC meets alone and on the second day there is a joint meeting with management representatives. An additional extraordinary meeting can be called by mutual agreement in the event of economic developments which have particular relevance for the existence of the company.

The EWC must be informed about the following matters: (a) the situation in the branch, (b) the economic situation and prospects for the group, marketing strategies, (c) investments in products and processes, orders and output figures for individual plants, (d) the employment situation (e) management decisions which at cross-border level have an effect on employment and working conditions. Point (e) represents a general clause which essentially covers the individual points listed in the subsidiary requirements to the Directive.

The agreement allows for two employee representatives (either from the EWC members or experts) together with representatives of group management to call the meeting and prepare the agenda. Minutes are taken for the second day's meeting and made available to all EWC members. (EWC members have a right to 32 hours of paid time off to attend the annual meeting and also enjoy the same protection provided for employee representatives by law and agreement in each of their respective countries).

Although the 1993 agreement proposed the establishment of a joint body, this was dropped in the final agreement. The body itself consists solely of employee representatives who then meet annually in a joint meeting with management.

Fields of Interaction of the EWC

EWC and Group Management

The Merloni EWC meets once a year for two days, one day of which is a joint meeting with management representatives. This represents the only contact with group management for employee representatives from the company's foreign subsidiaries. The Italian EWC representatives have a further opportunity to meet with representatives of group management in the context of national information and consultation procedures, at which they can also obtain information on Merloni's investment strategy abroad.

The only meeting held prior to the completion of the study was in July 1996 at the group's headquarters. Five representatives attended from Italian group management: the group head of personnel, the head of industrial relations and the directors of the three product divisions. No management representatives from the foreign subsidiaries attended. In addition there were 12 trade union representatives from four countries who attended as external experts.

Management representatives provided information on the history and future strategy of the company. In addition EWC representatives were also given documentary material, albeit only in Italian. Employee representatives were given an opportunity to raise questions, although the answers were very general and there was little time for discussion because of the length of the presentations. Finally the EWC agreement was officially adopted. However, in contrast to the requirements of the agreement, no formal minutes of the meeting were prepared.

Group management regards the European Committee as a body for dialogue – meaning a non-binding exchange of information and opinions. It sees two useful aspects.

Firstly, communication with employee representatives is considered to decrease adversarial attitudes and raise acceptance of management decisions. In this respect the European Committee constitutes an attempt to extend the positive experience of a 'participative culture' (to quote the Italian personnel manager) beyond national level and to lead employee representatives to an understanding of the global dimension to group strategy.

Secondly, management uses the joint meetings of the European Committee to obtain information from EWC members and to gauge the mood and climate at each of the various facilities. The importance which group management accords to the EWC meetings can be read off from the fact that it holds a review meeting afterwards at which the five management representatives assess the course and outcome of the session. Following this there is a broader meeting at which Italian group management as a whole takes part. Although representatives of the managements of foreign subsidiaries are not involved, they are kept informed by the divisional product managers. However, the personnel manager of the British subsidiary had not been informed about the content of the EWC meetings.

For the Italian employee representatives on the EWC, the main use of the forum consists in their improved access to information. They have a particular interest in details of the group's strategy, knowledge of which can enable them to judge the prospects for individual plants and reduce the uncertainties experienced by RSUs when dealing with local managements. However, the meetings of the European Committee have not been specifically useful as yet. The information which they obtained at the first meeting was interesting, but not especially relevant for local RSU activity.

Confronted on an everyday basis with the conflictual industrial relations of the UK Merloni subsidiary, the British EWC representative had a wider concern. He wanted to use the joint meeting as a forum to exert moral pressure on group management in order to secure a change in management conduct locally. And specifically, he wanted to extract an opinion from group management on the job cuts and curtailments of trade union rights in train at the British subsidiary. For example, although the EWC agreement at Merloni stated that representatives were entitled to 32 hours' paid time off, the British representative was only allowed 24 hours by local personnel management.

Only management felt that the first meeting had gone well and had confirmed the rightness of its decision to be open about information: group management had given a frank presentation of the critical situation at the British plant at the first meeting. However, the meeting had nonetheless passed off without conflict. Representatives of personnel management also felt confirmed in their view that making accurate and extensive information available could avoid disputes with employee representatives.

In contrast, EWC and trade union representatives present criticised the quality of the information provided by management at the first meeting, which they felt offered nothing new compared with the information available at national level. The information provided was also unsatisfactory for the British EWC representatives and had not gone beyond what had already been provided by British management. There was all-round criticism that the information was neither precise nor extensive.

Internal Interaction

It should emphasised that at the time this study was completed, the EWC had only met once for two days – of which one was an EWC meeting without management representatives. This meeting highlighted the differing interests and expectations of the Italian and foreign EWC representatives. The Italian representatives saw the EWC more as a cultural entity than an institution for pursuing employee representation. The EWC afforded an opportunity to become better acquainted with the industrial relations systems of other countries and the situation at other plants. However, they had no direct interest in using the EWC as a representational forum. Quite the contrary: as far as representation was concerned, they regarded national structures as both sufficient and more suitable since a 'participative culture' had already been established at national level. Moreover, they also regarded employee representation as a national matter since, in their view, the foreign strategy of the group was not intimately linked to the Italian situation. The effects of the company's foreign operations on the workforce in Italy have so far been both minor and generally positive.

In contrast, the foreign strategy of the group has had highly negative effects for employees in Merloni's foreign subsidiaries.[1] One British EWC representative wanted to use the EWC meeting to mobilise other EWC members to protest against the treatment of the employees at the British subsidiary. The French and Portuguese EWC representatives had supported this. However, the Italian EWC representatives and full-time trade union officials blocked this initiative. Their solidarity did not extend so far that they were prepared to jeopardise their national participative culture and provoke a conflict with management.

The members of the EWC are passive between meetings. None of them, for example, took any interest in the ongoing business of the EWC, such as establishing the date of the next meeting or the agenda. This task was exercised by the personnel department and a representative of the Italian engineering unions. And none of the EWC members felt responsible for the fact that no one had decided who should be the two co-ordinators for the employee side, as provided for in the agreement. According to one representative from FIM, the co-ordinators were supposed to prepare the standing orders and be the contacts for the EWC with management. In that sense the co-ordinators' task was to function as the driving force for the continuing development of the EWC.

As yet, the existence of the EWC has not lead to the establishment or intensification of informal contacts. No internal structure of communication between meetings emerged. At best, some of the groundwork for this has been laid inasmuch as all the participants were given a list of those who had attended the meeting with addresses and telephone numbers. There are many plausible reasons why no such internal structure has yet come about. The fact that group strategy continues to be highly focused on Italy has meant that the Italian representatives have not felt a particular need to build contacts with their foreign counterparts. And although foreign EWC representatives may have a need to establish contact with the Italian representatives, developing this presupposes building up the required trust and finding suitable partners – neither of which has been accomplished.

The fact that as yet no co-ordinators have been decided on – in line with the agreement – who could constitute the heart of an internal communication structure is a major problem for the foreign representatives. The most likely candidate for this role would be the trade union co-ordinator for the Merloni EWC from the national executive of FIM-CSIL. However, the blocking of the British EWC representatives' initiative has cast doubts on the solidarity which foreign EWC members can expect of their Italian colleagues. Finally, the absence of foreign language skills also makes it all the more difficult to establish and sustain informal contacts. In addition, the British EWC representatives lack access to basic equipment, such as telephone and fax.

EWC and National Employee Representation

The Merloni EWC rests on a structure of workplace employee representation within Italy which is passing through a period of profound transformation. In the first place, since 1990 industrial relations at company level switched from conflict to co-operation, with management and trade unions now operating on the basis of a 'culture of participation'. The RSU elections, held at Merloni for the first time in 1995, have also changed the basis of employee representation in the company. RSU representatives are typically inexperienced and initially concentrate on local representational tasks. The RSUs – not just the EWC – are both passing through a phase of development and consolidation, with roles that are not yet clearly defined.

As yet, trade unions have been the most active element in negotiations with corporate management. This was also the case with the establishment of the EWC, in which workplace representatives played scarcely any role. RSU representatives have also taken no active role in the EWC and have left co-ordination and organisation to the trade unions. However, this has meant that the EWC is only poorly integrated with the workplace level. Better integration should follow from the fact that before the next meeting the Italian EWC representatives will meet the co-ordinator of the engineering unions to agree proposals for the agenda.

In formal terms it is relatively unproblematic for the Italian EWC representatives to inform RSU members and workforces about the course and outcome of EWC meetings as all RSUs at Merloni send at least one EWC representative, ensuring that all the Italian plants are represented. However, information was not systematically passed down after the first meeting and only those who expressed an interest were informed. This was justified by the fact that there were no concrete problems affecting the Italian part of the business on the agenda at the first meeting and as a result neither the RSU members nor the employees would have been interested in the course of the meeting.

In the UK the situation is almost optimal inasmuch as the subsidiary is a one-plant company (with fewer than 300 employees) and has three EWC representatives (not including full-time officials). The channel for information passes through the workplace trade union organisation inasmuch as EWC representatives inform shop stewards. The workforce then depends on shop stewards to pass information on. The EWC representative interviewed – a member of NUDAGO, which is not affiliated to the EMF and has 3,000 members – stated that it does pass on information: in contrast, AEEU and MSF members have not yet received any information via the EWC.

EWC and Trade Unions

The three Italian engineering unions, FIM, FIOM and UILM, occupy a key position within the arrangements for employee representation at Merloni. The executives of the three unions work together in a co-ordinating committee set up at group level, the task of which is to operate a unitary strategy for employee representation within the group and to put forward joint negotiating claims. The negotiations themselves are also conducted by the executives. This position meant that they were involved in and controlled the process of the establishment of the Merloni EWC from the outset.

The agreement reflects the strong position of the trade unions, especially the provision which provides for the participation of seven trade union experts. At the first meeting there were as many as 12 trade union representatives. Group management allowed the upper ceiling to be exceeded to avoid any further delay in holding the constitutive meeting because of the need to accomplish the difficult task of getting agreement between the trade unions. The number was boosted so that all the trade unions represented in the group could send a full-time official. For example, two full-time officials attending from the UK only represented seven and 10 employees respectively at the British UK subsidiary. In contrast, no EMF representatives were invited.

The trade unions do not need to agree on seven representatives until after the next meeting. For the trade unions the presence of full-time officials from all the trade unions represented in the group opens up the possibility of establishing a basis for extensive informal contacts and co-ordination (for example, on training). However, as yet no discussions have taken place between Italian and foreign trade union representatives. In Italy, seats on the EWC are divided equally between the three main confederations FIM, FIOM and UILM, irrespective of their membership: that is, in practice each of these sends three RSU members to the EWC. Full-time officials from all three were present at the constitutive meeting and all three sought to pursue a common strategy towards the EWC. For example, they agreed on one individual to negotiate on their collective behalf and also appointed a central trade union co-ordinator for the Merloni EWC. In the UK the 'joint negotiation and consultative committee' established a procedure by which the trade unions represented in the company would have EWC and expert seats assigned to them. The committee is a joint committee of all the trade unions represented in the plant, and conducts single-table bargaining with management. Here too the principle has been applied that as many trade unions as possible should be treated equally, irrespective of their actual membership in the company.

Although the establishment of the EWC was initiated by the Italian engineering unions, they intend to draw back somewhat in the future in order not to dominate it: on the one hand this is a recognition that the sheer volume of work involved would make this impossible, and on the other is a function of their desire to allow more scope for employees who actually work at the company. However, the EWC representatives themselves have as yet taken few initiatives to develop the institution, for the reasons outlined above.

Both FIM and FIOM are not entirely happy about the way that the Merloni EWC has developed and concede that they have made mistakes. The FIOM representative complained, for example, that the trade unions had been poorly prepared for the establishment of the EWC. One of the reasons was the protracted period over which it was set up. They also conceded that they allowed management too much scope to dictate the course of the meeting. As a result the meeting had proved a depressing experience. The FIM representative felt that workplace and foreign employee representatives had not been sufficiently involved in the establishment of the EWC and contrasted Merloni with the positive experience of setting up a special negotiating body at Whirlpool. She regarded the 'German model', on which the Merloni EWC was based, as more likely to detract from participation. In contrast, joint bodies would force employee representatives and management into practical co-operation and allow employee representatives to learn management from managers. Moreover, although in general she felt that unions should have a more minimal presence in EWCs, she thought that a continuing involvement would be advisable at Merloni after the initial period as the RSU representatives had not shown themselves to be either sufficiently strong or active to drive the institution forward.

For their part, the Italian EWC representatives were critical of their lack of autonomy vis-à-vis national trade union executives yet at the same time felt that they had not had sufficient union support. They also thought that the unions had treated EWCs as a low priority matter, and considered that it was up to the unions to ensure that workforces were better informed about EWCs in general. Put somewhat pointedly, although the trade unions were the instigators of the Merloni EWC, they had left it in the lurch.

Overall Assessment

With only one meeting to its name, the Merloni EWC is still in the earliest stages of development. It was established during the phase of 'enforced voluntarism' and passed through a preparatory period of almost three years from the start of negotiations to the first meeting. The incorporation of an EWC provision in the company agreement at the Merloni group was a pioneer achievement.

The Merloni European Committee is solely intended to serve as a medium of information, and there are good reasons to suppose that this will remain its main function in the future. Transferring negotiating powers from the national to the European level has been rejected both by the Italian EWC representatives at Merloni and management, and is as a result highly unlikely to take place.

Group management intends to influence the behaviour of employee representatives through an information strategy aimed at communicating the company's global perspective and incorporating employee representatives as – based on its domestic experience – it considers that this will lead to less adversarial industrial relations. As such, it hopes to extend the culture which it has established with the trade unions in Italy to the European level. However, the criticisms made by employee representatives at the first meeting suggest that management has not succeeded in meeting this objective. This is not only attributable to an error of judgement about the effect of its conduct, but is also an expression of the contradictory character of management's approach. The company's 'participative culture' is still part and parcel of the paternalistic tradition of what remains a family business – but can only function to the extent that the trade unions and employee representatives are prepared to play along. In contrast, the toughness shown by British management would not appear to be reconcilable with such a culture. As long as group management permits these different 'cultures' to coexist within the group, their culture of participation will inevitably lose credibility.

The first meeting of the EWC revealed a difference of interests between EWC representatives from the home country and those from the foreign subsidiaries: this could presage conflict for the future. The Italian EWC representatives want to strengthen their negotiating position at national level by means of the EWC, and in particular they want to improve their access to group-level information. In contrast, representatives from the foreign subsidiaries want to use the EWC as an institution through which they can represent their interests by setting out their concerns to group management in order to exercise some influence over corporate-level decisions. The dominance of the Italian EWC representatives is a problem in this respect in that the interests of foreign representatives have been given little space; in consequence, they do not feel themselves to be represented by the EWC.

There is a danger that the development of the EWC could be blocked by the following constellation of circumstances. The Italian engineering unions occupy a key role in the Merloni EWC for two reasons. Firstly, they are tied into a culture of participation at national level and are regarded by management as competent and reliable negotiating parties. Workplace employee representatives have transferred the task of representing employee interests at group level to trade union representatives. And secondly, it was the Italian engineering unions who took the initiative to establish an EWC at Merloni. RSU representatives took no active role in this process. However, the trade unions do not have a strategy for advancing the development of the EWC, and want to pass on the initiative to the members of the EWC. What is problematic is that the Italian representatives on the EWC lack the experience needed to enable them to pursue employee representation independently without such external support.

Note

1. Clear evidence for this can be seen in the case of the UK subsidiary, New World. The French subsidiary was also being restructured, but the effects were not known.

16 The EWC at ENI: Building Block of a European Corporate Culture

ENI is a holding company, formerly a public corporation, with six main groups of businesses: in the energy field, Agip (oil and natural gas extraction), Snam (provision, transport and distribution of gas), Agip Petroli (refining and distribution of oil products), Snam Progetti (construction of plant and refineries), Saipem (assembly of plant and refineries); and in the chemical industry, Enichem (petro-chemicals). The core of the group's activities are in the energy field, which in 1995 accounted for 80 per cent of group turnover, 75 per cent of employment, and over 90 per cent of investment. Following the success of its 1992 restructuring programme, the Italian government decided to privatise and float the group in 1995. By 1997, ENI was 46.7 per cent privatised, with the remainder of the shares still in public hands.

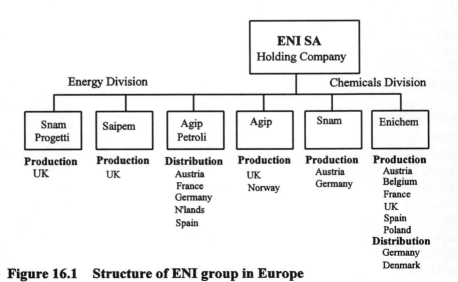

Figure 16.1   Structure of ENI group in Europe

ENI is still a highly nationally-focused group. Although 130 of the 228 companies in the group have their headquarters outside Italy, the distribution of employment in the group presents a quite different picture. In 1995 ENI employed more than 90,000 employees worldwide, more than 70,000 of which were in Italy and only 5,000 in the rest of Europe. The company's strategy is also primarily concentrated on the home market and is directed at winning and retaining market leadership in Italy. The internationalisation of ENI has two aspects. Dependency on raw material deposits means that the energy division is a global business; in contrast, the chemicals division is focused on Europe. Whereas the number of employees in the group fell from 131,200 in 1990 to 86,400 by 1996, turnover rose from L. 50.9 trillion to L. 57.6 trillion during the same period.

Over its history, the group has passed through a series of restructurings. The phase which began in 1992, and was in the main completed by 1995, was aimed at concentrating the group on core activities – primarily, oil and gas production and distribution. A restructuring of the petro-chemical business – another core activity – was also set in train. In the recent past, the chemical division made losses which were underwritten by the energy division. Although chemicals are now in profit, there is still considerable pressure for rationalisation, cost-cutting and more outsourcing. Businesses not deemed core will be sold. The restructuring has led to a sustained improvement in the group's profitability. ENI is now concentrating on developing those areas in which it already has market leadership. Decentralisation will also be carried out to facilitate more rapid decision-making and an improved flow of information. Strategic planning will be aimed at making the organisation leaner and exploiting the group's competitive advantages.

Overall this implies growth for the energy division and shrinkage of the petro-chemicals business. Some 90 per cent of planned investment will take place in oil and gas production. In the energy field, rising demand is expected from politically less-stable countries such as China, the former Soviet Union and South East Asia. Group strategy is aimed at opening up these markets while retaining market leadership in Italy. The companies are managed on a decentralised basis and indirectly controlled through strategic objectives. Within this framework, the undertakings within the group have a free hand in deciding how to meet their objectives – subject to investment approval from the holding company. Cohesiveness between all the member companies in the group is intended to be fostered through a common culture.

The French ENI subsidiary originally belonged to Rhône Poulenc and was only recently bought by Enichem/Grenoble. The most important supplier is an

Enichem plant in Italy and sales are also organised from Italy. In this respect, the French plant is entirely dependent on decisions made at the Italian parent company Enichem.

Origin and Structure of the EWC

The Origin of the ENI EWC

A written agreement on the establishment of a European Works Council at ENI was concluded on 19 April 1995 between representatives of ENI group management, the national executive of the Federation of Italian Chemical Unions (FULC), and a representative of EMCEF. The initiative was taken by FULC who were keen to gain a foothold in the Italian chemical sector. With a history of co-operative industrial relations and its dominant position in the Italian chemical industry, ENI was the obvious choice. As with Fiat in the metalworking industry, ENI dominates industrial relations in its branch. However, in contrast to Fiat, ENI has traditionally pursued a course of co-operation through the inclusion of the trade unions. Up until the early 1990s, ENI was a member of the employers association ASAP which – in contrast to Confindustria – also sought to foster co-operative industrial relations, enabling the trade unions to have recourse to established patterns of co-operation via the association. As a consequence of all this, ENI was favourably disposed to FULC's proposal. Negotiations were conducted by representatives of group management and FULC. On the employee side, an EMCEF representative was present from the outset, but no workplace representative or RSU member. Indeed at this stage, RSU representatives had not been informed by the unions about the course of negotiations.[1] The three chemical unions which make up FULC consequently played the central role in the introduction of the ENI EWC and dominated negotiations from the employee side. In contrast, the employers' association played no role at all.

The ENI EWC represented the first such agreement in the Italian chemical industry. The fact that it assumed this vanguard role also meant that the trade unions were very keen to control the negotiations in order to ensure that appropriate standards were set for subsequent agreements. Where the trade unions have not been able to do this, as at Pirelli, they have preferred not to sign an agreement at all.

The establishment of the EWC at ENI occurred during the phase of 'enforced voluntarism'. The preamble makes express reference to the fact that the agreement should be understood as implementing the Directive (that is, an Article 13 agreement). The EWC was established only at the level of the holding company, not the individual divisions.

The Agreement

The preamble contains three noteworthy points. Firstly, it defines the aim of the agreement as being:

> to achieve closer co-operation at the international level between the group undertaking and employees' *trade union* representatives. *(our emphasis)*

This formulation reveals the importance of the trade unions within industrial relations at the ENI group. Secondly, the preamble reaffirms that the establishment of the EWC represents:

> a significant contribution to a corporate strategy based on efficiency and productivity which – not least through the application of substantial investments – aims to secure growth, competitiveness and employment in the group.

These passages illustrate the fact that the EWC is dedicated to meeting core corporate objectives, with the interest of the company's employees accorded an essentially derivative status. And thirdly, the preamble notes that in establishing the EWC, ENI wishes:

> to affirm the tradition of social partnership established in Italy at the European level and extend this dialogue to trade union representatives of its employees working in companies operating in other countries of the European Union.

That is, national company-level industrial relations is taken as the benchmark and model for what should prevail at European level in the group, with the company hoping to export the tried-and-trusted model already operating at ENI.

Only employee representatives can be members of the EWC. The precondition is at least three years' service in the company. The EWC includes representatives from all national production facilities with more than 150 employees. Employees working in units which do not come up to this threshold are to have a dedicated information procedure established for them.

At present, there are 27 employee representatives on the EWC. Italian representatives, with 16 seats, make up an absolute majority, with the remaining

11 seats distributed as follows: three from the UK, two each from Austria, France and Spain, and one each from Belgium and Germany. As an experiment until the current agreement expires, the EWC has been expanded by three additional seats which are taken by FULC. This mirrors Italian dominance in the EWC, itself a reflection of the group's strong national focus.

Management representatives at the joint meeting include the group personnel director and divisional personnel directors. A representative of EMCEF may also be invited to meetings.

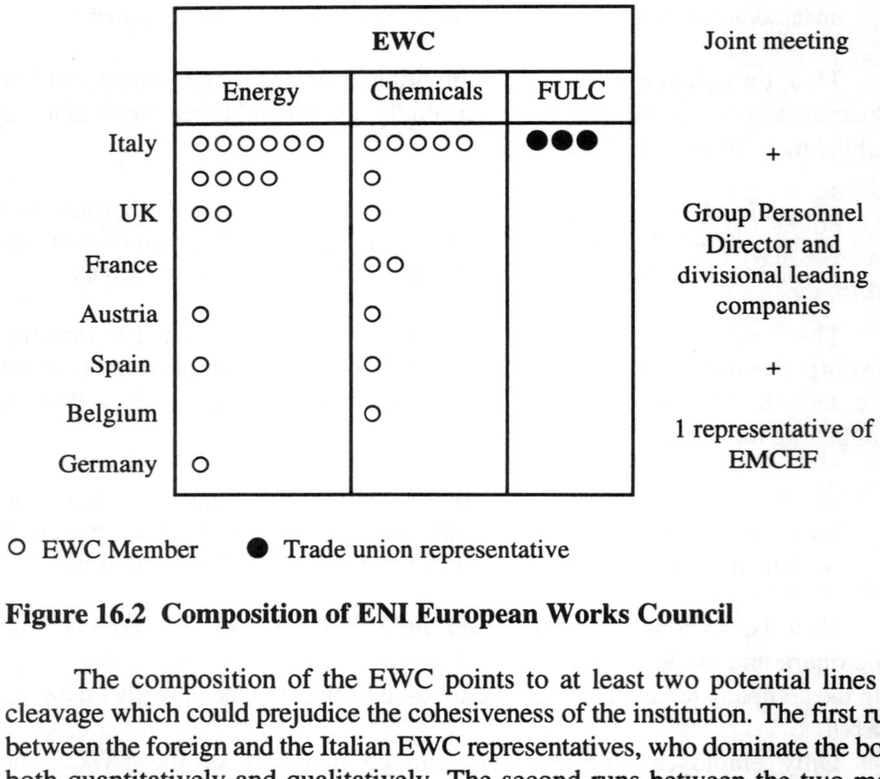

	EWC			Joint meeting
	Energy	Chemicals	FULC	
Italy	○○○○○○ ○○○○	○○○○○ ○	●●●	+
UK	○○	○		Group Personnel Director and divisional leading companies
France		○○		
Austria	○	○		
Spain	○	○		+
Belgium		○		1 representative of EMCEF
Germany	○			

○ EWC Member   ● Trade union representative

Figure 16.2 Composition of ENI European Works Council

The composition of the EWC points to at least two potential lines of cleavage which could prejudice the cohesiveness of the institution. The first runs between the foreign and the Italian EWC representatives, who dominate the body both quantitatively and qualitatively. The second runs between the two main divisions of chemicals and energy, given the differing problems faced by these businesses.

The EWC meets once a year. With the agreement of group management and submission of reasonable grounds, EWC members can call for an additional meeting. EWC members have the right to meet separately one day before the official meeting. Simultaneous interpretation is offered in French, Spanish,

English and German on both days. At the end of the meeting minutes are drawn up, translated into all these languages and sent to all the trade unions represented in the group.

Group management determines the time and location of the meeting, and sets the agenda. The agreement requires a secretariat to be established to deal with the preparation and organisation of meetings. EWC members merely have the right to ask the secretariat to put an issue on the agenda if it falls within one of the listed topics.

The following topics are listed in the agreement for inclusion in the information and consultation procedure: (a) the economic and financial position of the group; (b) corporate strategy and investment plans; (c) employment; (d) plans to reduce the scale of or close a company or facility with cross-border effects; (e) relocations of production outside the EU; (f) introduction of new working or production methods; (g) plans and issues related to the international mobility of employees in the group; (h) health and safety; (i) vocational training and further training; (j) positive action programmes.

Points (a)-(c) basically incorporate the subsidiary requirements to the Directive and points (g)-(j) reflect social and employment matters which fall within the scope of human resource management. They indicate a slight difference of emphasis to the Directive which places priority on information and consultation on commercial decisions made by group managements. This is also testified to by the fact that the personnel function is responsible for the EWC and represents group management on it.

The Italian trade unions have succeeded in consolidating a strong position for trade union representation on the EWC.

Fields of Interaction

EWC and Group Management

The ENI EWC meets once a year for one and a half days, of which half a day is taken up by a joint meeting with management. Contact with group management between meetings is maintained by a representative of FULC, and not a select committee within the EWC. ENI management is represented at meetings by the divisional heads of personnel and of the holding company. Managers from the group's foreign subsidiaries are not present. In order to retain control over the course of meetings, a representative of group management occupies the chair. This is meant, amongst other things, to forestall discussion of issues which are not included in the designated list of topics.

Up until the time at which this study was completed, two EWC meetings had taken place. The first – constitutive – meeting took place in Rome on 30 November 1995. This enabled EWC members to become acquainted and develop some sense of the purpose of the EWC. The discussion which took place on the perspectives for the EWC, as set out in the agreement, indicated that the EWC was intended to be a body which went beyond merely providing for an exchange of information.

Topics discussed at the second meeting, held in June 1996, were the group's investment strategy, prospects for development within the EU, and employment in the group. Health and safety were also discussed and a decision made to establish a European Observatory for Occupational Health and Safety. This new forum was conceived as a joint body with equal management and employee representation. The trade unions can send one expert from each of the countries for which there is EWC representation. Group management has the same number of representatives, drawn from the various divisions. Finally there are two representatives of group management and one each from EMCEF and FULC. The Observatory has control and monitoring functions and can make proposals for improving health and safety which it forwards to the EWC for discussion, not to group management. In this respect, the Observatory is formally controlled by the EWC. The aim is to achieve harmonisation of health and safety standards within the European parts of the group. This initiative can draw on the successful practice of participation in the sphere of health and safety already in operation in Italy and can build on the corresponding EC Directives. As such, it represents an extension of positive national experience to the European level.

Prior to this meeting, negotiations had already been in train between FULC and ENI group management on the establishment of the Observatory. The initiative came from management, with joint work subsequently undertaken with the unions on setting up the body. EWC members first heard about it at the second EWC meeting when they were presented with a draft of the agreement. And although the agreement was concluded within the context of the second meeting, the signatories on the employee side were not the members of the EWC but the three Italian chemical unions (FILCEA, FLERICA, and UILCER) and EMCEF. As far as RSU representatives are concerned, the Observatory presents them with a dilemma. Whilst welcoming the concrete benefits it offers, which include strengthening the EWC, they are critical of FULC's unilateral move and the fact that they were presented with a *fait accompli*. The second meeting also saw the presentation of draft standing orders for the EWC, again prepared by the trade union side.

Management's openness and enthusiasm about the EWC are rooted in its hopes that it will facilitate an extension of the co-operative relationships it enjoys with the trade unions in Italy to the European-level and with this foster a European corporate culture. The EWC is intended to trigger a 'multiplier effect' for a participative culture amongst workplace employee representatives and workforces in Europe, including those in Italy, and convince them of the mutual benefits to be obtained from co-operative and constructive relationships. As a consequence, group management regards training as an important means of improving the efficiency of the EWC. In addition to language courses, management also wants to develop a knowledge of the structure and culture of ENI, including the industrial relations culture which prevails at group headquarters.

The background to this strategic objective is the particular pattern of industrial relations in the Italian part of the group. The co-operative relationships between ENI management and FULC at union/employer association level also characterise relationships within the group. The main discussion and negotiating partners for group management are not workplace employee representatives - the RSUs - but FULC. There is no co-ordinating committee for RSUs at group level. The participation extended by management to FULC, is evidenced, for example, in the February 1996 agreement on FULC's involvement in the chemical restructuring plan. The group personnel manager at ENI group level regards the union has having taken a very responsible position. The agreement was the expression of a joint set of objectives and the outcome of a process of mutual understanding and agreement. Each side was able to put forward proposals which represented their respective interests, but on the basis of an understanding that they would not behave adversarially.

The EWC has also contributed to a permanent improvement in the flow of information between management layers. Previously, communication between the personnel function at holding company and divisional level was sparse. The establishment of the EWC and the decisions which it has made on overarching issues, such as setting up the Observatory, have led to a noticeable intensification of contacts. Relations between the EWC and group management are also likely to have effects within management, given the current unwillingness of middle-management to co-operate with employee representatives.

One further reason behind management's interest in the EWC is its desire to make use of the expert knowledge of EWC representatives and sound out the prospects for joint initiatives with the EWC. As a consequence it wants to give priority to those issues on which EWC members could act as experts and on which joint activity is possible (such as health and safety, and training). Group management's concern is to come to uniform European provisions on suitable issues with the aim, in the longer term, of concluding framework agreements with the EWC.

In contrast, management has no interest in dealing with the specific problems brought up by individual employee representatives and has sought to block any such issues arising by undertaking to give a written opinion on such matters. This is also undoubtedly the reason why the EWC was established at holding company and not divisional level. The detailed problems of foreign operations are not within the scope of group management and have to be put before divisional management. Management at holding company level wants to refer such problems back to the divisions and regards the EWC – as an institution spanning all the divisions – as an inappropriate forum for such matters.

Employee representatives on the EWC are primarily interested in obtaining information from group management and feel themselves a little overwhelmed by the adoption of joint initiatives and the treatment of specialised issues. They do not have the impression that the EWC is there for them and their interests, but that it is more an institution which serves to boost the image of both group management and the trade unions.

Their need for information is not met by the meetings. Although management is seen to have provided comprehensive information, its quality is not judged to be any better than that available from the company's annual report. In addition, employee representatives were critical of the fact that at the second meeting they were deluged with information about the company's future strategy without having any opportunity to respond. In future they want information to be sent out ahead of the meeting in order to be able to prepare themselves and work out what additional questions they might want to ask.

Although a programme was established for the EWC from the outset, there have been a number of practical shortcomings. For example, the French representative could not attend the meeting due to other engagements as the invitation only arrived two weeks before the meeting, despite the fact that the agreement specified that representatives had to be given at least 20 days' notice of the time, place and agenda. Moreover, she did not receive the minutes.

The lack of a secretariat has proved to be particularly problematic. A secretariat could function as a point of contact between group management and EWC representatives, and thus create a channel for information and the exercise of influence for representatives. The need for such a body is also testified to by the criticism expressed by one EWC member that one meeting a year was not enough and that the time for the meeting was too short. ENI's personnel management is aware of the problem of a lack of co-ordination between meetings and wants to establish a clear line of responsibility for contact to the EWC and its ongoing activities. It is planned, in line with the agreement, to entrust a manager from the industrial relations department at group level - who has already been designated - with the task of organising the business of the EWC. Her tasks will include serving as a contact for EWC members between meetings, receiving their proposals and questions, and preparing the meetings. This includes collecting agenda suggestions from EWC representatives and the trade unions and evaluating their relevance for the work of the EWC. FULC is in agreement with this solution.

Group management and employee representatives have differing expectations of the EWC. For group management - in conjunction with the Italian trade union representatives - the issue is to discuss concrete and qualitative issues with the EWC and agree joint proposals for the way forward. The paramount interest of employee representatives is to obtain information from group management. The course of the meetings is set by management and the Italian trade union representatives.

Internal Interaction

Communication between EWC members is confined to the period of the annual meeting. On the day before the official meeting, an EWC meeting takes place without management at which problems encountered in the individual countries can be brought together and any questions which emerge from this formulated for management to respond to. There is no subsequent review meeting.

Internal EWC communication during the meetings is seen as problematic by the Italian representatives because of the sheer diversity of problems experienced in the individual companies. These difficulties were compounded by language problems. Problems were also created by the differences in the industrial relations backgrounds of the members. Despite this, the atmosphere was seen as open and co-operative. As far as the French representative was concerned, the meetings were dominated by the Italians and in particular the representatives of the Italian chemical unions. She felt that she was not a fully enfranchised member, but merely had the task of reporting on the situation in the French part of the group.

There are no informal contacts between meetings either between the Italian EWC members or between foreign and Italian members. The French member had had contact with a Belgian member, suggesting that sporadic contacts might be maintained between the foreign members. The trade unions, which have the most frequent contact with management, do not serve as a distribution point for information between meetings.

As yet, FULC representatives have not built up an infrastructure to ensure that the information they obtain from management is forwarded to EWC representatives. And the latter do not see how they can obtain such information. The channel for information to group management remains confined to the FULC representatives.

The French EWC representative has sought to establish contact with the Italian representatives, but without success. She was repeatedly referred to FULC full-time officials. Instead of forwarding her requests for information to the Italian EWC representatives, they routed them direct to management. The French representative described an attempt to obtain information about a newly-appointed manager to the French subsidiary: her telephone enquiry to the Italian trade union representative was answered – by phone – by an employee of the group personnel department.

The Italian EWC members also complained about the inadequacies of internal communication. As an illustration they cited the fact that a French subsidiary had been sold between the first and second meetings without any anyone on the EWC finding out – the reason cited as to why the issue had not been raised at the subsequent EWC meeting.

One indicator of the state of internal communications is also the fact that the Italian EWC representatives did not know whether any practical steps had been taken after the second meeting to get the Observatory for Health and Safety up and running. They do not know who they should address any questions or proposals to, nor whether the members of the new body had been designated. This would have required contacting FULC at national level or EMCEF, neither of which they had done.

One major reported shortcoming was that it was not possible to discuss the agenda within the EWC. And as long as there was no clear line of responsibility, members did not know who they should address agenda proposals to. The Italian EWC representatives were obliged to tread the detour of going via the national executives of their trade unions and putting a request to them to add an item to the agenda. For the EWC members from the company's foreign subsidiaries, the route was even less transparent.

The Italian EWC representatives felt that one possible solution to the problems encountered in the internal communications structure would be the establishment of a co-ordination committee or secretariat, and have proposed this to FULC. In the absence of such a committee, they argued, EMCEF should take on the task of co-ordination and act as a central point of contact. They criticised FULC for not responding to their request. They would not be opposed to a secretariat being located within group management as, in their view, its task would not be political but essentially organisational in nature: this would also have the advantage of avoiding the problems associated with the composition of any internal EWC committee. A secretariat run from within group management would also serve to weaken the dominant position of FULC vis-à-vis EWC members without having to run the risk of an open conflict.

EWC and National Employee Representation

The ENI EWC is entirely separate from national workforces and arrangements for employee representation. In Italy the EWC is not integrated into the structure of workplace representation, the RSUs. Italian EWC representatives only inform 'their' workplace about the course and outcome of EWC meetings. There is no group-level co-ordination of RSUs, as is usually the case in other large concerns. At most, RSU members from the various ENI facilities within individual constituent companies in the group maintain telephone contact. As yet, there has been no meeting of all RSU members for the whole group. Only when negotiations are imminent will RSU members for one company get together to prepare their claim and negotiating strategy.

FULC, which is in close contact with group management and is much more aware of the strategic possibilities of the EWC then the EWC members themselves, does not lay great emphasis on communication with RSUs and the workforce, being more inclined to pursue a policy of indirect representation.

Despite the existence of a unified trade union structure, FULC, and a unified structure of workplace representation (RSUs), as yet no channel of communication has been established between the two levels. In contrast, communication takes place via the individual constituent unions which make up FULC (FILCEA, FLERICA or UILCER) and their members in the RSUs.

The French EWC representative has stopped passing on information to lower levels of representation because, in her view, she does not have any information about the EWC which is of any real significance. In her words: 'How would I look if had to tell people who work hard all year around that I'd just spent two days in Rome for nothing'. Conversely, employees in France were interested in information from group management as the plant had only recently been integrated into ENI and the implications were not, as yet, clear.

Overall, it appeared as if, of anyone, it was group management who were interested in ensuring effective communication with national employee representatives as they hoped that this would lead to a diffusion of co-operative industrial relations to the workplace level in Italy and elsewhere in Europe.

EWC and Trade Unions

The EWC agreement provides for three additional seats for FULC representatives, to be divided equally between the three main Italian union confederations - although UILCER has a much lower level of representation within ENI than FILCEA and FLERICA. In practice, FULC is in fact represented by four full-time officials as the national officer from FULC responsible for the EWC is also an employee of ENI and sits as an ENI EWC representative. The general secretary of EMCEF has participated in both meetings; as yet no full-time officials from other national trade unions have participated in the meetings.

The Italian trade union officials from FULC clearly exercise a predominant role within the EWC. They negotiated the agreement with management and *de facto* determine all the Italian EWC representatives: their nominations are in some cases subject to subsequent ratification by elections on the part of RSU members. They use their strength within the national part of the ENI group to model the EWC in accordance with their own strategic objectives. Because of its pioneering role, the ENI EWC is seen by FULC as offering a model for emulation elsewhere and has having a degree of strategic significance. FULC's main aim is to extend the powers of the EWC, subject to greater participation by the trade unions, and develop it into a negotiating body. FULC is eager to extend the practice of negotiation which it already has with group management to the European level. In contrast, they see the creation of an infrastructure and structure of communications as being of secondary importance. The EWC is presented by the union with *faits accomplis* – as with the plan to set up an Observatory for Health and Safety, which had already been negotiated between FULC and management prior to the EWC meeting.

FULC is attempting to use the EWC to extend its negotiating scope to the European level, but without taking full consideration of the interests of EWC members themselves. Both the Italian and French EWC representatives have criticised the appropriation of the EWC and control over it by FULC. In practice, the Italian EWC members have had contact neither with the national official of FULC responsible for the EWC nor with the representative of EMCEF between EWC meetings.

The French EWC representative maintains good contacts to her trade union, the CFDT, although they can do little to improve the position of French employee representatives in the EWC. Given the failure of her efforts to establish contact, she now puts her requests for information about ENI to the CFDT which passes them on to its Italian counterparts. However, so far this route has also proved unfruitful.

Overall Assessment

The development of the ENI EWC has been centrally shaped by the activities of FULC which has taken control of the body and sought to hold it up as a model for the rest of the Italian chemical industry. ENI has offered favourable terrain for this in two respects. Firstly, the Italian trade unions could look back on an established culture of negotiation at group level and a strong position within industrial relations arrangements at ENI. And secondly, the pronounced national focus of the group meant that there was a good prospect of extending FULC's strength at national level onto the European plane as the risks of losing control were minimal, both for the Italian trade unions and ENI management – given the marginal significance of the company's foreign subsidiaries.

FULC's priorities have been problematic. Its main aim has been to be able to show some demonstrable results from the EWC's activity as quickly as possible. In contrast, it has lost sight of the fundamentals of constituting the EWC as a body. Little attention has been paid to integrating foreign EWC representatives, the needs of EWC representatives for information, or building up the required infrastructure. The criticism expressed by EWC representatives that the EWC is primarily there to improve the image of both ENI management and FULC are understandable, even if this in fact misunderstands the strategic aims which each is pursuing.

Group management is using the EWC as a 'soft' instrument of managerial control over a highly decentralised structure of subsidiaries and divisions. The EWC is intended to diffuse the industrial relations culture which prevails at the centre to the subsidiaries. The establishment of the European Health and Safety Observatory is not only aimed at achieving uniformity across Europe but also across the divisions in order to set a common framework for the various corporate cultures within the divisions and establish greater cohesiveness.

The establishment of the ENI EWC at the level of the holding company is problematic for EWC representatives inasmuch as this does not fit with their need for information at divisional level. This is a particular problem for foreign EWC representatives whose need for information is both country- and division-specific – indeed involves subjects of such specificity that there is little general interest in management's response at the joint meetings. Moreover, the EWC is conceived of as a consultation forum for specifically personnel and employment issues, and much less as a source of information on commercial and business matters. This can be seen both in the fact that the sole representatives of management are from the personnel department, and not from commercial functions, and in the interest on the part of personnel management in using the joint meetings to discuss specific personnel and employment questions.

Note

1. This picture is also confirmed by a questionnaire completed by an RSU representative: 11 of the 14 questions asked by us on the preparation for and establishment of the EWC were not answered and two were answered incorrectly.

PART V:
CONCLUSIONS AND
PROSPECTS

17 Implications of the Case Studies

A: EWCs and Management – From Acceptance to Recognition

The relationship between EWCs and management is not a static one, but develops through a process of mutual interaction. Although it can be reasonably assumed, at least for those EWCs established by voluntary agreement, that their existence is accepted by management, this does not mean that managements fully acknowledge the legitimacy of EWCs' need for information and consultation. For the most part, EWCs have had to struggle to obtain recognition as institutions to which information should be disclosed and, going one step further, as bodies for the representation of employee interests. Extending the scope of their activity has usually been the end result of a step-by-step process.

The path from acceptance as a recipient of information to recognition as an institution of company-level employee representation is a complex process with many interrelated stages. EWCs develop from being a purely information forum to a consultative body; at the same time, they attain autonomy from management. EWCs also acquire the status of an industrial relations actor inasmuch as they no longer simply articulate specific or local interests but represent interests and put forward demands which have been collectively elaborated within the EWC itself, functioning as an institution and with its own views on employment and corporate issues. In the optimum scenario, management then gradually realises that it must consider the interests of the EWC in order to be able to realise its own interests.

Differing Constellations of Interests

In their early stages, EWC representatives simply want to obtain information which can help them exercise their duties as agents of their respective national systems of representation. Their prime concern is to acquire information which can enable them to come to a better informed assessment of prospective developments at group level and their local consequences. The EWC consists of a group of individuals with differing interests, depending on which part of the group they represent – with marked differences between representatives from the parent company and those from subsidiaries. Representatives of employees in subsidiary companies have a much greater interest in information than those from the group's home base who can often satisfy their need for information through national arrangements and their proximity to group management. As a consequence, EWC members from the group's headquarters are more interested in maintaining existing power relations – that is, their own institutionalised dominance. The position is somewhat different in the United Kingdom as the majority of companies have no corporate-level representational arrangements. British EWC members have often, therefore, sought to use EWCs as a substitute for the lack of an appropriate national forum. These diverse interests constitute latent – but at times also manifest – barriers to the establishment of a cohesive European body.

EWC representatives can only begin to develop and articulate common interests once they have built up sufficient trust and experience. This does not mean, however, that every EWC which has been in existence for some time is capable of articulating collective interests. In fact, such capacities can also sometimes be found in new EWCs, as at ICI in the form of the demand for a European provision on compensation for expenses for employees working from home, or at GKN in the organisation of preparatory meetings at which members exchange information and views.

In contrast, managements invariably rapidly develop their own agendas for EWCs. Their main interest has been to use EWCs to raise the acceptance of corporate decisions on the part of employees and their representatives in order to minimise the 'frictional losses' experienced during restructuring operations. One indicator of this is senior management's interest in participating in EWC activities – intended as a signal that the EWC is a 'top management issue' and that employee interests are taken seriously. The presence of group management is also a sign of management's interest in the EWC as an instrument of control. Management may also be eager to build a European corporate culture or transpose the experience of co-operative industrial relations in one jurisdiction to the European level. Where this is the case, EWCs are usually assigned to the human resources department. Group management always attend every meeting. EWCs can also be viewed as an instrument for internal communication and management of the group – often indicated by the attendance of management representatives from foreign subsidiaries.

National managements may also have an interest in the EWC as they frequently receive little direct information on group strategy. In none of the companies looked at in this study was there any provision for a European meeting of national management representatives. And although some companies do hold meetings of national personnel managers, they are not as well-informed as EWCs.

From Information to Consultation

With the exception of Bull (with two meetings a year) all the EWCs in the study meet once annually in a joint meeting at which EWC representatives have an opportunity to obtain information from group management. Since fresh information on current developments is emerging constantly, the meetings can only provide limited scope for dealing with such matters. All the agreements allow for extraordinary meetings to be called to deal with current developments, although ICI represents the only instance to date in the case-studies in which such a meeting had been called.

One possible solution to this problem is to create an information network to ensure that EWC representatives receive information from group management between meetings. The most highly-developed instance of this is in the case-studies is at Schmalbach-Lubeca, where the EWC praesidium meets representatives of group management every two months and where the EWC also has the right to request information from national managements.

The information needed to carry out the tasks of employee representation was not made available to all the EWCs in the study from the outset: rather, EWC members had to win the right to information – a stage at which the Italian and UK EWCs were still at when this study was completed. There were repeated and substantial conflicts in the French examples until management met the EWCs' desired standard. And in one of the German EWCs, management first had to be 'educated' until the information was of the required quality. In the other cases, the quality of information provided did improve, but was still not regarded as satisfactory by all EWC members.

In the initial phase, EWC members found it difficult to judge what information they needed, what they could ask for, and how to assess what they were given. In part this lay in the fact that the establishment of the EWC was not at the instigation of workforce representatives but was rather bolted on from the top. And in part, it was due to the frequently inadequate structures and practice of national industrial relations. In order for an EWC to develop into a cohesive body, it is necessary for a common standard to emerge as to how information is to be dealt with. Managements were also often not always aware of what employee representatives expected during the early stages. The dissatisfaction of EWC members with management approaches to information during this phase may often, therefore, be attributable to mutual uncertainty about the expectations of the other party. One indicator of the quality of information is the amount of written information made available before the joint meeting. Written information is provided at Schmalbach-Lubeca, GKN and Bull; in two instances, the EWC does not receive written information until the joint meeting (Hoechst, Rhône Poulenc), and in other cases no information was provided in advance or only of an inadequate kind.

What is of importance for the influence of employee representatives at the joint meeting is less who sits in the chair – which is essentially a formality in more long-standing EWCs but can play a role in the early stages – and more the preparation of the agenda and the specific subjects to be addressed. In the case-studies, the EWC is barely involved in determining agenda items in the Italian groups. In the other countries a steering committee establishes the agenda, in consultation with management.

Parallel to the achievement of a desired standard of information disclosure, EWCs can also be seen to have developed formal organisational structures. This process is closely related to information disclosure in that a formal structure enables information to be secured and processed more efficiently, and in some cases is the prerequisite for some sorts of information becoming available at all. In their early stages EWCs are often dominated by management, with the administrative unit responsible for organising meetings and for communication with management located within the group personnel department. Although this is a unit with no formal political function, this decision nonetheless has a political side to it which can easily be underestimated. Contact amongst EWC members between meetings is made more difficult, the exchange of information in these periods is subject to management control, and the influence of management on the content of the statements which emerge from EWCs, such as minutes, increases. Moreover, a dedicated and formal structure creates a basis on which EWCs can develop into autonomous bodies with a formalised and independent relationship to management. Such autonomy presupposes that the EWC has access to its own resources, as at Bull in the case of its budget or at Schmalbach-Lubeca with its own administrative facilities. More extensive provisions, such as time-off for EWC members, which harmonise national differences in resources for employee representatives and raise the independence of the EWC, can be found embryonically at Schmalbach-Lubeca.

The independence of the EWC as an actor is indicated by the fact that it can conclude agreements, albeit in most cases only on provisions affecting itself. EWCs have tended to conduct negotiations with management and sign agreements where existing EWC agreements need re-negotiation. In such instances, management is prepared to recognise the EWC as a negotiating partner. The EWCs at Bull and ICI are on the way to concluding agreements going beyond this with group management.

EWCs normally interpret consultation as meaning that employee representatives can put questions to group management. In some cases, as at ICI, this entails lists of prepared questions. This very restricted notion of consultation has already given rise to dissatisfaction. Management either provides answers which avoid the issue (Merloni) or postpones having them raised (ENI).

Consultation in the sense that the EWC is informed and consulted before a management decision is taken has generally been rejected by group managements. One particular area of management concern is that sensitive data has to be given to employee representatives, without the corresponding degree of trust having developed between the EWC and management. Although almost all agreements contain a section dealing with the treatment of confidential information, the lack of effective sanctions means that such clauses cannot guarantee that information will be kept confidential. Moreover, managements are only willing to engage in serious consultation if they consider that employee representatives have sufficient expertise. Achieving consultation procedures therefore requires, to a greater degree than in the case of information, that the EWC is recognised as an independent actor by management. One path in this direction is the issuing of opinions by the EWC as a European body. Such initiatives can be seen at Schmalbach-Lubeca and at Bull. Consultation on how to respond to the social impact of corporate decisions would, however, go a good deal further than what has been seen so far in most cases.

One other line of development aims at concluding agreements with management on specific, precisely-defined subjects which lend themselves to negotiation. In fields such an environmental protection, safety at work and the like, on which management and employees have some coincidence of interest, managements have sometimes been more willing to inform the EWC and seek discussion and agreement than in those areas envisaged by the Directive. This approach can become problematic, however, if the EWC is seen merely as an instrument of human resource management and where such themes dominate the meetings. The EWC will be concentrating on the wrong level if issues of group strategy become overshadowed. Nonetheless, such projects can have a positive effect on developing the capacity of the EWC where they contribute to the process of its internal constitution and the establishment of an organisational structure. Moreover, the interests of the employees will be effectively represented: putting a high value on high safety standards will raise the legitimacy of the EWC.

Summary

Although in most cases information and consultation might not have come up to expectations when measured against the standards of national information rights, EWCs have, however, advanced beyond the level of representation provided for by the Directive. The first steps in the direction of the development of EWCs into an active body, into a forum for European interest representation, are clearly evident in the case-study examples.

EWCs could develop into a European forum via a number of possible routes. Three main options can be identified.

Firstly, the status quo can be preserved: that is, it does not prove possible to overcome the blockages to the development of the EWC – either from within the EWC itself or from management – as these actors simply do not have a sufficiently strong interest in its development. In contrast, the other two developmental paths exhibit their own unfolding dynamic.

One path runs from the EWC as an information body mainly used for purposes of national employee representation via the creation of a distinctive structure in the form of a steering committee and the establishment of an administration independent of the employer through to the constitution of the EWC as a European body, informed 'comprehensively and in good time' by management and recognised for negotiating purposes. The other path begins with negotiation on issues on which consensus is possible, with the EWC constituting itself as an institution through its involvement in projects; broader questions of group strategy are initially accorded a much lower priority.

Both paths have their strengths and weaknesses. The danger with the first is that management might lose interest in the EWC, which then suffers a loss of recognition as a consultative body. In the second, the risk is that EWC could lose sight of the fact that it must also serve as an information intermediary for the group's employees. The strength of the first path lies in the directness of the route to becoming a European body; the advantage of the second is that the EWC can move fairly swiftly to occupy and work within a distinct sphere of activity.

B: Relationships within EWCs – *En Route* to a European Forum?

The conclusion of an EWC agreement confers neither the capacity to act or form policies nor inner coherence. An agreement is merely the starting point, not the end of the EWC's development. Rather, development proceeds through an internal process of constitution through which the EWC must unlock its potential and build its strengths. This internal process of constitution can take a radically different course from case to case and may succeed to a greater or lesser degree. Three dimensions are of particular importance:

1)   The communicative dimension: is the EWC establishing internal communicative relationships and the structures which can promote and stabilise these relationships?

2)   The socio-cultural dimension: are EWC members developing the individual competencies needed to advance the EWC and develop it in the above sense?

3)   The institutional dimension: has it been possible to create internal organisational structures which can secure the EWC's continuity and capacities?

The Communicative Dimension

In general, structures to facilitate communication do not develop prior to the conclusion of an EWC agreement. This applies at least for those cases in which agreements were struck before the phase of 'enforced voluntarism' where only a few individuals were involved in the negotiations, which for the most part remained a purely national affair. At best a representative of one of the European trade union industry federations was brought in. Broader involvement in the run-up period was only possible once EU funds became available to finance European meetings (Budget line 4004). However, in the case-studies considered here, these meetings were not used to establish informal contacts. In the British examples a type of special negotiating body was formed, as provided for by the Directive. But this also failed to generate informal contacts on any scale. The development of informal and formal structures of communication was and is a primary and urgent task for EWCs.

EWCs meetings are not only concerned with facts but also with social relationships. They constitute the framework in which employees from different countries can become acquainted and participate in mutual exchange. Contacts can be established, mutual trust – often the prerequisite for communication between meetings – generated, and the need to sustain contacts fostered.

In the final analysis, structures of communication are less determined by individual compatibility than by the needs of interest representation – that is, the degree of genuine interest in the EWC. The central indicator for this is that the structure of communication in the majority of cases is markedly radial in form – or is at least a blocked radial structure: blocked in the sense that the centre of the star is not transparent. This radial structure is almost a necessary outcome of the interest of employee representatives from subsidiary companies in obtaining the sort of information which is only available at groups' headquarters: as a rule, annual joint meetings cannot satisfy this need. A radial structure represents a substitute solution to this problem. However, it is not without its own problems since the centre of the star is also the eye of the needle through which the flow of information must pass.

A radial structure presupposes that EWC representatives from the home base have access to information about the group – a prerequisite not typically met in the case of British parent companies (ICI represents an exception to the broader pattern of British industrial relations). It also presupposes that basic infrastructural requirements, such as telephone, fax or e-mail, are also available. Most EWCs have access to the first two, and e-mail is becoming more widespread. A further prerequisite is that the centre is adequately staffed with one or more individuals responsible for the distribution of information – a task which will grow over time. Our case-studies show that this requirement is not always met, and that EWC representatives from foreign subsidiaries are often helpless when confronted with this deficiency (ENI, Merloni). Occupying the central position within the star is not only a labour-intensive, but also a highly responsible role as EWC representatives from foreign subsidiaries rely on the flow through the eye of the needle being sustained. Conversely, this also puts the information distributers at the centre in a powerful position. They determine which information will be passed on, and which will be held back. All information passes through their hands, and they retain an overview. They can use this power to control the flow of information for their individual (national, local, political-trade union) interests and also to secure their own position within the EWC. As a consequence, this function presupposes either a high degree of personal integrity or mechanisms to ensure collective control.

One possibility for improving internal communications is that of transferring responsibility for distributing information to an institution. As a rule, this role is exercised by the steering committee.[1] This can mitigate the problem, but does not eliminate it as individual EWC representatives from the home country retain the more intensive contact to group management. Nonetheless, such institutionalisation signifies an intensification of communication in two respects. Firstly, it institutionalises, intensifies, and consolidates the flow of information between employee representatives with access to group management and group-level information and members of the steering committee. It is desirable for a more intense traffic of information to flow between group management and the steering committee as this will ensure that the steering committee acquires its own independent right to information from group management. In any event, procedures should be established to regulate how the EWC members will be informed by the steering committee. Our case-studies noted a number of initiatives in this respect which might be worth emulating. Of all the examples, the communication arrangements at Bull are the most developed. Here EWC members are divided into country groupings, with detailed provisions as to which steering committee member is responsible for which grouping. EWC members also have access to a data-bank on which all information considered relevant for the EWC and employee representation is stored and available.

The coherence of the EWC can only be established by means of a dense structure of communications. The significance of internal communications will also grow once the EWC moves on from being only a recipient of information to acting as an institution of employee representation. Internal communication then ceases to be simply the passing on of information provided by group management, but serves to aggregate interests, and establish a common EWC position and strategy.

The Socio-Cultural Dimension

The EWC imposes high individual demands on its members. For many, not being able to communicate directly in their mother tongue is an unaccustomed experience. However, EWC members are required not only to establish an understanding across language barriers but also across the traditions of differing political and industrial relations cultures. All this can lead initially to uncertainty as to how to behave, to the formation of factions, and to inequalities of power.

Communication in a variety of languages was seen as a problem in all the EWCs examined. At the meetings themselves, individual contributions are simultaneously translated. In the majority of cases, this also applies in meetings of the praesidium or steering committee. However, language remains an obstacle to informal contacts, obstructs the building up of trust and promotes the formation of sub-groups. A number of means to mitigate this have been tried. For example, employees, employee representatives, trade union representatives and secretaries and administrators have been drawn on as interpreters and translators. Such solutions remain improvised and contain an element of chance: communication can become neglected in those languages for which no translator can be found. Moreover, such a process does not establish direct contact.

Communication is wearisome and difficult. In most cases, high priority is accorded to language training, but with considerable variation in how this is delivered, ranging from the possibility of participating in in-house language training to language courses tailored to an individual EWC member and based on their pre-existing skills.

One consideration is that of offering training to the EWC as a team. The reasoning behind this is that communication problems are not simply caused by language difficulties but also by the lack of knowledge about the differing industrial relations systems represented at meetings. Translation implies far more than rendering meaning from language into another. It entails understanding specific national logics and patterns of behaviour, and the problems these can generate. Different industrial relations systems also bring with them differing styles of politics – some of which may be perceived to be incompatible, with consequent conflicts and factionalism within the EWC. Being able to put such different political styles – which can range from co-operative and informal approaches to demonstrative and conflictual displays of power – to good use presupposes an understanding of the sources of power which employee representatives draw on in their respective national systems of industrial relations.

Operating on such a comparatively unknown terrain means that EWC representatives initially can be deprived of certainty of expectations and trust. However, confidence in an abstract system (Giddens, 1990) – the trade union – can establish a basis for trust. And conversely those who lack this prerequisite may be treated with greater distance: for example, the French representatives of the CGT (as a non ETUC union) who have to work against the suspicion of importing a radical political agenda, or representatives of enterprise-based unions, who are suspected of being too close to the employer.

EWC representatives from the parent company enjoy much more favourable preconditions for involvement in, and action through, the EWC than those of representatives of foreign subsidiaries: they have a 'home advantage', although its extent can vary substantially. It can be broken down into the following components.

As a rule, EWC representatives from the home country form the single largest contingent – a dominant position which endows a feeling of security. They also usually have recourse to national structures of representation to obtain information and influence on group-level decisions. As a consequence, they are not as dependent on the EWC as their foreign colleagues and also have an information and negotiating advantage, rooted in established relationships with group management. And finally, the fact that meetings are held in their mother tongue and in their own country offers benefits which should not be underestimated. (See, 'Internal Features of EWCs' in the Appendix.) This 'home advantage' can lead to dominant behaviour by the 'home team', including intimidating foreign EWC representatives or blocking consideration of their interests.

The establishment of mutual trust is a necessary prerequisite for an open exchange of information within the EWC. Trust becomes more important where the EWC is no longer simply a recipient and distributor of information but sees itself as an active institution of employee representation, confronted with the need to achieve a balance of interests internally and then vis-à-vis management. Not all EWC members will feel themselves equally well-served. This can become a problem when one individual or group feels persistently disadvantaged and loses confidence in the EWC, or fails to establish it at all. Trust on the part of EWC members in the institution is the means through which the EWC achieves consistency and stability, and becomes able to survive crises and protracted periods of difficulty.

The case-studies show that confidence-building measures by those who dominate the EWC can lead to surges of institutional development – and conversely that where this does not happen, development can be obstructed. Such measures can include voluntary relinquishment of positions of dominance – such as the EWC chair (Rhône Poulenc, Bull) or support for EWC representatives in the event of national conflicts (Schmalbach-Lubeca, Hoechst).

The Institutional Dimension

The formation of institutions is subject to two evaluative criteria: efficiency and degree of democracy. The process should both raise the capability of the EWC and create a European forum in which equal consideration is given to the interests of EWC representatives from all European locations.

The composition of the EWC in all the case-studies was the result of the application of the principle of 'qualified proportionality' – that is, countries with larger workforces are under-represented and those with smaller workforces over-represented. This means that representatives from the home country have not always insisted on representation in strict proportion to their workforce numbers. Such restraint has served to forestall one potential source of conflict over the issue of representation. In one case, however, votes on the EWC are weighted in accordance with workforce numbers when decisions are taken (Hoechst) and in all cases employee representatives from the home country remain the largest contingent and sometimes retain an absolute majority (ICI, ENI).

'Opponent free' EWC meetings are gaining in importance. During the initial phase they were predominantly used to prepare the meeting of the joint committee (putting together a list of topics for consideration). Over time these meetings can acquire a significance of their own, especially once it becomes evident that problems can be discussed more openly in the absence of management. In two instances EWC meetings were held without the attendance of the employer between the annual joint meetings. In contrast, review meetings after the joint committee tend to be regarded as less important, although they may offer a better opportunity to understand issues than spontaneous individual responses to information provided by management because of the scope for mutual discussion. However, a collective opinion presupposes a process through which the EWC can arrive at a consensus following the disclosure of information by management.

Every EWC – explicitly or implicitly – posseses a leadership and operational structure. The internal structure can be found set out in the agreements, in EWCs' standing orders, in minutes and in supplementary agreements. The main internal EWC forum is the steering committee, which exercises both leadership and operational functions. The establishment of a steering committee puts leadership, operational and decision-making structures on a broader and international basis. However, steering committees were not found in all our case-study examples (for example, ENI and Merloni) and even where they are established they do not always lead to a change in the structure (Hoechst). The range of tasks of the steering committee also varies considerably: in some cases it merely serves to prepare the agenda for the joint meeting; in others it represents possibly the most important forum, meeting between EWC and joint committee meetings, both with and without management, in order to obtain information and reach mutual agreement. The greater the importance of the steering committee, the more important will be the issues of information exchange between the two bodies and the nomination procedure for steering committee members. Conflicts and dissatisfaction can arise on the part of those not represented on the steering committee if the procedure is not felt to be properly democratic.

The establishment of additional, subject-based committees or working parties allows a larger number of EWC members (and possibly non-members) to become actively involved in the work of the EWC. A variety of individuals can be drawn on for limited periods and for specific issues.

Building internal structures is also always a question of resources, specifically of the time which EWC representatives can make available and the financing of the EWC – that is, the costs assumed by the employer. In the long term, only a dedicated EWC budget can ensure that the EWC is independent of national representative arrangements and that representatives from foreign subsidiaries can be more actively involved in its work.

Summary

The case-studies suggest that EWC representatives from the home country usually initially dominate the EWC and give it its particular shape. The customary starting point is the transfer of the national model and national modes of behaviour onto the European body. This applies in particular in situations where the agreement has been negotiated solely by employee representatives from the parent company. Only through further interaction can the learning take place which – ideally and, as far as the case-studies are concerned, in practice – will lead to the creation of a European body. The prerequisite for this is that EWC representatives from the home country consciously refrain from exploiting their 'home advantage' to secure and extend their own power on the EWC but rather use it to strengthen the EWC as an actor at group level: that is, they recognise that in the long term they may also become reliant on the EWC as their national capacity for action shrinks.

Involvement of employee representatives from outside the parent company's home country in the establishment of EWCs and the negotiation of EWC agreements was helped by the financial support available under EU budget line 4004 and continues to be ensured through the requirement under the Directive to establish a Special Negotiating Body. Such involvement creates conditions under which the emerging EWC can begin its work with a high level of international communication.

C: EWCs and National Employee Representation – Integration Still in its Infancy

At least since the early-1990s, the pursuit of 'lean production' has gone hand in hand with a rationalisation of structures of information and consultation. Whilst this has emphasised the decentralisation of information and decision-making, it has devoted less attention to the issue of which decisions should continue to be made at the centre and what new possibilities are created by reorganisation.

These processes also impinge on every level of workplace employee representation as customary decision-making hierarchies and structures of information are turned upside down. At workplace level, representatives are confronted with new forms of direct participation; at the same time these self-organising groups are no longer controlled by local management but are placed in a framework established at a higher level which both fosters competition between production units but also requires a high degree of co-ordination between them. The result is contradictory: increasing scope for shaping processes within the framework is combined with diminishing scope for influence on the structure of the framework itself. How closely individual units are tied to the centre varies between companies. (This is also one reason for the varying assessments of the scope available at the immediate workplace which simultaneously gains and loses in autonomy.)

Effective employee representation presupposes a capacity to intervene and prevail at every level within an organisation. Forums at company or group level - such as the EWC - not only constitute points at which information relevant for local activity can be collected and distributed, but must themselves become a factor in shaping local strategies. This is only possible if the EWC and national structures of employee representation are properly integrated.

When an EWC is first established, such links are initially improvised and depend on the personal engagement of individuals. Formal and informal structures exist only in embryonic form. Equally, the actors only develop a sensitivity for the significance of information exchange and even for the EWC itself once they have gained some experience of its practical operation. In our case-study examples, the EWCs are on the road to integration but are still far from achieving it. Undoubtedly, the need for such integration will only become apparent once EWCs are accorded a higher significance. Or rather: development of the field of interaction between EWCs and national structures for employee representation presupposes that the process of constitution has already been completed to some degree in the other fields of interaction described above.

The specific features of national industrial relations systems mean that the prerequisites for successful integration vary considerably between countries (see the table 'EWCs and National Structures of Representation' in the Appendix).

Despite a pre-existing structure of representative institutions in France, political trade unionism means that there is no single channel of information to employees, but rather a divided stream running through each of the trade unions. Moreover, the problem of competition between the *comité de groupe* and the EWC can serve to lower support from French EWC representatives where the parent company is French.

The structured formal arrangements for employee representation in Germany create fairly favourable preconditions for a cascade of information from the EWC to workforces. The existence of a large number of works council members with time-off, who usually also make up the EWC, and the institutional competencies acquired within the German system, also favour such integration. However, this complex structure of representative bodies can lead to the problem of the accumulation of offices which, despite extensive time-off rights, overburdens multiple office holders and concentrates power in the hands of a few leading officials – with possible counter-productive effects on foreign EWC representatives. Moreover, the persistent problem of competition between group works councils and EWCs is a serious one. EWCs are at risk of becoming no more than an instrument through which group works councils gain information.

In Italy the formation of EWCs is proceeding hand in hand with a recasting of national structures of employee representation. Both EWCs and workplace bodies – the RSUs – are still engaged in the process of establishing themselves as institutions. Workplace employee representatives have yet to develop an awareness of their own role and identity. Moreover, not all groups have elected representative bodies at national level. The division of labour between trade unions and workplace employee representatives can mean that workplace representatives lack the competencies to deal with issues of group strategy.

In the UK, EWCs are being used to build national structures of employee representation within groups as no such body usually exists in British companies: in comparison, the European dimension is less significant. The EWC at ICI represents an exception to the British rule in this regard.

In many instances, the EWC remains an information committee, a body from which information can be drawn at European level for use within national representative activities. EWC representatives are confronted with the question as to what to do with the information they receive at the joint meetings, which information should be passed downwards and how they should do this. In theory, they can make use of the same tools as management,[2] albeit with fewer resources. These are: (a) cascading oral or written information via existing national bodies, (b) directly informing employees through workforce meetings (although this is precluded in systems in which such meetings are not part of workplace industrial relations - as in France) and other direct methods such as leaflets, articles in company newspapers, or via an electronic bulletin board.

In most cases, EWC representatives use existing representative arrangements to pass on information orally through the various institutional levels. Because only information regarded as relevant is passed on, the flow tends to thin out as it moves downwards, with EWC and national representatives acting as filters for the next level. The fact that the EWC is seen as a passive forum for receiving information means that the absence of information for employees further down the line is not seen as a political problem.

In some cases, there is no top-level national employee body through which information can be routed (notably in the UK, but also in Italy in some companies). In a few instances, this has prompted efforts to set up communication structures specifically dedicated to EWCs (Hoechst in Italy, Merloni in Italy, Rhône Poulenc in the UK). In addition, there are also methods for directly informing workforces. As a rule, information is passed on unsystematically at regular workforce meetings. In one case, the EWC has committed itself to make a presentation at meetings to promote the EWC. Minutes of EWC meetings may also be pinned up on union or works councils notice boards – although it is not always EWC representatives who actually draft them. At GKN, for example, EWC and management prepare a joint communiqué. Articles on EWC matters in company newspapers are also usually written by management. In one case, there is an EWC database which can be accessed by all employees.

In general, EWCs do not regard informing workforces as a high priority, and in some cases leave the task to group management. Such an approach neglects the fact that the transmission of information also simultaneously communicates judgements, perceptions and an image of the company and of the EWC which is shaped by a particular set of interests: in other words, they could use the process of informing the workforce as a political instrument.

Only a few EWCs see it as a political task to ensure that the EWC is firmly anchored in national structures of representation or to campaign for acceptance amongst employees. This will not be achieved by simply passing on information obtained from management or by only reporting concrete results, although this is what happens in most cases. EWCs can only be understood by employees if they are informed about its progress, its setbacks and difficulties, and when the individual learning which EWC representatives experience through their activity can be passed on, and multiplied.

Nonetheless, the acceptance of EWCs would be raised by their ability to demonstrate results. Projects which have a limited life-span, which are confined to a single issue, and which are not inordinately demanding in terms of the work required, could be one way of tackling this. It is worth considering the extent to which projects (or working parties) could draw on the expertise of ordinary employees rather than EWC representatives - as with the ENI Health and Safety Observatory which is staffed by health and safety specialists. This creates a broader basis for European-level representation and exchange and allows productive use to be made of the expertise available in the workforce. However, the EWC should still exercise control over the composition and work of such projects, as happens with the ENI Observatory.

D: EWCs and Trade Unions – The Search for Efficient Co-operation and Strategic Focus

Effective employee interest representation at European level can only take place if certain preconditions are met. The most important of these is close co-operation between EWCs and trade unions, without which EWCs can barely be established at all or achieve sustained existence. However, the relationship between EWCs and trade unions needs active intervention – it will not emerge spontaneously. Although most EWC pilot projects came about with the support of the European industry federations, and indeed often at their instigation, national trade unions, with the exception of the French CFDT, were often reserved about or, where they preferred a statutory regulation, even critical of such efforts. National unions only took on a larger role in the establishment of EWCs during the 'pioneer phase' which followed the first projects. As a rule, they then took the initiative. Either workplace trade union representatives approached management with a request to set up an EWC or management, following an agreement with a union, initiated contact with employee representatives. Only rarely has the initiative been taken by the employer. Trade unions have also been able to prepare the ground at branch level – in some cases through an accord with an employers' association and in others through including the demand for the establishment of EWCs into conventional sectoral collective agreements – sometimes by-passing workforce representatives altogether.

With the dual strategy pursued during this phase, in which voluntary agreements were intended to lend weight to the demand for a legal provision, the trade unions concentrated primarily on setting up as many EWCs as possible. Two further motives could be discerned in the case of the British unions. In the first place, following their turnaround on Europe they did not want to lose contact with developments at other European trade unions; and secondly, they could use the establishment of EWCs to construct a mechanism for maintaining contacts above the immediate workplace level. The desire to set up a large number of EWCs did, however, have the disadvantage – which was consciously accepted – that voluntary agreements would have lower provisions than the standard which the trade unions had set for themselves. This was the only way to ensure that agreements could be struck with willing managements, whose interest in anticipating the Directive often lay in concluding a 'quick and dirty' deal. It meant, however, that the dual strategy weakened the trade union aim of using the Directive as a lever to set high standards for employee information and consultation at European level, even though the Directive, under pressure from the trade unions, went beyond the provisions of the earlier agreements and held out the prospect of further improvements through its revision clause. As a consequence, in those more long-standing EWCs there were negotiations on aligning the voluntary agreements with statutory standards, at the latest by the time the Directive was transposed into national law.

Pursuing the priority of establishing as large a number of EWCs as possible – at least up until the adoption of the Directive in 1994 – also had an impact on the forms of feedback between EWCs and trade unions. The fact that trade unions were in most cases only indirectly involved in setting up EWCs, usually via participation in preparatory meetings and attendance as special advisers, meant that they have remained dependent on information provided by EWC representatives (the notable exceptions to this are the two Italian cases and the one German engineering company). Formally established structures and procedures to ensure this are, however, still in their infancy, and also frequently exclude EWC representatives from subsidiary companies. Although the unions have been attempting to put their support for EWCs on a more regular footing – for example, in the form of the working groups of full-time officials from European industry federations such as EMF and EMCEF – the fact that only one representative per country is delegated puts pressure on the trade unions in France, Italy and especially in the UK to agree a common position at national level on EWC issues. However, the fact that not all unions are members of the ETUC (notably the CGT) means that such national co-ordination cannot be rounded off at European level.

Efforts have also been made at national level by industry trade unions to co-ordinate the work of EWCs through working groups or projects, and to provide for an exchange of information. However, how this support should be delivered, what its precise role should be, and who is responsible has not been definitively resolved in all cases. In addition to the agreement that the large trade unions at companies' headquarters should take on this responsibility, the EMF and EMCEF have also insisted that each EWC should have a full-time official responsible for support. This had not been achieved in all the case-study examples, in particular because the growing number of EWCs stretches trade union resources and not all unions had been able to establish regular access to EWCs. Communication also remains patchy where workplace trade union representatives already enjoy a high degree of autonomy – in Germany by law and in France in practice – or where there is a gulf between workplace and trade union representation. In contrast, the integration between EWCs and trade unions is close in those instances in which, as in France or the UK, EWC representatives are also simultaneously trade union office holders. The exchange of information can also be regarded as formally secured in those cases where full-time officials are represented on the EWC through an agreed provision or participate in EWCs and joint sessions on a continuous basis as external advisers.

The Functional Dimension: Trade Unions - From Initiator to Service Organisation?

Even where procedures exist for exchanging information between EWCs and trade unions, and trade union support for EWCs in the form of seminars, training and other material, is formally established, problems can crop up in the maintenance of working relationships. Whilst national trade unions can help during the 'foundation period' of the EWCs which they initiated and supported, especially at companies' headquarters, contacts with EWC representatives often subsequently become more patchy. Whilst the trade unions find it difficult to sustain regular support, the logic of workplace representation tends to push company-specific aspects into the foreground for EWC members, despite the fact that they are defined via their membership of trade unions.

In addition to offering general advice with model agreements and legal help, trade unions also want to train EWC representatives to become 'experts in their own cause'. This embraces language training and the provision of information on the particular aspects of each participating country, as well as training in how to interpret the information provided by group managements. These services are also called for by EWCs, and EWC representatives from subsidiary companies have drawn attention to the ground which still needs to be made up. Beyond this, EWC members report a need for knowledge about different systems of industrial relations in Europe and an interest in exchanging experiences with other EWCs.

In contrast, the issues dealt with by EWCs and joint meetings are often seen as excessively focused on the individual company, with insufficient consideration to the sector in which the company operates. Although more general issues, such as health and safety or environmental protection, look beyond the immediate corporate context, and although the contact groups organised by the European industry federations for national trade union delegates offer potential discussion forums for such issues, these are primarily concerned with the organisational aspects of establishing EWCs and also lack a corresponding national underpinning for further exchange and discussion. However, if the main substance of EWC work becomes detached from broader trade union concerns, there is a danger that the support offered to EWCs by the unions will be reduced to training - and in that sense no more than a service role.

The Strategic Dimension: Uncertainties in Setting Priorities

The gap between the technical and organisational help provided by unions in establishing EWCs and ongoing substantive and strategic support can be attributed, in the first instance, to the limited resources which national and European trade unions can make available and the continuing focus of trade union policy on setting up additional EWCs. However, it is also indicative of shortcomings in the debate within the trade unions as to the status and role of EWCs within their overall strategy. In addition, the fact that this discussion cannot be conducted solely at national level, but requires a direct cross-border exchange encompassing the European industry federations, contributes a further difficulty. There is an urgent need to resolve the question as to whether EWCs should become an institution empowered to negotiate and conclude agreements with group managements at European level. Without such clarification there is a danger that the pace of development of EWCs could slacken markedly.

In the case-studies considered here, the trade unions concerned exhibit widely varying views on the issue of group-level agreements, although in most cases all have already been confronted with the agreements concluded between EWCs and group managements which adapted pre-existing voluntary agreements to national statutory provisions following transposition of the Directive into national law. In France, the CGT vigorously rejects the idea of any agreement being concluded between EWCs and group management. Even supplementary negotiations in companies headquartered in France continue to be regarded as a task for the French trade unions, not an EWC. Behind this view is, on the one hand, the fear on the part of the CGT that the involvement of EWCs could breach the 'favourability principle', according to which company agreements can only improve on and not worsen sectoral agreements, and these in turn can only improve on the law. And on the other, the CGT only sees scope for emphasising trade union rights and standing via legal means at national, but not at European, level. In addition, the CGT views the differences in trade union practices as an enduring obstacle to closer co-operation at European level. Concrete experience with EWC work and French case-law in the case of Renault have, however, strengthened the position of those in the CGT who are more open-minded about the possibility of negotiating powers being granted to EWCs.

The French FO is also opposed to the transfer of negotiating powers to EWCs. During the transposition of the Directive into national law, it successfully opposed giving a seat in EWCs to the European industry federations, fearing that the presence of European trade union representatives would impel EWCs towards becoming a negotiating body. In contrast, the CFDT favours such a development. The FUC-CFDT has also used its contacts to Italian and Spanish chemical trade unions to raise the status of EWCs. However, this position is not entirely uncontroversial within the CFDT. Movement by EWCs in the direction of becoming a negotiating forum have been viewed with concern by the FGMM-CFDT, as it regards this as a move towards relocating the locus of negotiations from the sectoral to the workplace level. As far as the FGMM is concerned, European level negotiations must be firmly anchored in sectoral and national framework agreements.

In Italy the sectoral unions in the chemical and metalworking industries are unambiguously in favour of EWCs acquiring negotiating powers and regard their own presence in EWCs as preparing for and guaranteeing such an extension of their powers. In the view of the chemical industry trade union confederation FULC, the transfer of negotiating powers to EWCs should, however, only take place if they can be linked to agreements concluded at sectoral level. The metalworking and chemical trade unions in Germany also favour negotiating powers, not so much as a strategic objective but more in recognition of the inevitability of the European-level within community-scale groups becoming a negotiating arena. In our case-studies, the British trade unions, which have the most experience of workplace-level negotiations and which could easily integrate EWCs into their customary negotiating arrangements, also favour extending the powers of EWCs.

Such a step would confront the trade unions with a host of new problems as it would imply an upheaval in established national structures. One of the consequences would be that responsibility for an EWC – located with the largest trade union at the group's headquarters – would no longer coincide with the geographically-defined national negotiating powers of trade unions. Trade unions, whose geographical scope may embrace many multinationals but only a few corporate headquarters, would find themselves confronted with a substantial European presence within their bargaining area. The question of the legitimacy of EWCs and their integration with national collective bargaining is one which will only be raised once EWCs have become a European, group-level negotiating forum, the results of which feed back into the national negotiating arena. For example, the Italian trade unions are concerned about an ebbing away of negotiating rights in their national arena because of agreements applicable in multinational companies in which they do not have direct representation at group level.

Locating support and service for EWCs with the largest union at groups' headquarters raises additional problems of its own. For example, EWCs have on occasions equipped themselves with an internal structure which does not fit well with the form of support offered by trade unions. If EWCs free themselves from their 'national bias' – for example, by locating the steering committee at a subsidiary – then the flow of information to the supporting national trade unions becomes more problematic than in cases where the geographical scope of the two coincide. The danger that the formalities of trade union support are established but that the procedure lacks real substance is also very real, leading to a widening gulf between EWCs and trade unions. Bridging this would require close contact between trade unions with members represented on EWCs combined with flexible forms of support which are not confined by considerations of 'territoriality'. Close co-operation between national trade unions might also ease a second problem associated with trade union support for EWCs by securing more support for representatives in subsidiary companies and ensuring that the interests of the workforce at the group's home base do not confront them twice over without any intermediate filtering – first in the shape of the local EWC representatives and second in the shape of the local trade union.

Notes

1. The term 'steering committee' is used to denote that institution responsible for the current business of the EWC. It operates under a variety of designations, such as 'Praesidium', 'Secretariat' or 'Agenda Committee'.
2. Gold (1994) cites the following forms for direct information and communication with employees on corporate activities at European level: written communication, such as company annual reports; special reports; letters to employees; news bulletins; employee mass meetings, of varying frequency (annual to daily/weekly), at varying levels (top management to office/workplace/shift) and using varying methods (direct briefings or cascading information).

18 EWCs in the 'European Social Model' - From Information Committee to Social Actor

Growing economic internationalisation and cross-border corporate restructuring within the Single Market have generated a new impulse for integration in the sphere of social policy in the European Union, not least by virtue of the mobilisation of Europe's trade unions to ensure that market integration is matched by a social dimension – a movement reflected in the incorporation of the Agreement on Social Policy into the Amsterdam Treaty and an intensification of the Social Dialogue between the Commission, the European employers' associations and trade union organisations. However, within this framework, employers and trade unions are driven by differing interests. Employers' associations want further deregulation within the Single Market and greater flexibility on labour markets; they are opposed to the construction of a system of European industrial relations, a higher status for the Social Dialogue, and the extension of EU powers into social policies. As such, they remain an uncomfortable partner for the trade unions.

In contrast, there is growing readiness by the trade unions to pursue closer co-ordination at European level. The establishment of EWCs in 'community-scale' undertakings and the initiatives towards the co-ordination of national collective bargaining strategies can be seen both as an expression and a consequence of this. Both elements are amenable to further development. For instance, in contrast to earlier Commission proposals, EWCs do not currently possess co-determination rights, but simply rights to participation in the form of information and consultation.

EWCs are frequently viewed as bodies composed of both employer and employee representatives. A difference is then drawn between a French variant, in which management has a substantial influence because the body is chaired by group management, and a German variant, in which employees are guaranteed a high level of autonomous representation through their occupancy of the chair (Rivest, 1996). On this criterion, according to a study of 111 agreements, some 75 per cent could be classified as 'French' and 25 per cent 'German'

(Carley/Geissler/Krieger, 1996). Following Wortmann and Dörrenbacher (1996, p. 9), 'one can differentiate between those EWCs in which employer representatives are represented, and those composed solely of employee representatives'. However, at the same time they also note that 'the difference between the two formal models is less important for their practical activity than how the specific powers and interrelationship between the two sides are structured in reality'. The formal differentiation between models diminishes in significance once EWCs develop greater autonomy. An analysis of how EWCs have become established shows that management influence on EWCs should not be assumed to be static but is rather the expression of differing phases of a process of dynamic development. Nonetheless, the duration and intensity of this development can vary considerably.

There was a strong mutually reinforcing interaction between the establishment of EWCs via voluntary agreements and the passage of the EWC Directive. In the first place, this affected the spread of EWCs. Whereas it would have been impossible to build up the trade union and political pressure needed to ensure the passage of the Directive without the pioneer projects, faced with the frequent refusal of direct contacts to employee representatives by managements, conversely without the Directive it would have been impossible to have achieved the Community-wide extension of EWCs. The practical operation of EWCs also anticipated the procedural provisions of the Directive via voluntary agreements and made these possible. This practice was reflected in legal norms, just as the establishment of legal norms has influenced EWC practice. It is, therefore, appropriate to view the development of the institution of the EWC as a mutually interacting process of constitution.

The Constitution of a New Industrial Relations Actor at European Level?

From Information Committee to Interest Representation

The first European bodies at group level for employee information and consultation were established purely for the purpose of information disclosure. Whereas management often saw such bodies primarily as an instrument for communicating corporate policies, employee representatives hoped for 'an "authentic picture of corporate reality" ' (Nagel et.al., 1996, p. 171) - that is, for information on the position and strategy of the group which could be used to improve the quality of their local work. Although bodies were on occasions used to raise concrete issues concerning individual sites through direct contact with group managements, the first information committees were initially barely more than an assembly of employee representatives from different company sites in a number of European countries, called together by management on the basis of an agreed delegation procedure. They served group management in their self-professed aim of providing information to employees. As a consequence, from the standpoint of employee representatives, committees functioned initially as a European component of their national activity.

However, these narrowly circumscribed aims were soon exceeded. On the one hand, the aspirations of employee representatives as far as the quality and quantity of information, the timing of its disclosure and its presentation in writing, were only met by group managements after resolving initial disagreements. On the other, employee representatives were able to use information committees both for direct contacts with group management – short-circuiting local management – and as a body for dealing with current conflicts of interest within the group. Both developments presupposed, and led to, a need for employee representatives to intensify, formalise and institutionalise their internal communications. The emergence of this European component in employee representation was manifested in demands for autonomous preparatory and review meetings and an independent steering committee, the establishment of which became a standard element in voluntary agreements.

In addition to their information function, joint committees were also able to obtain an – albeit limited – consultative and participative role which had been necessitated by the occasional need for employee representatives to vote and agree on issues, and hence for the formation of a collective identity as a representative institution. The fact that the majority of EWC representatives in the case-studies were trade union members and active as employee representatives at national level created a favourable set of preconditions for the development of an independent body with its own structures and procedures, and distinct from group management – despite their origins in differing systems of industrial relations. One of the key factors in the emergence of a collective and institutional identity as a body for European employee representation has been the effort to draw back national political styles in favour of a common approach – something observable as a quite deliberate strategy in some cases, but never one undertaken everywhere as a matter of principle. Developing the capacity to act collectively as an EWC was especially important in negotiations to improve on earlier voluntary agreements. The fact that such a capacity could not always be established was less to do with ability of the EWC to arrive at a compromise internally than with the differing views of the trade unions involved as to the current and future function and capabilities of EWCs.

EWCs - En Route to Becoming a Social Actor ?

EWCs are venturing into the uncharted terrain initially opened up through voluntary agreements. Information and consultation rights still have to be tested and put into practice, and formal acceptance of information rights still has to be turned into actual recognition as a form of employee representation. In view of the many practical problems which have to be dealt with in the construction of a functioning European body and which – like language problems – are likely to continue in the medium-term, and given the attempts by group managements to incorporate EWCs into corporate strategies, EWC representatives are called on to demonstrate a high and sustained level of motivation and legitimacy. Two potential hazards could become especially serious: the first is the risk of disillusionment and frustration should the input of energy fail to correspond to any tangible outcomes; the second is the risk that EWCs become detached from the broader trade union legitimation of their activity, which can favour the formation of productivity coalitions at group level. This applies in particular in 'dual systems' where workplace or company-based representation might become detached from the framework of collective bargaining conducted by unions. These risks can be reduced if unions are able to develop their own structures, as well as those of workplace employee representation at national and European level, such that they can provide effective service, advice, training and a strategic direction for EWCs and anchor their operation in workplace representation and collective bargaining. Integration between EWCs and trade unions also presupposes that national and European union work is developed more through transnational projects than formal representative structures. EWCs which are closely integrated with trade unions will be better able to withstand conflict and crises and secure their stability and continuity in the event of corporate restructuring – which can presage a recomposition of the EWC.

Building up internal organisational effectiveness is no less important than integration with trade unions. At the heart of this lies the creation of institutions and procedures for communication – that is, for mutual information and collective discussion. The skills must also be made available for evaluating the information received, establishing what information is needed and on what issues consultation is required, and identifying the issues on which negotiations might take place with group management. This confronts EWC representatives with a dual task: firstly, to establish a collective European operational routine and integrate this into their national everyday activity. This is important because the capacity to link up with national systems of employee representation is crucial to guarantee feedback to the workplace, not least in order to ensure that EWCs are seen as legitimate. In the case-studies looked at here, this has been achieved, at least in the parent companies. Too close a link to national structures of workplace representation can, however, court the risk that an EWC becomes excessively modelled on the industrial relations arrangements which prevail at the group's headquarters. Such dominance by a national model can lead to a neglect of the interests of employees in subsidiaries – inevitably detracting from the effectiveness of the EWC.

EWCs are restricted, not least by the Directive, to information and consultation. However, to some extent the logic of development of EWCs allows for this boundary to be overstepped since many EWCs have already had cause to negotiate with management when bringing existing agreements into the line with the standards set by the Directive. The trend towards the decentralisation of industrial relations to workplace level and the creation of cross-border trade union structures would suggest that the trade unions ought to support an extension of the negotiating powers and capacities of EWCs. Projects defined and carried out jointly with management could form an important link between information and consultation, on the one hand, and negotiation on the other. They could demarcate a terrain of issues on which both sides could gain from joint action. Assuming they succeeded, joint projects could contribute to stabilising joint committees in that managements might perceive added-value in the EWC. In the most favourable scenario, joint projects could promote EWC influence over group management decisions. Limiting the activity of the joint committee to the transmission of information and the carrying out of (social and environmental) projects would, however, narrow the terrain, pushing it below the strategic horizon which represents the specifically European level of employee representation. This can only be regarded as having been properly established once EWCs have developed a form of information, consultation and negotiation which offers the prospect of exercising some influence over the social, commercial and financial decisions made by group managements.

The adoption of the Directive in 1994, and its transposition into national law in 1996, brought about a fundamental change in the circumstances for the establishment of EWCs. This no longer depends solely on the strength of employee and trade union representatives and the willingness of managements to inform and consult with their employees. The 'struggle for information' has been decided, and the result enshrined in law, subject to the revision of the Directive in 1999. The fundamental social right of employees to information, consultation and participation – long since guaranteed in most EU Member States – can now become a reality throughout the operations of multinational businesses in the EU.

Despite the strengthening of employee information and consultation rights by the Directive, newly-established EWCs are likely to face similar problems in becoming established as those seen in the case-studies considered here. The mere right to information and consultation does not ensure that the quality of information is invariably good. Even if the effects of corporate decisions on employee interests are 'significant', what this actually means may have to clarified in specific cases. A set of information and consultation standards accepted by both sides has to be developed through practice. Equally, any newly developed EWC has to built up the trust, knowledge and organisational capacity needed to allow an open flow of information and communication despite the serious problems of communication between employees with different languages and diverse industrial relations backgrounds. The integration between EWCs and national trade unions and systems of employee representation required for effective and legitimate representation also has to be fashioned for each new EWC.

However, the rich experience already available to EWCs from workplace employee representation at national level is likely to reinforce the tendency for EWCs to go beyond the provisions of the Directive. Although the involvement of employees in the Directive is restricted 'to the thinner branch of the development of employee participation, namely information and consultation' (Höland, 1997, p. 60), our eight case studies, as well as Höland's 'practical reports from EWCs' indicate that the 'processes of establishing new procedures and institutions initiated by such agreements will not necessarily stop at the conceptual and legal limits' (*ibid*). This applies, for example, to the restrictive interpretation of 'consultation' , as proposed by the French employers' association CNPF in the drafting of the Directive, which limits consultation to 'an exchange of views and the establishment of dialogue between employees' representatives and central management or any more appropriate level of management' (EWC Directive, Article 2). It also applies to the capacity of EWCs to negotiate agreements, which has already progressed through the experience of negotiating with group managements 'in its own cause' to improve on existing voluntary agreements.

19 The EWC Model as Political Objective

The EWC case-studies set out above have shown that information and consultation can offer a jumping-off point for an active strategy of employee representation. This raises the question as to what conditions must be met to allow an EWC to 'function' well from the standpoint of employee interests. There is no straightforward answer to this since the employee side itself consists of a number of different constituencies - workforces, trade unions, national and supra-national institutions, and trade union confederations. Any evaluation will also depend on the objectives set for the EWC and what models can be held out for emulation. Such a model must also take into account the standpoint of management - that is, embrace the issue of what would constitute success from their standpoint. Initially, an EWC can be no more but no less than a body for the exchange of information (management - employee representatives, amongst employee representatives, and in relation to national representatives) and for information and consultation with the employer side at European level. It then develops its own unique properties in relation to national structures of representation: that is, a supra-national dimension and identity. Such a positive model can also be counterposed to other - negative - possibilities: the EWC as a travel opportunity, as a passive committee to satisfy the image requirements of management, or worse still a mere mouthpiece for management.

Such a model can only be general in nature - a type of political outline. We might therefore ask how the eight EWCs considered here could be measured against such a model, with the aim of gauging whether practice conforms with the outline. If this fails to occur over the medium- and longer-term, then there would be grounds for revising the model. Such a revision could take the form of an iterative procedure: the model 'wanders' around the practice, and the practice 'wanders' around the model - each shaping and approximating to the other.

The model presupposes that the EWC will develop a degree of autonomy from management, from national arrangements for employee representation, and from the trade unions. As noted above, this may only be possible if all three sides perceive some gain in such autonomy. Below we compare the development of EWCs in the eight case-study companies with this model. In addition, we look at the interrelationship between EWCs and collective bargaining, which continues to be overwhelmingly conducted at national level.

Finally, we address the question of the significance of EWCs for European politics more broadly. EWCs are one element in the Europeanisation of industrial relations, and hence of the general political landscape of Europe. Is Europeanisation in the sphere of industrial relations through the creation of EWCs simply a step on the road to globalisation in line with the neo-liberal pattern, leading to a 'levelling down' of standards in Europe, or will EWCs be a motor for an autonomous European political, economic and social development, offering the prospect of emancipation from the nation state as an alternative to the stagnation or re-nationalisation of politics.

One can compare the process of attaining a supra-national quality in industrial relations with the take-off of an aircraft. The aircraft may fail to become airborne – that is, industrial relations remain a national concern. The take off may prove to be abortive – that is, the aircraft stalls or has to return: this would imply a re-nationalisation of industrial relations. Or the aircraft may fail to reach its assigned cruising height – success in which would signify the realisation of the model.

- At *Schmalbach-Lubeca* the take-off has been successful. The starting point was the agreement between management and the two most important national groups of employee representatives, the German and the Dutch. Management wanted a unitary European corporate strategy – both outwards and internally in relationship to the workforce. As far as the employee side was concerned, they wanted to overcome the difficulties which had previously hindered co-operation between Dutch and German employee representatives. The EWC's supra-nationality therefore served the interests of both sides.

- At *Hoechst*, the aircraft is flying low. The EWC remains an annex of the German system of co-determination. The chair of the EWC has allowed representation to become concentrated in his own person. There is even a risk of re-nationalisation. On the other hand, the prospects for developing a more comprehensive approach have not (yet) been entirely eliminated.

- At *Bull* the machine is airborne. However, support for the EWC by national representatives at the company's headquarters is not sufficient. They regard the meetings more as a routine than as an opportunity to reconcile mutual interests and develop a supra-national approach to information and consultation. It may be that the anticipated benefits to the French EWC members are insufficient because they already have access to most of the information before meetings begin. As a consequence, in order to 'tackle the long haul', a representative of a subsidiary ought to take on the task of secretary of the EWC.

- At *Rhône Poulenc*, take-off has been obstructed. Management and employee representatives are both responsible. Management does not inform in the appropriate way, at least on occasions: and the French employee representatives continue to pursue their national political differences 'by other means'. Because the EWC is 'only' concerned with information and consultation, this conflictual approach is not understood by EWC members from other countries. The entire take-off phase has become protracted.

- At *GKN*, the aircraft has just left the ground, principally because employee representatives at the German subsidiary, which also supplies the EWC's chair, want it and management supports it. Employee representatives at the British parent company gain from this solution through the possibilities it offers for obtaining national information. British management also perceives a benefit in that the local German management, with its experience of working in a dual system of employee representation, has taken on operational responsibility for the EWC. However, the situation is not entirely stable because of problems of employee representation arrangements within the UK.

- At *ICI* the aircraft is also about to become airborne, again because both management and British employee representatives see benefits in internationalisation. However, developments are in their early stages. As yet, the only factor favouring the success of a supra-national EWC model is the experience of the British parent company with a national information and consultation procedure.

- At *Merloni* – to stay with our analogy – take-off has been delayed. Although management hopes to derive benefits from the EWC, it is not in a position to implement its ideas about information and consultation. As yet, Italian employee representatives have not identified any advantage to them in internationalisation, and national managements – as in the UK – appear to be either obstructing or ignoring the initiative.

- *ENI* is in much the same position as Merloni. The formally enshrined presence of the the Italian chemical trade union confederation FULC in the EWC has so far led it to dominate the body. Moreover, as well as centralised negotiations, the Italian system of collective bargaining also provides for group- and company-level bargaining. Negotiations therefore require a high-level of co-ordination. This can absorb much of the efforts of both the employer and employee sides, especially as the system of workplace representation, the RSUs, is still relatively new. The joint Observatory project, already under way, could speed up the take-off.

This model, as it emerges from an analysis of the eight case-studies, is still very static: it is concerned with information and consultation within the framework offered by the Directive. What is questionable is whether EWCs which restrict themselves to this will be fit 'for the long haul'. The introduction of a dynamic element might yield the following EWC model. Where changes in corporate strategy take place, the EWC must be capable of tackling projects in which the interests of employees in Europe as a whole can be articulated. EWCs can only acquire this capacity where the flow of information not only passes to the representatives of national workforces but where steps are taken to ensure that information gets to the workforces themselves – that is, to individual employees. As a consequence, an EWC will be nothing without functioning and effective national structures of employee representation. Conversely, in the wake of the transnationalisation of undertakings, it is conceivable that national workforces will also be nothing, or at least not very much, without the overarching co-ordinating influence of an EWC. This may sound a trifle far-fetched at present, but as the conflict at Renault showed, matters can change extremely swiftly.

To remain with our analogy: getting airborne and reached 'normal' cruising altitude are no guarantee that the aircraft is flying on the correct heading. This raises the question as to whether the objectives set by the advocates of EWCs and the creators of the EWC Directive have been attained and are likely to be attained. The key question is: is an appropriate flow of information from management to employee representatives, and from these to workforces, possible or probable? How will relationships between EWCs, trade unions and employer associations develop? Will EWCs develop coherence and autonomy? Will they be able to develop their own projects in which aggregate European employee interests will be articulated? Another, less congenial, comparison was drawn by one interviewee: 'An EWC and management - that's like going for a drive together but without a map and with a trade unionist in the back seat'.

EWCs and the Social Dialogue

The operation of EWCs could also lead to new demands being placed on the Social Dialogue at European level. Within the triangle of 'Social Dialogue - Sectoral Dialogue - Workplace Dialogue', which constitutes the initial elements of a system of European industrial relations, EWCs currently represent the most dynamic pole. Following the transposition of the Directive into national law, the number of EWCs is growing in every branch. This raises the issue of the link between EWCs and prospective sectoral Social Dialogue as the precondition for their development as an institution in European interest representation. If the weak link in the development of a European industrial relations is Social Dialogue at sectoral level, could EWCs serve as an opening to sectoral collective bargaining? The Community-wide establishment of EWCs in line with the criteria set out in the Directive will gradually create a negotiating space between EWCs and company central managements. Employee representatives – both on EWCs and trade union representatives – are not faced with the problem of the lack of a negotiating partner. Networking EWCs at branch-level could offer a feasible route towards sectoral agreements, at the time lifting some of the burden from the actors at workplace level. What would need to be established is what issues have to be addressed and regulated at corporate level and whether these could be dealt with at sectoral level. One of several possibilities could be that in linking EWCs and sectoral dialogue, the exchange of EWC experience and objectives could fulfil an important mediating function between the concerns of companies and those of their respective branches, especially where national trade unions responsible for sectoral negotiations have an interest in transnational co-ordination at industry level. In the long-term, EWCs could become a component of a European network of 'arms length' bargaining (Marginson/Sisson, 1996) in which both transnational co-ordination and vertical-international co-ordination between the European, the national and the workplace level takes place.

EWCs and the European Company Statute

The most difficult issue to forecast is that of the relationship between EWCs and official policy. The particular features of the legislative process in the EU mean that the present EWC Directive can only be improved on, not worsened – a step for which no majority could be found. On the other hand, legislative processes are so protracted that there is little prospect of any immediate improvement, despite the impetus which the Renault affair gave to such a development. The

EU as a community based on the rule of law is also able to sanction breaches of the meaning and letter of the Directive. As a consequence, the core objective behind the Directive – that is, the establishment of EWCs in all undertakings and groups which meet the criteria – is likely to be achieved.

In answer to the question as to whether the EWC Directive has acted as a stimulant for politics more broadly, and in particular for EU provisions in the sphere of industrial relations, one can cite one concrete example – alongside numerous non-verifiable speculations – which is closely connected with the EWC Directive. This concerns the proposals for a European Company Statute (Societas Europeae, SE) which has been given a new impetus through the EWC Directive and its successful transposition (the 'Davignon Proposal')[1]. This model adopted the proposals for employee information and consultation set out in the EWC Directive in that it gave priority to the achievement of a negotiated solution. A subsidiary requirement would only take effect if negotiations broke down: this would provide for 20 per cent of the seats on a company's group supervisory board or administrative board to be taken by employee representatives. No institutionalised participation rights were granted to trade unions.

Further attempts to take the measure forward took place during the UK Presidency of the Council in the first half of 1998 in the form of a compromise text in which board-level participation would not be guaranteed in all SEs but would depend on the practice of employee representation in the countries which participated in an SE. The UK's proposal did not find majority support on the Council of Ministers, with countries such as Germany – where board-level representation is highly developed – concerned that their companies might be excluded from joint ventures culminating in an SE because of a desire to avoid the more stringent provisions.

A further important measure which is seen by its promoters as complementing EWCs is the proposal for provisions on information and consultation of employees at national level intended 'to bridge the gaps in national legislation by establishing a consistent Community framework'.[2]

In general, there is as yet no concrete answer to the question as to whether the EWC Directive will serve as a stimulant for broader policies in Europe. The example of the European Company Statute cannot yet be cited as an example, given the current state of development of the proposal. Broadly the same can be said for the proposals for national information and consultation. It is at best conceivable that EWCs will bolster the trend which is already observable in the European Parliament: that is, the dominance of political groupings, versus the national blocs which play the dominant role in the Council of Ministers. If

EWCs are to develop a supra-national dimension – that is, if the aircraft is to take off – then this tendency could become more pronounced: the nation-state would play a lesser role and the road to a united Europe would become broader.

The research conducted here is not sufficient to give a well-founded answer to the question as to whether the employment and social structures of the EU's Member States are converging or diverging. Our provisional prognosis can only be very speculative, but suggests that there are signs of convergence. There is gradual Europeanisation of industrial relations in the Member States and the emergence of a European, transnational level of industrial relations, in which EWCs – strengthened by national court rulings – constitute a highly dynamic element.

Notes

1. The Davignon Proposal was submitted in May 1997 and restarted legislative activity on the European Company Statute after several years of stagnation.
2. Second consultation document to the social partners, 5 November 1997; cited in *European Industrial Relations Review*, 287, p. 3.

20 National Prospects: EWCs in Italy, France, the UK, and Germany

Any consideration of the relationship between EWCs and trade unions in the light of the model's requirements for a flow of information to national workforces and EWCs' capacity to engage in consultation and carry out projects must begin by establishing the preconditions under which such a relationship can emerge at all. One evident precondition is that the EWC must possess a distinct identity, taken here to mean enjoying a degree of autonomy or independence. EWCs are fundamentally an employee body. The French practice, under which the chair is occupied by the 'patron', does not necessarily imply a breach with this concept. All the case-study examples have separate employee-only pre-meetings which serve to nourish such a sense of relative autonomy. There is also no reason why the participation of 'external' trade union representatives in EWC meetings should compromise their independence. Under voluntary agreements concluded under Article 13 of the Directive, trade union representatives may also be full-members of EWCs with voting rights. However, apart from the exceptional case of Italy, as a rule they do not generally dominate EWCs in which they participate.

What does require clarification is whether and how the relative autonomy of EWCs, once achieved, feeds back onto national trade union collective bargaining activity. In Germany, there is a particular fear within the trade union movement that the principle of industry collective bargaining – already the focus of controversy – could be further weakened. On the other hand, there are those who would argue that since some additional flexibility ought to be introduced into German collective agreements, the injection of a degree of 'syndicalist' company-based bargaining via EWCs might be seen as a positive contribution. We cannot explore all the ramifications of this debate here, but would draw attention to the observations made by Saul Revel (1994, pp. 130ff). He resists the temptation to join the 'mainstream' in the current neo-liberal debate and propose a wholesale decentralisation of bargaining. In his view, this would lead to greater segmentation of the labour market. Where trade unions succeeded in

248

establishing and sustaining a presence, wages would be relatively high and market entry for those offering labour would be restricted through closed shops or comparable practices. Non-unionised areas of the labour market would have to absorb a higher factor input, leading to a further relative fall in factor incomes compared with unionised segments. Revel (1994, pp. 51ff) notes that those supplying labour would be able exercise a major impact on productivity through making use of job-specific knowledge and developing a variety of workplace strategies. The institutions of decentralised collective bargaining could make use of these mechanisms. According to the empirical material presented by Revel, countries with centralised collective bargaining perform better from a macro-economic standpoint than those with decentralised bargaining. We accept this argument here inasmuch as we also view the trend to 'workplace syndicalism' with great scepticism, both in macro-economic and broader social terms.

Trade union activity in the field of collective bargaining could also be weakened if unions become overburdened by demands from EWCs for advice and support. Our case-studies suggest that there is considerable need for such advice, but that the trade unions lack the resources to offer anything approaching an entirely satisfactory solution. The problem which trade unions have in meeting this need is also connected to the fact that full-time officials have not yet come to terms with the need to delegate tasks which they cannot perform themselves – that is, the impending reality of trade union 'outsourcing'. This also offers one answer to the possible threat to trade union collective bargaining activity. EWCs' need for information and advice constitutes a challenge to the trade unions to change their structures. One part of the solution may lie in strengthening the European industry federations. If the trade unions fail to do this, then EWCs are at risk – to use our earlier analogy – of abandoning or having to postpone take-off.

The prospect that EWCs might actually strengthen rather than weaken collective bargaining is rooted in the argument that the improvement in international co-operation at workplace level fostered by EWCs could also promote an improvement in international trade union co-operation. Such a process would certainly reduce the currently almost insurmountable hurdles to European-level collective bargaining. Lean production and lean management techniques also call for international co-operation within undertakings, and for closer relationships between suppliers and purchasers. The associated development of participative management approaches and improvements in corporate cultures may also create a more favourable set of preconditions for EWCs. And because competition between different European locations within a group is seen as no less problematic and worrying by workforces as competition between their own and other companies, co-operation between EWCs and different national trade unions, even co-operation between managers, EWCs and trade unions, is more likely now than a few years ago.

The biggest danger for national systems of industrial relations and trade union collective bargaining activity probably continues to lie in how industrial complexes are structured. These consist of a circular disposition of a number of different actors around a small number of key international companies, the 'spiders' in a complex web of relationships (Dörre et.al., 1997, p. 53). Dual systems of industrial relations could fit well with this, also creating scope for a major role for EWCs. Collective bargaining by national trade unions, supported by the European industry federations, would concentrate on concluding framework agreements, which would then need to be fine-tuned to group-, company-, or workplace-level. In this scenario, the supplier companies grouped around a key enterprise would have either no, or only a weak, EWC. They would be confined to workplace, company, regional or national bargaining. Their domination by the central enterprise would leave them little room for manoeuvre on pay. National trade unions would have to strive to do the best they could for employees in such enterprises using industry or company-level agreements – although workplace employee representatives would be under pressure to agree to undercut such agreements.

An associated question is whether and how EWCs become diffused into national systems of industrial relations – a step which would represent a Europeanisation of industrial relations. On the assumption that EWCs represent a – tentative – step towards the acceptance of a dual system of employee interest representation at European level, the question is raised as to what this might mean for trade union activity at national level, and in particular for collective bargaining. One initial step for the trade unions would be to establish a strong base for information and consultation with EWCs in order to be able to influence agreements concluded at European level. This would also have an impact on the trade unions themselves, as co-operation with EWCs will lead to a change in their established structures.

It would, however, be overhasty to see such a decision for a dual system as tantamount to a transposition of the German model of co-determination to Europe as a whole. The decision is simply one which sets the direction towards a dual system, with the substance still to be developed. The case-studies considered here have shown that EWCs can develop in a wide variety of ways, and that there is no reason to suppose that the German structure of co-determination will become dominant at European level. National diversity will continue to prevail, albeit possibly in a weakened form.

The Italian Perspective

Classifying the two Italian case-studies is difficult because of the very small number of EWCs established there overall: in fact, the two represented the only functioning examples at the time the fieldwork for this study was carried out. As a consequence, the only possibility for making comparisons is restricted to the preparatory and establishment phase. We nevertheless venture the thesis, with some reservations, that these case-studies will prove to be representative - a position justified by the fact that Italian industrial relations are subject to a highly-structured framework which leaves little scope for alternative approaches.

One crucial given is the strong control over EWCs exercised by the trade unions, and the acceptance of this by companies and employers' associations. As yet, for example, there has been no attempt by an employer to establish an EWC by circumventing the trade unions. Following the conclusion of the national agreement transposing the EU Directive into Italian law, such attempts would now be virtually impossible. The strong role of the trade unions corresponds to a comparatively weak status for the institution of workplace representation, the RSU, and as a consequence of the EWC members which it appoints. RSUs are a fairly recent institution, and although they have greater formal autonomy than their predecessors (works councils and factory delegates), they have not yet been able to take advantage of this in practice.

Within this framework there are, nonetheless, differing trade union approaches to EWCs - as seen in our case-studies in the approaches of the metalworking and chemical unions. Whereas the chemical industry unions prefer a highly-structured approach, retaining a good deal of control, the metalworking unions have so far been more experimental, albeit with an ambivalent outcome. As far as EWCs in companies or groups with their headquarters abroad are concerned, the situation of EWC members is likely to closely resemble that of those in Italian-owned businesses.

The overburdening of those responsible for national EWCs and the absence of alternative trade union support strategies have meant that Italian EWC members in foreign subsidiaries have had to exercise their role to some extent in isolation and in accordance with their own judgment, with only weak linkages and little - if any - scope for feedback .

Compared with the position of mutual trade competition seen in France, Italy's pluralistic trade union structure has become more unified in recent years. The relaxation in the political fronts between unions and co-operation between them at branch-level in the implementation and support of EWCs are likely to ensure that the problem of trade union competition does not become a serious one. What is more important is that 'old' factory delegates are still often represented in the 'new' RSUs: their relationship to the grass-roots is traditionally so strong that they will probably find it difficult to come to terms with the EWC. Where this is the case, a degree of differentiation within RSUs, and possibly within the EWC concerned, can be expected into a more dynamic and more retarding element. Because of the guaranteed trade union presence in RSUs, the danger of a serious gulf opening between trade union and workplace representation, always latent in a dual system, has been institutionally averted. As a result, the trade unions are more willing to view EWCs as a promising opportunity for the Europeanisation and internationalisation of industrial relations. On the other hand, the structural dominance of trade unions in EWCs can lead to frustration on the part of 'ordinary' RSU members, which could detract from their legitimacy in the longer term.

The recent move towards a system of workplace employee representation which draws together both elements – the strong position of the trade unions and the withering away of union rivalries – has created a favourable context for the successful operation of EWCs within Italy and their integration into the supra-national European level, despite the problems referred to above.

The French Perspective

In view of the weakness and fragmentation of the French trade unions, the work of EWCs will not be straightforward. In the first place, in all probability EWCs in France will consist of both employee and management representatives. Employee representatives in previous voluntarily agreed EWCs are partly delegated direct by the trade unions, reproducing the practice seen in the *comité de groupe* and partly by elected bodies such as the *comité d'entreprise*. Whilst the chair of the EWCs is customarily occupied, in accordance with French tradition, by a representative of the company, as with the *comité d'entreprise* employee representatives usually appoint the secretary. This at least ensures that the everyday work of the secretariat – in the sense of the French, political function of the secretariat – and, where agreed, the preparation of EWC meetings (including the agenda) does not bypass employee representatives.

One especially important decision for the future operation and effectiveness of EWCs in France will be whether existing information and consultation procedures, which are fairly well-developed and formalised at establishment level, should be transposed to the EWC. Despite the weakness of the French labour movement, it should prove relatively unproblematic to conclude formal agreements on information and consultation procedures at EWC level. What will be critical is their practical implementation - with workplace experience in France not so far the most positive. Such consultation procedures do not match the co-determination rights provided for under German works councils legislation. In the context of traditional French industrial relations, such forms of co-determination are almost inconceivable for the vast majority of French workers and employers.

The issue of whether EWCs should have a bargaining mandate is a fairly open one, given these workplace realities. Although bargaining, in formal legal terms, remains the sole prerogative of the trade unions, the erosion of representation at workplace level could open up negotiating possibilities for EWCs, despite their adversarial composition. It is not surprising, for example, that an agreement on this issue has been concluded at Danone – previously BSN – where one of the first EWCs was established. What will be critical will be whether trade union delegates and representatives of the *comité d'entreprise* respond to such possibilities and how they include their 'back office' organisation (trade unions and employees at company and workplace level).

It will always be difficult to find a satisfactory formula to regulate trade union representation in EWCs, given the minimum of five, and sometimes more, trade unions. The task is made all the more difficult by the fact that the CGT, which is closely aligned with the French Communist Party, is still not a member of the ETUC. However, the need for co-operation in existing EWCs has shown that practical co-operation between CGT representatives and ETUC-affiliated unions is possible and does take place.

The British Perspective

Three problem areas are likely to emerge in the establishment of EWCs in the UK. Given the traditional lack of development of 'supra-workplace' structures of employee representation, especially at regional and sectoral level, shop stewards and other workplace union representatives generally have only poor access to the kind of information which is pertinent to this level. This is likely to create a problem in the transmission of information for EWCs which lack the support of a developed information network at workplace level. This is not only a structural but also a substantive issue, as the socialisation and activity of lay union representatives is almost wholly built on, and restricted to, the workplace.

One further problem will emerge from the UK's single channel system of employee representation via trade unions which is that British trade unions can often no longer speak for a majority of employees at any given workplace. More and more cases can be expected in which trade unions represent workplaces or entire companies on EWCs, in which only a small proportion of the workforce is unionised. This applies traditionally, and recently increasingly, to multi-national companies - which account for some 60 per cent of large UK companies (parent or subsidiary), the highest proportion of any European country (Marginson et.al., 1995).

The principle of multi-trade unionism also creates a problem of legitimation in the appointment and election of employee representatives to EWCs which could lead both to complication and competition. The decision as to whether full-time trade union officials or lay representatives should attend EWCs, and in what proportion, will need to be judged on it merits in each case, with no easy solution. This will also not make it easy for their representatives on EWCs to co-operate with management on the basis of the 'spirit of co-operation' required by the Directive. Against the background of trade union competition in workplaces with more than one union - albeit a receding phenomenon given the recent spate of trade union mergers - the Directive's injunction for 'co-operation in a spirit of trust' has a second aspect: that of co-operation between trade unions. The degree to which national trade unions can establish a cohesive position will have a critical impact on the scope for inter-trade union co-operation within and with the EWCs at European level (Traxler and Schmitter, 1995).

The German Perspective

As far as the diffusion of EWCs into the German system of industrial relations is concerned, there already exists a well-honed system of co-determination with rights extending well beyond those envisaged for EWCs. As a result, the problem is less one of how an existing system of national industrial relations - with its specific shortcomings - can be better adapted to EWCs, but rather the converse: how a relatively highly developed dual system can be protected against dilution by the shortcomings in the field of co-determination exhibited by EWCs.

For example, there could be multiple overlapping of the information and consultation roles of the economic committee in larger companies, the group works council, the central works council, employee supervisory board members and the future EWC. Employee representatives on all these bodies need to ensure a very high degree of co-operation between their institutions, based on an agreed division of labour and full exchange of information (Nagel et.al., 1990). Based on the established and customary 'spirit of co-operation' between group works councils and management, national tried-and-tested channels may also continue to be regarded as the preferred option, even where an EWC exists - a development which could risk the further marginalisation of EWCs. This could produce an asymmetry between national and international approaches to how information is dealt with: German EWC members could request and obtain information on establishments and companies outside Germany, but be less forthcoming in delivering information on their own operations. Although such a problem could arise in any EWC, irrespective of the nationality of the parent company, the established industrial relations arrangements and economic power of Germany in the EU could make this into a particular concern in German companies.

21 Will EWCs Promote the Europeanisation of Industrial Relations?

A Europeanisation of industrial relations can take place in three arenas: the Social Dialogue between the European umbrella organisations for the employers and the trade unions, which can culminate in European-level quasi-'Eurostate' regulations following negotiations and the legislative response of the Council of Ministers; transnational co-ordination and growing practical integration between sectoral and regional collective bargaining; and procedures for information and consultation in large companies, with a trend toward the conclusion of agreements at the level of the newly-installed EWCs. There are a number of reasons why EWCs are likely to become one of the key pillars of a Europeanisation of industrial relations. Their introduction in line with the requirements of the Directive will open up a negotiating space between EWCs and group managements. Initiatives on issues which lend themselves to a consensual solution, such as health and safety, training or workplace environmental protection, are already in evidence. Our case-studies have also shown that in Italy and Germany in particular, there is a discernible willingness on the part of managements and EWCs to engage in negotiations and, ultimately, to arrive at agreements on these and other issues. Examples include ENI, Hoechst and Schmalbach-Lubeca. An agreement has already been reached between group management and the EWC at Danone on the initiation of such negotiations. And in contrast to the sectoral level, employee representatives (either EWCs or potentially trade unions) are not faced with the lack of a negotiating partner. One pragmatic and necessary initial step for the trade unions would be to establish good communications with EWCs in order to be able to define the choice of issues and substance both of consultation and future negotiations at European level.

By the year 2000, some 1,500 undertakings operating across Europe are expected to have an EWC. This means – put conservatively – that some 40,000 employees will be involved in the practical operation of EWCs. These 40,000 individuals represent a potential multiplier effect for the Europeanisation of industrial relations. And depending on how their relationships to the trade unions are structured, these 40,000 EWC members – both as individuals and EWC members – could influence the development of the collective bargaining dimension to EWCs. Given the continuing absence of structures for industry bargaining at European level, there is a danger that EWCs could either become syndicalistic bodies solely focused on 'their' companies or disguised agents, to a greater or lesser degree, of group managements. Such a development would be especially problematic as it would run in parallel with the further erosion of national industry-level collective bargaining. This problem could be exacerbated by the fact that agreements between a European group management and an EWC, based on the economic dominance and power of multinational companies at least in the peripheral regions of Europe, might achieve better conditions of employment on a localised basis than has been achieved under national collective bargaining.

In view of this situation, it would be logical for trade unions in Europe to make intensive efforts to involve themselves in the establishment, development and operation of EWCs. This could take place via the participation of trade union experts through advice and consultation to EWCs - a process requiring a stable network of links between EWCs and the trade unions represented in multinational companies. This could also serve to spread 'best practice' at sectoral level. In all likelihood, such an approach would raise the following questions.

- How and with what intensity will links between EWCs and trade unions be established?

- Will the problem of co-ordination between different trade unions be satisfactorily resolved for all sides?

- What is the significance of trade union co-operation within European groups for the Europeanisation of the remainder of their organisations and their activities?

- Can 'best practice' models be developed and made binding at sectoral and transnational level?

- How can the 'nationalisation' of EWCs, as can happen almost 'naturally' given the weight of the EWC at the parent company, be prevented?

Despite all these unresolved issues, there are grounds for believing that a positive scenario is possible. If the trade unions can succeed in building close and stable network to EWCs at both national and at European industry-level, then 'good' company agreements with EWCs - initially on 'soft' issues - could acquire a dynamic role for national collective bargaining in which best practice could be emulated. The number of employees in such 'community-scale' undertakings matches the scope of most national industry or regional collective agreements, and exceeds a good many.

What is certain is that without close interaction between EWCs and trade unions the EWC as an institution will not become a motor for the development of a European-level of industrial relations. However, even trade unions with strong national memberships, and a corresponding organisational capacity, will experience problems in servicing EWCs. A networking strategy places enormous information and co-ordination demands both on national trade unions (and not principally their international departments) and on the European sectoral trade union federations. Trade unions are currently so overburdened that they cannot guarantee continuing support once an EWC has become established - especially where EWCs become engaged in real consultation and establish enduring working relations, for example through projects. As a consequence, there is a major risk that trade unions will not be able to go much beyond the routine obtaining of information, the choice of which will be dominated by group managements. Under such conditions the relationship to the national workplace 'substrate', so crucial for the legitimacy and efficiency of EWCs, will be additionally handicapped and EWC representatives from subsidiaries will be threatened with marginalisation.

These potentially serious risks need to be set against a number of opportunities, some of which have already been referred to. EWCs provide a jumping off point for international co-operation at group and workplace level, not only between employee representatives but also between the trade unions represented in these companies. The simultaneous movement in the organisation of production towards greater decentralisation (focus on the workplace, direct involvement, participative management) and globalisation (Europeanisation of the organisation of production, corresponding corporate restructuring and cross-border corporate culture with a European identity in the context of 'triadic' competition) lay out the main dimensions along which EWC models can be developed and introduce new scope for greater international trade union co-operation. It is especially important that trade unions maintain close relationships with EWCs as competition between the European locations of individual companies is often felt to be as much of a problem by workforces as external commercial competition. The externalisation of such intra-company conflicts to trade unions and group-level managements could assist in moving towards that 'objectification' of conflict which is regarded an important positive aspect of dual systems. The precondition for this is that the 'extensive' industry-level agreement - the core of industrial relations in most EU Member States - is not subjected to any further erosion but is accepted as a rational basis for developing the work of EWCs and European management within a European model of industrial relations.

The influence of EWCs on the development of European industrial relations cannot be forecast precisely, and could vary enormously between industries and companies. However, it may well be that a fundamental decision has already been made for a 'dual system', a decision which will not be without its effects on monistic systems such as those in Italy and the UK.

The Revision of the EWC Directive

The 1994 EWC Directive provides for a revision to take place in 1999. This examination of the Directive will provide an opportunity to incorporate EWC practice, which may go beyond the formal provisions, and experience into the revision process and enable these to make a productive contribution to any extension or concretisation of participation rights. Material rights would follow procedural rights, and practice would 'prove to be the first stage in the movement towards more strongly established substantive regulations' (Höland, 1997, p. 67). At the same time, the revision process will allow a degree of uniformity to be brought into both the diversity of provisions at company level, which originally arose with the voluntary agreements, and the underlying legal foundation, although this could serve to cap the degree of openness which has so far characterised the development of EWCs. An 'offensive' revision of the Directive would, nonetheless, presuppose a political debate both in the Member States and at EU level on the form and extent of fundamental social rights to information, consultation and participation - a debate in which the trade union capacity to generalise from individual EWC experiences should play an important role.

Seen from the current standpoint, this could lead to a modest strengthening of the powers of EWCs. On the one hand, a link could be established to existing employee rights in the event of collective redundancies, especially as regards the time at which information must be available. On the other, steps could be taken to specify procedural norms more precisely and secure the position of EWC members, especially on the issue of time-off, with the aim of achieving some uniformity on EWC members' rights across Europe. Finally, there must be a guarantee of adequate office facilities equipped to current technical standards, with access to the possibilities for information and communication offered by e-mail and fax. EWCs are established on the basis of co-operation, which embraces co-operation with management and with trade unions. This co-operation can only be developed on a secure basis of material and procedural rights, and not if these rights constantly have to be fought for and over. In the medium-term an extension of these rights will be unavoidable.

According to the current state of the draft Directive on a European Company Statute, information and consultation rights are clearly defined. In particular, employee representatives are granted a period in which to respond to a disclosure of information or issue an opinion. The understanding of participation in the draft goes beyond that of merely informing and consulting. These proposals could also offer a benchmark for the revision of the Directive on European Works Councils.

APPENDICES

APPENDICES

Appendix I: Comparative Overview of EWCs

EWC Interaction with Management

	Hoechst	Schmalbach-L.	Bull	Rhône Poulenc
Relationship EWC-Management	Co-operation	Negotiation	From co-operation to negotiation	Co-operation with some negotiation
Joint meetings	annual	annual	twice-yearly	annual
Chair	EWC President	EWC President	Management	Management
Management reps. at joint meeting	Group management, national personnel heads from countries represented	Group management, German personnel manager and others on specific issues	Initially group management, later French head of personnel	Group CEO and heads of personnel from countries represented
Information	Esp. on group developments	Group developments and specific problems	Group developments	Group developments
Consultation	Questions in connection with presentations; no impact on management decisions	Common EWC opinions in specific cases; case-by-case impact on decisions	Refused by management; common EWC opinions in specific cases; case-by-case impact on decisions	Refused by management; no impact on decisions
Resources and organisation	No own resources; secretariat within management	Independent of management and own organisation	Own resources (budget)	No own resources; meetings prepared by management
Contact with management outside meetings	EWC President	Praesidium	Secretariat, which also prepares meetings	'Annual Report & Accounts Committee'
Autonomy of EWC	First steps	Already developed	Achieved after hard struggle	In development

EWC Interaction with Management (cont'd)

	ICI	GKN	Merloni	ENI
Relationship EWC-Management	Co-operation	Still open; negotiations conceivable	Co-operation	Co-operation
Joint meetings	annual, two extraordinary meetings	annual	annual	annual
Chair	Management	Management	Management	Management
Representatives of management at joint meeting	Board members, group personnel director, UK divisional managers	Top group management, personnel managers from countries represented	Head of Group Personnel, divisional managers from Italy	Personnel management from Italy
Information	Esp. on group developments	Esp. on group developments	Esp. on group developments	Esp. on group developments
Consultation	Refused by management; indirect influence on group decisions	As yet no need; no influence on corporate decisions	No consultation; no influence on corporate decisions	Consultation on areas of possible agreement; no influence on corporate decisions
Resources and organisation	No own resources; secretariat within management which has strong involvement	No own resources; secretariat within management; steering committee never meets without management	No own resources; management dominates EWC meetings	No own resources; secretariat within management
Contact with management outside meetings	Steering committee for preparation of meetings	Steering committee for preparation of meetings	FIM representative	FULC
EWC autonomy	First stages	First stages	No autonomy	No autonomy

Internal Characteristics of EWCs

	Hoechst	Schmalbach-L.	Bull	Rhône Poulenc
Basis of communication	EWC President as competent interlocutor	EWC President as competent interlocutor	Differentiated communication structure: EWC electronic database	Good technical infrastructure (e-mail); established communication structure
Actual communication	EWC President is hub of radial structure	EWC President is hub of radial structure	Secretariat is hub of radial structure	'Report & Accounts Committee' hub of radial structure
Allocation of seats domestic/foreign (largest foreign contingent)	7 / 22 (4)	5 / 17 (3)	10 / 20 (3)	15 / 21 (4)
National access to group management	Central Works Council, Econ. Committee, Supervisory Board	Central Works Council, Econ. Comm. Super-visory Board: access to VIAG management	comité de groupe	comité de groupe
Established relationship to group management	Yes, 'consensus culture', esp. Group Works Council chair	Yes	Yes	Yes
Language of meeting	HQ mother tongue	HQ mother tongue	HQ mother tongue	HQ mother tongue
Location of meeting	Home country	Antwerp and rotating	Home country	Home country
Steering committee	Praesidium	Praesidium	Secretariat,	'Accounts Committee'
Leadership structure	Dominated by German EWC President	Four-person praesidium	German EWC secretary	rotating chair
Administrative structure	Secretariat of personnel dept. and Group Works Council	Own secretariat located at EWC President	Secretariat of personnel dept. and Group Works Council	None

Internal Characteristics of EWCs (cont'd)

	ICI	GKN	Merloni	ENI
Basis of communication	Address list, as yet no communication structure	Address list, as yet no communication structure	Address list, as yet no communication structure	Address list, non-transparent communication structure
Actual communication	As yet, barely any EWC internal communication	As yet, barely any EWC internal communication	As yet, no EWC internal communication	As yet, no EWC internal communication
Allocation of seats domestic/foreign (largest foreign contingent)	18 / 10 (2)	13 / 16 (6)	9 / 9 (3)	19 / 11 (3)
National access to group management	Consultation forum	No	Collective bargaining	only FULC
Established relationship to group management	Yes	No	Yes, 'participative culture'	Yes, 'participative culture'; only FULC
Language of meeting	HQ mother tongue	HQ mother tongue	HQ mother tongue	HQ mother tongue
Location of meeting	Home country	Home country (+ Brussels)	Home country	Rotates
Steering committee	Agenda preparation committee	Steering committee	Election of two co-ordinators planned	No
Leadership structure	British EWC Chair	German EWC Chair	Not fixed	Not fixed, in practice, domination by FULC
Administrative structure	Use of secretariat of personnel dept.	Use of secretariat of personnel dept.	None	Planned secretariat in personnel dept.

EWCs and National Employee Representation

	France	Germany	Italy	UK
Flow of information	Despite structure of representative bodies, flow divided by separate (political) trade unions	Structure of representative bodies offers precondition for information cascade: question of political will	Representative bodies above RSU-level not present in a form suitable for information transmission	Absence of national bodies for employee representation: shortcomings in downward flow - ICI an exception
Legitimacy of representation	Nomination by TUs according to negotiated formula and partial consideration of other criteria (e.g. divisions). Problems in subsidiaries because TUs must agree on 1/2 reps.	Election or appointment from Group Works Council, with some consideration to other criteria (divisions); not seen as a problem because it simply represents extension of national arrangements	At parent companies, nomination by TUs based on agreed formula; RSU not so established that elections sought; irregularity at Hoechst (appointed by management and subsequently endorsed by RSU) - in future election by own committee	Nomination by TUs in accordance with agreed formula; at Rhône Poulenc EWC rep. elected by consultation body the legitimacy of which was questioned by EWC rep. interviewed
Capacities and competences	Accumulation of offices leads to failure to meet EWC deadlines on some occasions	Recruitment from full-time works council reps; issue of multiple office-holding and hence capacity limits; accumulation of power can be a problem; know-how in politics of representation	Less with RSU than TUs; RSUs still in phase of constitution; dominance of TUs and/or excessive demands on RSU reps. on EWC	Workplace orientation, as only few group level bodies; no legal right to time-off
Status/Link to national structure	Competition of other bodies with *comité de groupe* leads to lack of motivation by French EWC reps.	Danger that EWC simply seen as information provider of the Groups Works Council and hence restricted	RSU reps. need body at group level but EWC does not meet this need - hence status is low	At GKN substitute for missing national forum; joint meeting used as opporunity to talk with group management

Appendix II: Interviews Conducted

Companies

Company	Country	Function	Comments
Schmalbach-Lubeca	D	EWC President	2 interviews
- engineering	F	EWC Member	
- German parent	D	Group personnel manager	
- French subsidiary	F	Personnel manager	
Hoechst	D	EWC President	2 interviews
- chemicals	I	EWC Member	
- German parent	D	Group personnel manager	
- Italian subsidiary	I	Personnel manager	
Bull	F	EWC Member (CGT)	
- engineering	F	Deputy EWC Secretary (CFDT)	
- French parent	D	EWC Secretary	
- German subsidiary	F	Group personnel manager	
	D	Personnel manager	
Rhône Poulenc	F	EWC Member (CGT)	
- chemicals	F	EWC Member (CFDT)	
- French parent	GB	EWC Member	
- UK subsidiary	F	External adviser to group personnel manager	
	GB	Personnel manager	
GKN	GB	Deputy EWC Chair	
- engineering	D	EWC Chair	2 interviews
- UK parent	GB	Group personnel manager	by telephone
- German subsidiary	D	Managing Director - German subsidiary	
ICI	GB	EWC Chair	
- chemicals	I	EWC Member	
- UK parent	I	EWC Member	by telephone
- Italian subsidiary	D	EWC Member	
	GB	Group personnel manager	
	I	Personnel manager	
Merloni	I	EWC Member	
- engineering	GB	EWC Member	
- Italian parent	I	Group personnel manager	
- UK subsidiary	GB	Personnel manager	
ENI	I	EWC Member	
- chemicals	F	EWC Member	
- Italian parent	I	Group personnel manager	
- French subsidiary	F	Personnel manager	

Organisations

Country	Function	Institutions	Country/branch	Comments
Germany	Trade union	IG Metall IG CPK	Engineering Chemicals	
	Employer association	Gesamtmetall BAVC	Engineering Chemicals	Telephone
France	Trade union	FGMM-CFDT FUC-CFDT CGT CGT-FO	Engineering Chemicals Confederation Confederation	
	Employer association	CNPF	Confederation	
UK	Trade union	AEEU TGWU TUC	Engineering Chemicals Confederation	
	Employer association	CIA	Chemicals	
	Consultant Consultant	 EWC Study Group	Engineering	
Italy	Trade union	FULC FIM-CISL FIOM-CGIL	Chemicals Engineering Engineering	
	Employer association	FEDERCHIMICA CONFINDUSTRIA	Chemicals Confederation	
Europe	Trade union	ETUC ETUI EMF EMCEF ECF-UIF	Confederation Confederation Engineering Chemicals Food	2 interviews 2 interviews
	Employer association Consultant	UNICE	Confederation	
	Parliament EU Commission	EP DG V		

Bibliography

Albert, M. (1993), *Capitalism against Capitalism*, London.

Altvater, E. (1993), *The Future of the Market*, London.

Altvater, E. and Mahnkopf, B. (1996), *Grenzen der Globalisierung. Ökonomie, Ökologie und Politik in der Weltgesellschaft*, Münster.

Armingeon, K. (1998), 'The persistence of differences between national industrial relations systems in Europe', in W. Lecher/H.-W. Platzer (eds.), *European Union – European Industrial Relations?*, London, pp. 72-80.

Armingeon, K. (1996), 'Regelungen der industriellen Beziehungen in Europa. Chancen und Risiken der Globalisierung', MSS, Duisburg.

Armingeon, K. (1997), 'Produktiver Zwang', *Mitbestimmung*, 1/1997, 22-24.

Beck, U. and Beck-Gernsheim, E. (1994), *Riskante Freiheiten. Individualisierung in modernen Gesellschaften*, Frankfurt a.M.

Blank, M., Geissler, S. and Jaeger, R. (1996), *Euro-Betriebsräte: Grundlagen – Praxisbeispiel – Mustervereinbarungen*, Cologne.

Bispinck, R. (1995), 'Tarifpolitik in der ersten Hälfte der 90er Jahre – Eine zwiespältige Bilanz', in R. Bispinck, (ed.), *Tarifpolitik der Zukunft – Was wird aus dem Flächentarifvertrag?*, Hamburg, pp. 24 ff.

Bonneton, P., Carley, M., Hall, M., and Krieger, H. (1995), *Review of Current Agreements on Information and Consultation in European Multinationals*, Social Europe, 5/1995, Luxembourg.

Brand, R. (1992), ' "European Information Meeting": Ein Modell des europäischen Dialogs der Sozialpartner im Hoechst-Konzern', in J. Deppe (ed.), *Euro-Betriebsräte. Internationale Mitbestimmung – Konsequenzen für Unternehmen und Gewerkschaften*, Wiesbaden.

Buda, D. (1998), 'On course for European labour relations? The prospects for the Social Dialogue in the European Union', in W. Lecher/H.-W. Platzer (eds.), *European Union – European Industrial Relations?*, London, pp. 21-46.

Burchardt, H.-J. (1997), 'Die Globalisierungsdebatte: Ahistorisches Ringelreihen und reduktionistische Prophezeihungen', *Gewerkschaftliche Monatshefte* 7/97, S. 397-409.

Carley, M., Geissler, S., and Krieger, H. (1996), 'The contents of voluntary agreements on European level information and consultation: preliminary findings of an analysis of 111 agreements', in *European Works Councils in Focus*, Dublin, S. 1-14.

Couëtoux, M. and Di Ruzza, R. (1990), *Les relations sociales en Europe*, Montreuil.

270

Crouch, C. (1993), *Industrial Relations and European State Traditions*, Oxford.

Crouch, C. (1995), 'Exit or Voice: Two Paradigms for European Industrial Relations After the Keynesian Welfare State', *European Journal of Industrial Relations*, Vol. 1, S. 63-81.

Däubler, W. (1997), 'Entwicklung und Perspektiven des europäischen Arbeitsrechts', in H.-W. Platzer (ed.), *Sozialstaatliche Entwicklungen in Europa und die Sozialpolitik der Europäischen Union. Die soziale Dimension im EU-Reformprozeß*, Baden-Baden, pp. 101-117.

Danis, J.-J. (1996), 'Der Europäische Betriebsrat bei Elf Aquitaine. Ein Kurzportrait', in *Fallstudie für das Europäische Gewerkschaftsinstitut (EGI)*, Brüssel, S. 58-74.

Danis, J.-J. and Hoffmann, R. (1995), 'From the Vredeling Directive to the European Works Council Directive – some historical remarks', *Transfer* 2/1995, pp. 180-187.

Deppe, F. and Weiner, K.-P. (eds.) (1991), *Binnenmarkt '92. Zur Entwicklung der Arbeitsbeziehungen in Europa*, Hamburg.

Deppe, J., Hoffmann, R. and Stützel, W. (eds.) (1997), *Europäische Betriebsräte Wege in ein soziales Europa*, Frankfurt/New York.

Dörre, K. (1995), 'Postfordismus und industrielle Beziehungen', in E. Bulmahn, P. v. Oertzen and J. Schuster (eds.), *Jenseits von Öko-Steuern. Konturen eines ökologisch-solidarischen Reformprojektes im Übergang zum Postfordismus*, spw Jahrbuch 1995/96, Dortmund, pp. 145-172.

Dörre, K. (1996), 'Globalstrategien von Unternehmen – ein Desintegrationsphänomen. Zu den Auswirkungen grenzüberschreitender Unternehmensaktivitäten auf die industriellen Beziehungen', *SOFI-Mitteilungen*, 24/1996, pp. 15-27.

Dörre, K., Elk-Anders, R. and Speidel, F. (1997), 'Globalisierung als Option: Internationalisierungspfade von Unternehmen, Standortpolitik und industrielle Beziehungen', *SOFI-Mitteilungen*, No. 25, pp.43-70.

Dufour, C. and Mouriaux, M.-F. (1986), 'Comités D'entreprise: Quarante ans après'. *Les Dossier de l'IRES*, 4.

Dufour, C. (1993), 'Frankreich', in R. Bispinck and W. Lecher, (eds.), *Tarifpolitik und Tarifsysteme in Europa*, Cologne, pp. 105 ff.

Ebbinghaus, B. and Visser, J. (1994), 'Barrieren und Wege "grenzenloser Solidarität": Gewerkschaften und europäische Integration', in W. Streeck (ed.), *Staat und Verbände*, PVS Sonderheft 25/1994, Opladen, pp. 223-255.

Elsenhans, H. (1996), 'Gegen das Gespenst der Globalisierung', in W. Fricke, (ed.), *Zukunft der Industriegesellschaft*, Jahrbuch Arbeit und Technik 1996, Bonn, pp. 25-36.

European Commission (1996), *Employee Representatives in Europe and their Economic Prerogatives*, Social Europe, 3/96, Luxembourg.

European Industrial Relations Review (1996), The Changing Face of Collective

Bargaining, Nr. 268, May, p .1.

Falkner, G. (1996), 'European Works Councils and the Maastricht Social Agreement: towards a new policy style?', *Journal of European Public Policy*, June 1996, pp. 192-208.

Flecker, J. (1996), 'Globalisierungsprozesse und industrielle Arbeitsbeziehungen', in U. Steger (ed.), *Globalisierung der Wirtschaft: Konsequenzen für Arbeit, Technik und Umwelt*, Berlin, pp. 155-176.

Flecker, J. and Schulten, T. (1996), 'Arbeitsbeziehungen in Europa und die Zukunft des "europäischen Sozialmodells"', Mss., Vienna/Hannover.

Fulton, L. (1995), 'Neue Kraft nach zwei Jahrzehnten Rückschlags', *Gewerkschaftliche Monatshefte* 4, pp. 238-244.

Fulton, L. (1996), no title, (Beitrag für das Europäische Gespräch der Hans-Böckler-Stiftung), Ms., Duisburg.

Gerum, E. (1992), 'Führungsorganisation und Mitbestimmung in der europäischen Unternehmensverfassung', *zfo* 3, pp. 147-153.

Gerum, E., Steinmann, H. (1984), *Unternehmensordnung und tarifvertragliche Mitbestimmung, eine sozioökonomische Untersuchung zur vergleichenden Unternehmensverfassungsforschung am Beispiel Schweden*, Berlin.

Giddens, A. (1994), *Beyond Left and Right. The Future of Radical Politics*, Cambridge.

Giddens, A. (1990), *Consequences of Modernity*, Cambridge.

Gold, M. (1994), *Direct Communications in European Multinationals: a Case Study Approach*, Dublin.

Gold, M. and Hall, M. (1992), *Report on European Level Information and Consultation in Multinational Companies – an Evaluation of Practice*, Dublin.

Guarriello, F. and Jobert, A. (1992), 'L'Evolution des Relations Professionelles dans les Groups Transnationaux', *Dossier de Recherche*, No. 46, September.

Härtel, H.-H. et al. (1996), *Grenzüberschreitende Produktion und Strukturwandel: Globalisierung der deutschen Wirtschaft*, Baden-Baden.

Heidenreich, M. (1990), *Nationale Muster betrieblichen Strukturwandels*, Frankfurt/M., New York.

Heidenreich, M. (1991), 'Verallgemeinerungsprobleme in der international vergleichenden Organisationsforschung', in M. Heidenreich and G. Schmidt (eds), *International vergleichende Organisationsforschung*, Opladen, pp. 48-66.

Héritier, A., Mingers, S., Knill, C. and Becka, M. (1994), *Die Veränderung von Staatlichkeit in Europa*, Opladen.

Hirsch, J. (1994), 'Vom fordistischen Sicherheitsstaat zum nationalen Wettbewerbsstaat', *Das Argument*, 203, pp. 7-21.

Hirsch-Kreinsen, Hartmut (1997), 'Globalisierung der Industrie: ihre Grenzen und

Folgen', *WSI-Mitteilungen*, 7/97, pp. 487-493.

Höland, A. (1997), 'Mitbestimmung und Europa – Expertise im Rahmen des Projektvorhabens "Mitbestimmung und neue Unternehmenskulturen – Bilanz und Perspektiven" ', Bremen (mimeo).

Huffschmid, J. (1994), 'Globalisierung oder Blockbildung? Zur Struktur kapitalistischer Internationalisierung', *Blätter für deutsche und internationale Politik*, Heft 8, pp. 1008-1013.

Hyman, R. (1994), 'Changing Trade Union Identities and Strategies', in R. Hyman and A. Ferner (eds.), *New Frontiers in European Industrial Relations*, Oxford.

Jansen, P., Kißler, L., Kühne, P., Leggewie, C. and Seul, O. (1986), *Gewerkschaften in Frankreich – Geschichte, Organisation, Programmatik*, Frankfurt/New York.

Javillier, J.-C. (1984), *Les Reformes du Droit du Travail depuis le 10 Mai 1981*, Paris.

Jessop, B. (1992), 'Regulation und Politik. Integrale Ökonomie und integraler Staat', in, A. Demirovic, H.-P. Krebs and T. Sablowski (eds), *Hegemonie und Staat. Kapitalistische Regulation als Projekt und Prozeß*, Münster, pp. 232-263.

Jobert, A. (1990), 'La négociation collective dans les entreprises multinationales en Europe', in G. Devin (ed.), *Syndicalisme: dimensions internationales, La Garenne-Colombe* (Eds. Européennes ERASME).

Junne, G. (1996), 'Integration unter den Bedingungen von Globalisierung und Lokalisierung', in M. Jachtenfuchs and B. Kohler-Koch (eds.), *Europäische Integration*, Opladen, Pp. 513-530.

Kaelble, H. (1987), *Auf dem Weg zu einer europäischen Gesellschaft. Eine Sozialgeschichte Westeuropas 1880 bis 1980*, Munich.

Kastendiek, H. (1990), 'Convergence or a Persistent Diversity of National Politics', in C. Crouch and D. Marquard, *The Politics of 1992. Beyond the Single European Market*, Oxford, pp. 68-97.

Keller, B. (1996a), 'Sozialdialoge als Instrument europäischer Arbeits- und Sozialpolitik?', *Industrielle Beziehungen*, Heft 3, pp. 207-228.

Keller, B. (1996b), 'Nach der Verabschiedung der Richtlinie zu Europäischen Betriebsräten – Von enttäuschten Erwartungen, unerfüllbaren Hoffnungen und realistischen Perspektiven, *WSI-Mitteilungen*, 8, pp. 470-482.

Keller, B. (1997), *Europäische Arbeits- und Sozialpolitik*, Munich, Vienna.

Klak, A. (1998), ' European industrial relations: an employer's viewpoint' in, in W. Lecher/H.-W. Platzer (eds.), *European Union – European Industrial Relations?*, London, pp. 148-156.

Koch, C. (1995), *Die Gier des Marktes. Die Ohnmacht des Staates im Kampf der Weltwirtschaft*, Munich.

Kohler-Koch, B. (1992), 'Verbände und europäische Integration. Die Rolle organisierter Interessen im Integrationsprozeß', in M. Kreile, *Die Integration Europas*, Opladen, pp. 81-119.

Kohler-Koch, B. (1996a), 'Die Gestaltungsmacht organisierter Interessen', in B. Kohler-Koch and M. Jachtenfuchs (eds), *Europäische Integration*, Opladen, pp. 193-219.

Kohler-Koch, B. (1996b), 'Politische Unverträglichkeiten von Globalisierung', in U. Steger (ed.), *Globalisierung der Wirtschaft: Konsequenzen für Arbeit, Technik und Umwelt*, Berlin, pp.83-114.

Kohn, M. L. (1987), 'Cross-National Research as an Analytic Strategy', *American Sociological Review*, No. 52, pp. 713-729.

Kotthoff, H. (1994), *Betriebsräte und Bürgerstatus. Wandel und Kontinuität betrieblicher Mitbestimmung*, Munich.

Koubek, N. et al. (1996), *Unternehmensstrategien in der Triade*, Baden-Baden.

Krieger, H. (1996), 'Partizipation der Produzenten. Mitbestimmung am Arbeitsplatz', Ms., Duisburg.

Küchle, H. (1996), 'Deutschlands Position auf dem Weltmarkt', *WSI-Mitteilungen*, 5/1996, pp. 295-303.

Küchle, H. (1997), 'Ökonomische Globalisierung und die europäische Zukunft des Nationalstaats', in H.-W. Platzer, *Sozialstaatliche Entwicklungen in Europa und die Sozialpolitik in der Europäischen Union*, Baden-Baden, pp. 15-22.

Lecher, W. (1992), 'Elemente eine europäischen Arbeitsbeziehungsmodells gegenüber Japan und den USA', *WSI-Mitteilungen*, No. 12, pp. 807-812.

Lecher, W. (1994a), 'Die reale Situation der Vertretung der Arbeitnehmerinteressen in den Betrieben in Frankreich und Deutschland – ein empirischer Vergleich', *Wirtschaft und Gesellschaft* 3, pp. 399-414.

Lecher, W. (1994b), 'Euro-Betriebsräte – ein empirisch gestützter deutsch-französischer Vergleich', *WSI-Mitteilungen*, 2, pp. 108-116.

Lecher, W. (1995), 'European Works Councils and Direct Participation: the "Dual Shift" as a Challenge to the German Industrial Relations System', in R. Hoffmann, O. Jacobi, B. Keller and M. Weiss (eds), *German Industrial Relations under the Impact of Structural Change, Unification and European Integration*, Düsseldorf, pp. 108 ff.

Lecher, W. (1996a), 'Forschungsfeld Europäische Betriebsräte', *WSI-Mitteilungen*, 11, pp. 710-715.

Lecher, W. (1996b), 'Supranationale Tarifpolitik: ihre Möglichkeiten und Grenzen in der europäischen Union', *Internationale Politik und Gesellschaft*, 1/1996, pp.36-46.

Lecher, W. (1997), *Labour Relations and Social Model – a Triadic Comparison*, Working Paper of the ETUI, Brussels.

Lecher, W. and Naumann, R. (1994), 'Italy', in W. Lecher, (ed.), *Trade Unions in the European Union*, London, pp. 56 ff.

Lecher, W. and Platzer, H.-W. (1996), 'Europäische Betriebsräte: Fundament und Instrument europäischer Arbeitsbeziehungen? Probleme der Kompatibilität von nationalen Arbeitnehmervertretungen und EBR', *WSI-Mitteilungen* 8, pp. 503-512.

LeGoff, J. (1997), 'Europas Systeme gleichen sich einander an – Der Gesundheitsmarkt', *Le Monde diplomatique* (supplement to *tageszeitung*), 16 July 1997.

Leibfried, S. (1996), 'Wohlfahrtsstaatliche Perspektiven der Europäischen Union: Auf dem Wege zu positiver Souveränitätsverflechtung?', in M. Jachtenfuchs and B. Kohler-Koch (eds), *Europäische Integration*, Opladen, pp. 455-477.

Leibfried, S. and Pierson, P. (1995), 'Die soziale Dimension der Europäischen Integration,' ZeS-Arbeitspapier No. 12, Bremen.

Leibfried, S. and Pierson, P. (1997), 'Der Wohlfahrtsstaat in der europäischen Mehr-Ebenen-Politik: Die Rolle der Mitgliedstaaten', in H.-W. Platzer (ed.), *Sozialstaatliche Entwicklungen in Europa und die Sozialpolitik der Europäischen Union. Die soziale Dimension im EU-Reformprozeß,* Baden-Baden, pp. 77-92.

Leibfried, S. and Rieger, E. (1995), 'Wohlfahrtsstaat und Globalisierung, ZeS-Arbeitspapier', No. 15, Bremen.

Luttwak, E. N. (1994), *Weltwirtschaftskrieg. Export als Waffe – aus Partner werden Gegner*, Reinbek b. Hamburg.

Lutz, B. (1991), 'Die Grenzen des "effet sociétal" und die Notwendigkeit einer historischen Perspektive. Einige Bemerkungen zum vernünftigen Gebrauch internationaler Vergleiche', in M. Heidenreich and G. Schmidt (ed.), *International vergleichende Organisationsforschung*, Opladen, pp. 91-105.

Majone, Giandomenico (1996), 'Redistributive und sozialregulative Politik', in M. Jachtenfuchs and B. Kohler-Koch (eds), *Europäische Integration*, Opladen, pp. 225-248.

Marginson, P. et al. (1995), 'The Second Survey of Industrial Relations in Large Companies', Warwick Papers in Industrial Relations. Coventry: IRRU, University of Warwick.

Marginson, P., Gilman, M., Jacobi, O., Krieger, H., *Negotiating European Works Councils: an analysis of agreements under Article 13*, Dublin (forthcoming).

Martin, A. (1996), 'European Institutions and the Europeanisation of Trade Unions: Support or Seduction?', ETUI Discussion and Working Paper 96.04.1, Brussels.

Martinelli, P., Rubino, A., Stanzani, C. (1992), 'Informazione e la Consultazione dei lavoratori e del Sindicato in Gruppi italiani operanti in più paesi communitari', *Quaderno Sind Nova*, No. 9.

Millward, N., Stevens, M., Smart, D. and Hawes, W.R. (1992), *Workplace Industrial Relations in Transition*, Aldershot.

Müller, H.-E. (1997), 'Heimatlose Weltbürger?', *Die Mitbestimmung*, 1/1997.

Müller-Jentsch, W. (1996), 'Theorien Industrieller Beziehungen', *Industrielle*

Beziehungen, No. 1, pp. 36-64.

Müller-Jentsch, W. (1997), *Soziologie der Industriellen Beziehungen - Eine Einführung*, Frankfurt/M, New York.

Münch, R. (1993), *Das Projekt Europa – Zwischen Nationalstaat, regionaler Autonomie und Weltgesellschaft*, Frankfurt/M.

Nagel, B. (1996), 'Entwicklungsperspektiven von Euro-Betriebsräten und deutsche Mitbestimmung', *WSI-Mitteilungen*, 8/1996, pp.494-503.

Nagel, B., Riess, B., and Theis, G. (1990), *Der Lieferant on line, Just-in-Time Produktion und Mitbestimmung in der Automobilindustrie*, Baden-Baden.

Nagel, B., Riess, B., Rüb, S. and Beschorner, A. (1996), *Information und Mitbestimmung im internationalen Konzern*, Baden-Baden.

Narr, W. D. and Schubert A. (1994), *Weltökonomie. Die Misere der Politik*, Frankfurt a.M.

Neyer, J., Seeleib-Kaiser, M. (1995), 'Bringing the Economy Back In: Economic Globalizarion and the Re-Commodifikation of the Workforce', ZeS-Arbeitspapier No. 16, Bremen.

North, D. C. (1990), *Institutions, Institutional Change and Economic Performance*, Cambridge.

Perlitz, M. (1993), *Internationales Management*, Stuttgart/Jena.

Platzer, H.-W. (1991), *Gewerkschaftspolitik ohne Grenzen? Die transnationale Zusammenarbeit der Gewerkschaften im Europa der 90er Jahre*, Bonn.

Platzer, H.-W. (1991), 'Sozialpolitik und soziale Integration in der Europäischen Union. Bedingungen, Perspektiven und Grenzen im Spannungsfeld von Markt- und Politikintegration', in B. Dietz (ed.), *Die soziale Zukunft Europas,* Gießen, pp.41-63.

Platzer, H.-W. (1996), 'Die Umweltpolitik der Europäischen Union: Ordnungs- und integrationspolitische Konflikte, Steuerungsprogramme, Entwicklungstrends', in E. Leicht-Eckhardt et. al. (eds), *Öko-Audit- Grundlagen und Erfahrungen*, Frankfurt am Main.

Platzer, H.-W. (1998), 'Industrial Relations and European Integration. Patterns, Dynamics and Limits of Transnationalization', in W. Lecher and H.-W. Platzer (eds), *European Union – European Industrial Relations*, London.

Porter, M. E. (1989), Der Wettbewerb auf globalen Märkten: Ein Rahmenkonzept, in M. E. Porter (ed.), *Globaler Wettbewerb*, Wiesbaden, pp.17-68.

Rehfeldt, U. (1992), 'L'expérience des comités de groupe européens', Paris (GIP Mutations Industrielles) (Cahier de recherche N° 62).

Rehfeldt, U. (1998), 'European Works Councils: an assessment of French initiatives', in W. Lecher/H.-W. Platzer (eds), *European Union – European Industrial Relations?*, London, pp. 207-222.

Reich, R. B. (1991), *The Work of Nations*, New York.

Rens, J. van (1991), 'Europaweite Bündelung der Kräfte in gewerkschaftlichen Joint-Ventures', *Die Mitbestimmung*, 4, pp. 291-293.

Revel, S. (1994), *Tarifverhandlungen in der Bundesrepublik Deutschland. Eine Untersuchung der Bedeutung verschiedener Verhandlungsebenen für die sozioökonomische Entwicklung*, Baden-Baden.

Rivest, C. (1996), 'Voluntary European Works Councils', *European Journal of Industrial Relations*, pp. 235-253.

Roth, B. (1984), *Weltökonomie oder Nationalökonomie? Tendenzen des Internationalisierungsprozesses seit Mitte des 19. Jahrhunderts*, Marburg

Ruyesseveldt,. J.v. and Visser, J. (eds) (1996), *Industrial Relations in Europe – Traditions and Transitions*, London/New Dehli.

Schmidt, E. (1997), 'Beteiligung an betrieblichen Umweltschutzmaßnahmen (insbesondere Öko-Audits) als Gestaltungsaufgabe für Europäische Betriebsräte in der Chemischen Industrie', Unpublished final report of a research project for the Hans Böckler Foundation, 97/755/2, Düsseldorf.

Schulten, T. (1995), ' "Europäische Betriebsräte" – Stand und Perspektive einer europaweiten Regulierung der Arbeitsbeziehungen auf der Ebene transnationaler Konzerne', in M. Mesch, *Sozialpartnerschaft und Arbeitsbeziehungen in Europa*, Vienna, pp. 335-363.

Schulten, T. (1997), 'Europäische Modernisierungskoalitionen? Der Beitrag Euro-päischer Betriebsräte zur Neuordnung der Arbeitsbeziehungen in Europa,' in Flecker, J. (ed.), *Jenseits der Sachzwanglogik – Arbeitspolitik zwischen Anpassungsdruck und Gestaltungschancen*, Berlin.

Simons, R. (1997), 'Kein Nullsummenspiel', *Die Mitbestimmung*, 1/97, pp. 12-17.

Stanzani, C. (1996), Der Europäische Betriebsrat bei Merloni. Ein Kurzportrait, in Fallstudie für das Europäische Gewerkschaftsinstitut (EGI), Brüssel, pp. 50-57.

Stoop, S. (ed.) (1994), *Der europäische Betriebsrat: einen Schritt voraus. Eine Untersuchung zum Erfolg von Euro-Betriebsräten*. Study commissioned by the FNV Centrum Ondernemingsraden, SOMO.

Streeck, W. (1996), 'Gewerkschaften zwischen Nationalstaat und Europäischer Union', MPIFG Working Paper 96/1.

Streeck, W. and Vitols, S. (1993), 'European Work Councils Between Statutory Enactment and Voluntary Adopation', WZB Diskussion Paper FS I 93 – 312, Berlin.

Telljohann, V. (1995), 'Das wiedergewonnene Selbstbewußtsein der italienischen Gewerkschaften', *Gewerkschaftliche Monatshefte*, 4, pp. 227-244.

Traxler, F. (1996), no title, (Beitrag zum Europäischen Gespräch der Hans-Böckler-Stiftung), Ms., Duisburg.

Traxler, F. and Schmitter, P. C. (1995), 'Arbeitsbeziehungen und europäische Integration', in M. Mesch (ed.), *Sozialpartnerschaft und Arbeitsbeziehungen in*

Europa, Vienna, pp. 231-256.

Weidenfeld, W. and Turek, J. (1996), *Standort Europa: Handeln in der neuen Weltwirtschaft*, 2. edn., Gütersloh.

Weinmann, H. (1992), ' "European Information Meeting": Grenzüberschreitende Information europäischer Belegschaftsvertreter der Hoechst -Gruppe', in J. Deppe (ed.), *Euro-Betriebsräte. Internationale Mitbestimmung – Konsequenzen für Unternehmen und Gewerkschaften*, Wiesbaden.

Welge, M.K. (1992), 'Strategien für den internationalen Wettbewerb zwischen Globalisierung und lokaler Anpassung', in B. N. Kumar and H. Haussmann (eds), *Handbuch der internationalen Unternehmenstätigkeit*, Munich, pp. 569-589.

Wendt, B.-J. (1991), *Die britischen Gewerkschaften heute – Strukturen und Strategien*, Rheinfelden/Berlin.

Wilke, H. (1992), *Ironie des Staates. Grundlinien einer Staatstheorie*, Frankfurt a.M.

Economic and Social Committee (1997), *Opinion on Employment, Competitiveness and Economic Globalisation*, CES325/1997, Brussels.

Wortmann, M. and Dörrenbächer, C. (1997), 'Multinationale Unternehmen und der Standort Deutschland', FAST-Manuskript, Berlin.

Zürn, M. (1996), 'Zum Verhältnis von Globalisierung, politischer Integration und politischer Fragmentierung', in W. Fricke (ed.), *Zukunft der Industriegesellschaft. Jahrbuch Arbeit und Technik 1996*, Bonn, pp. 9-24.